LEADERSHIP

LEADERSHIP

strategies for
organizational effectiveness

James J. Cribbin

A Division of American Management Associations

Library of Congress Cataloging in Publication Data

Cribbin, James J
  Leadership : strategies for organizational effectiveness.

  Bibliography: p.
  Includes index.
  1. Leadership.   2. Management.   I. Title.
HD57.7.C74   658.4'092   81-12722
ISBN 0-8144-5726-6   AACR2

©1981 AMACOM
A division of American Management Associations, New York.
All rights reserved. Printed in the United States of America.

First Printing

preface

The outstanding characteristic of organizations today is the number of antagonistic forces that are colliding head-on: stringent corporate requirements versus employee aspirations; sophisticated technological systems versus the social system; integrated production processes versus worker expectations; impersonal jobs versus subordinate satisfactions; neat interfacing networks versus human needs; intricate structures versus a sense of identity; cost and profit pressures versus personal progress and growth; stability versus innovation; uniformity versus change; conformity versus creativity; company growth versus constrictive regulations; corporate profit seeking versus demands of society. The clash of thesis and antithesis goes on unendingly.

How can practicing managers evolve a new synthesis from these opposing phenomena so that the organization's inherent potential energy can be made kinetic, not only for their own benefit but also for that of their subordinates and the organization? The simplest, least expensive, and most realistic strategy is to become both effective managers *and* effective leaders. Management is largely an action-oriented cerebral process. Leadership is principally an action-oriented interpersonal process. Assuming that you are already intent on increasing your managerial skills, this book seeks to help you improve your leadership competence.

There are five possible approaches to becoming a more

adept leader. You can rely on your own experience; the errors may far outnumber the trials. You can plow through the more carefully done research; most executives lack the luxury of time for this laudable endeavor. You can study how proven leaders have acted; helpful as this can be, it assumes that what worked well for one person, in his or her unique situation, will work equally well for another. You can read non-books that promise you salvation without effort; this is usually a self-deceptive venture in pep talks and puffery. Finally, you can examine some of the more significant research findings, reflect on how different leaders have coped with a variety of situations, and formulate a leadership-development program custom-tailored to you and your milieu. The chapters that follow facilitate your efforts to do just this.

I express my genuine appreciation to a number of people who assisted in the preparation of this book: to the managers who forced me to sharpen my ideas; to the editor who transmuted the manuscript into something far better than it was originally; to Claire Chrystal and Mary Mullaney, who transformed my hieroglyphics into intelligible prose; and to those publishers who permitted me to use copyrighted materials.

James J. Cribbin
Professor of Management
St. John's University
President
Cribbin Management Associates

contents

the real meaning of ROI: why shortchange yourself?

The Realities of Managerial Leadership

Competition is keener than ever before within and between industries. Productivity is a nettlesome problem. Scarce organizational resources are diffused because of legislative and social considerations, rather than focused on the primary purpose of the firm. Darman and Lynn, of the John F. Kennedy School of Government, estimate that 40 percent of corporate capital investment decisions are determined by factors other than the interests of the company, its shareholders, or its employees.[1]

At times, corporations are unduly influenced by specialists in law, accounting, and finance, some with limited or no line experience. Such specialists are absolutely essential. But the Olympian numerical perspective from the 30th floor of headquarters sometimes distorts the manufacturing, marketing, sales, and human realities at the operating levels, as many a sour acquisition has demonstrated. Abernathy and Hayes, of the Harvard Business School, contend that a new breed of manager is needed to reindustrialize and revitalize America: one adept at nurturing new technologies, building dynamic organizations, opening new markets, and developing more productive people; one who, in a nutshell, "is willing to sweat and bleed to make things happen." [2] Some interesting data support their viewpoint. From 1968 to 1978, the number of patents issued in Japan increased by 372 percent, while the number issued in the United States declined by 10 percent. In the past 15 years, Japan and West Germany have doubled their numbers of scientific personnel, but the number of those trained in similar disciplines in America has declined between 5 percent and 10 percent. However, during the seventies, our lawyer output increased by 83 percent.[3] Small wonder that legal fees are now approximately 1 percent of the GNP!

What is needed is leaders at all levels who will be sensitive to the 12 realities listed below.

Leading in Times of Changing People

The manager-leader might ponder six realities regarding the work force today.

People Think. For the first time in the history of the world, management must cope with employees who have been trained to think for themselves rather than to bow low before someone else's say-so. We no more know how to manage such people than we know how to educate them.

People Are No Longer Meek. Put succinctly, the meek are weary of waiting to inherit the *dirt!* The middle class, which makes any country prosperous, is becoming more restive. For instance, one study indicates that honors students seek the following characteristics in their future careers: interesting work, self-development, high-quality work, respect, and freedom on the job.[4] Such employees are disinclined to be docile or passive.

People Are Self-Interested. To an extent unknown 25 years ago, subordinates ask, "What's in it for me?" This is not selfishness but an all-too-human self-centeredness. Small wonder that career loyalty takes precedence over corporate fidelity, that competent subordinates are opportunistic and mobile. Psychologically, no relationship that satisfies primarily the needs of only one party can endure long. In light of this, it is amazing that more strident demands for an improved quality of work life surprise some managers!

People Expect to Be Heard. A supportive culture prompts employees to voice ideas and opinions with the expectation that they will be heeded. Interestingly, the culture has run ahead of research. It has been found that when a system exists for employees to influence their managers, productivity and morale almost always improve.

People Are More Expensive Than Ever. When labor was cheap and readily replaced, the main criterion for hiring labor was low cost. Today, a company like IBM invests over $2,000,000,000 annually just on fringe benefits. Under such conditions, the main criterion must be value received, not low cost. Labor must be efficient and more productive, not cheap.

People Have Great Potential. Experts have estimated that the average person is actualizing about 10 percent of his or her human potential. Not one study indicates that the average worker is working at anything near his or her true capability. Here is a key challenge of leadership—to unleash and channel the untapped talent that exists at every level in any organization.

For some managers, the changing values of the work force are discomforting; for others they are a threat. They yearn for the "good old days." Such reactions are not for you. Leaders, like therapists, confront reality with a clear eye. They accept it even when it is unpleasant and have strategies for capitalizing on it or at least coping with it. It is as simple, and as difficult, as that!

Leading in Times of Turbulence

More often than not, people change in response to a changing environment. The following societal trends are crucial for the manager-leader to understand.

The Knowledge Explosion. A baby is born tonight. By the time he or she attains the age of 50, knowledge will have multiplied a nimumum of 32 times. Take any field with which you are familiar, and consider the possibilities for growth. It would be difficult to make too farfetched a projection.

The Technological Implosion. Centuries ago Bacon claimed that knowledge was power. Today this is a fact. The rate of technological change is mind-boggling. No longer can the manager-leader expect to use yesterday's experience to give today's answers to tomorrow's opportunities.

Agglomerates and Alienation. The trend is clear: the strong are getting stronger, and the weak are being merged out of existence. This may bring joy to those who wield power in the executive suite, but its impact at the lower levels may be less than motivating.

> In the course of a dinner talk to the sales force of a large company, I asked, "What is your greatest problem?" Out of the dark came a cry, "Does anyone know I'm out there?" This was followed by another shout, "Does anyone give a damn?"

What employee wants to feel like a helpless cog in a complex organization that he or she neither understands nor influences? Here is a challenge for you as a leader: to preserve the human touch, to make work feel meaningful and contributions feel valid, to engender identification with a purpose, not merely with an organization.

Vague Value Systems. The sixties were the "me decade," the seventies the "helpless decade," and the eighties may well be the "faithless decade." Richard C. Gerstenberg, former chairman of General Motors, once noted, "I am concerned about a society that has demonstrably lost confidence in its institutions—in the government, in the press, in the church, in the military—as well as in business." [5] Interestingly, the *Harvard Business Review* surveyed upper management and discovered that 70 percent preferred traditional business ideology—entrepreneurship, individualism, competition, and minimum government intervention. But 73 percent felt that by 1985 communitarianism would prevail—concern for the community, power equalization, government-business coordination, and participatory democracy. [6] On the other hand, one is reminded of Adam Smith's comment, "I have never known much good done by those who affected to trade for the public good." Be that as it may, leaders must have sound values which serve as their North Star, wheel, and rudder, preventing them from yielding to the pressures of the moment.

Economic Imperatives and Moral Mandates. Each day the manager walks the fine line between economic musts and ethical oughts, at times with little guidance from the organization. To complicate the situation, some firms tend to reward those who attain outstanding short-term results, perhaps at the expense of long-term goals, or ignore the means whereby short-term objectives are achieved. When this happens, managers are tempted to abide by the 11th Commandment, "Don't get caught."

The two different viewpoints are brought out clearly in the following quotation from Donald Ephlin, head of the UAW's Ford department:

> "Top management is really convinced of the need for quality, but the pressure at the local level is for productivity and the foremen will cheat a bit to get the numbers. But if they do it now, we're going to raise hell." [7]

Administrative, Technical, and Human Systems. Complex organizations require managerial skills of a polished quality. Technology has brought an inflow of experts, each group with its own territorial imperatives, provincial allegiance, jargon, and trained incapacities. Technical sophistication often brings the hidden costs of lessened collaboration. Undergirding the administrative and technical systems is the social system consisting of group and individual needs, perceptions, attitudes, norms, behavior patterns, pressures, aspirations, mores, goals, and reward-punishment codes—all interacting within the matrix of the formal and nonformal organizational structures. The interaction of these factors constitutes an interesting potpourri for the manager, at times supportive, at times bothersome, at times frustrating.

The Manager-Leader and the 12 Realities

What can you do about these realities, most of which are beyond your power to control or even influence? You can do the *essential* thing, which is to reflect on how these realities affect *your* people, in *your* work environment, in *your* organization, in *your* community. You can take into account not only the constraints that these realities impose, but more importantly, the opportunities they present. At least then you will be reality-oriented—no mean achievement in any endeavor!

The True Meaning of ROI

If leaders are to capitalize on the realities we have described, they must adopt a new interpretation of ROI. To finance specialists, this term means return on investment. But to the leader, these initials have more significant meanings that go beyond the hackneyed bottom line.

Return on Ideas. Organizations probably need idea transplants more than society needs heart transplants. Good ideas are not hard to unearth, but profit-producing ideas are more difficult to come by. The Japanese with their quality circles and some European and North American firms have shown the wealth of ideas that lie dormant in any firm. The job of the leader is to build a system to identify and act upon profit-oriented ideas. This matter is discussed more fully in Chapter 15.

Return on Improvement and Innovation. If an organization is to avoid the stigma of being a mere "me-tooer," it must create a climate that boldly declares: (1) the worst enemy of the best is the good enough, and (2) people can improve anything that has been devised if they are let free and rewarded for doing so. This is also discussed in Chapter 15.

Return on Individuals. A Polish worker on strike commented, "If you stand up and work, or lie down, you get paid the same." How many managers in their daily behavior demonstrate a genuine belief in the potential of employees to grow and contribute? How many strive day in and day out to help their subordinates actualize their potential more fully? How many are convinced that apathy and creativity are both results, not causes, and have strategies to minimize the former, to enhance the latter? No one knows, but you can answer these questions for yourself with respect to your people.

Return on Interaction. Friction and cooperation, conflict and collaboration, jurisdictional disputes and respectful interdependence are all forms of interaction. Answer for yourself the return on interaction that each organization is getting, judging by the comments of lower-level managers in two different companies: "One thing I like about this place is that if you need another department's help, you're pretty sure to get it." Contrast this remark with the statement of another manager, "Ask another group for help around here and you get the reaction, 'It's not our job.' We use position descriptions largely for defensive purposes." Leaders realize that jealousy, infighting, and parochialism represent money falling through the organizational cracks.

Return on Interface. The purpose of the nerve ring of the starfish and that of the manager are similar, as Maier has pointed out: both enable the subunits to work more effectively together than they could separately. Sever the ring, and the rays of the starfish churn away vigorously but with little coordination. Let managers forget their accountability for maximizing interdependence through effective coordination, and the same phenomenon occurs. This all sounds like theory until one calculates the profit dollars lost in the following incident.

Things were going well in constructing a new 17-story, $30 million office building in Minneapolis. Then an errant computer served up 12,056 windows, all the wrong size. To make matters worse, because of the way they were made, the windows could not be cut to size.[8]

Return on Integrity. Emerson said it all when he remarked, "What you are thunders so loudly, I cannot hear a word you say to the contrary." Managers who refuse to try to model in their own behavior what they wish to engender in their people are no leaders at all.

Return on "Inthusiality." One part enthusiasm and one part vitality, "inthusiality" connotes a contagious spirit that the manager has for the importance of the work done. Likert's studies have shown this to be one of *the* characteristics of effective supervisors. "Inthusiality" does not mean the frenetic activity best described as energetic stupidity. Rather, it implies a conviction that the work done is meaningful, though hardly dramatic; contributing, though hardly glamorous.

The leader agrees with the finance experts that ROI refers to the bottom line. He or she, however, is more concerned with those intervening variables that produce the bottom line. Surely, any organization with a climate that stresses the importance of a rich return on ideas, improvement, innovation, individuals, interaction, interface, integrity, and "inthusiality" will have but one problem with its bottom line: it will be surprisingly large!

Myths Regarding Organizational Leadership

If clear notions regarding the real meaning of ROI are essential, it is no less important to get rid of some of the rubbish still surrounding leadership. Here are some of the more common forms of rubbish:

You Gotta Have Personality. Even today, one finds an occasional manager questing for those magical traits that will make him or her a leader. This continues in spite of the fact that, as Jennings concluded, "Fifty years of study have failed to produce one personality trait or set of qualities that can be used to discriminate between leaders and nonleaders." [9] Certainly it is favorable if the manager has, or at least is working on, those behavioral characteristics which Stogdill's massive review of the research shows to be commonly found in leaders: ability to enlist cooperation, administrative ability, attractiveness, cooperativeness, nurturance, popularity, interpersonal skills, social participation, and tact. Task-related traits are also significant: need for achievement, drive for responsibility, initiative, responsibility in pursuit of objectives, and task orientation.[10] It is far more important, however, to actualize more fully those assets that you already possess, to prevent irremediable limitations from causing you to waste time and energy, and to acquire those skills which will make you more effective. This is a far more challenging and rewarding task then chasing some will-o'-the-wisp called personality characteristics.

You Gotta Be Democratic. The contributions of the competent should be sought out. It is essential that people be involved and feel responsible for a decision and its outcome. But democracy is a political philosophy. It is not a theory of management. Besides, there is a danger that a pseudodemocracy, where everything must be reduced to a vote, will take over. As one manager said, "We discuss everything around here unendingly. We discuss and discuss and then come up with a mediocre decision so everyone will be satisfied." Participatory democracy is excellent if it does not degenerate into a popularity contest and if it results in better courses of action. But at times it becomes a "wet-finger" approach to leadership: whichever way the wind blows, the manager bends. One wonders about those managers who are reluctant to take a lonely position based on convictions when such a posture is called for.

You Gotta Have Genes. Whether leaders are born or made is a futile question. One cannot ignore heredity and the blessings and banes that it imposes. Unfortunately, nothing can be done about one's antecedents. More important is the determination of the leader to make the most of what has been inherited. When P. G. Wodehouse was asked how he became such a fine writer, he replied, "I haven't the foggiest notion. But I can assure you of this: I wanted to awfully much." William Penn once said, "No cross, no crown." More important than genes is a willingness to pay one's dues for professionalism. There are no quick fixes in leadership.

You Gotta Be Cute and Clever. This is ths advice of the climber, the manipulator, and the Machiavellian. It is bad advice. There are no truly stupid people, even though we all do stupid things at times. Even people who may be dull in school tend to be bright in life. Trick them once and the relationship is poisoned.

You Gotta Have Charisma. Vince Lombardi, Muhammad Ali, John F. Kennedy, and such folk are fascinating because of that animal magnetism called charisma. There are three things wrong with charisma: (1) no one really knows what it is, (2) no one knows how to acquire or increase it, and (3) it makes the followers dependent and docile, not interdependent and self-assertive. Besides, if you have charisma, you certainly do not need this book.

You Gotta Have the Right Situations. All leadership is situational. The situation is a necessary arena in which the leader must operate. To a considerable extent it can make or break the leader, but to attribute too much to the situation is a mistake. It's better to think of the matter as a pair of scissors. One blade represents what the leaders bring to the situation—their philosophy, education, experience, talents, competence, skills, attitudes, and so on. The other blade represents the situation that provides the leaders with both constraints and opportunities. The skill resides not in the situations but in the managers' deftness at making their behavior congruent with the realities.

You Gotta Be Aggressive. The fact of the matter is that aggressiveness is often the first overreaction of the basically weak. Strong people rarely find it necessary to be more than prudently assertive. Leaders are like experienced physicians. They have a repertoire of behaviors on which they can call to meet the contingencies of a given task or situation. They are flexible rather than the rigid victims of habit. If there is a time for forcefulness, there is also a time for a more subtle approach.

Facts About Organizational Leadership

What the Leader Is Trying to Be

What managers seek to be can be summed up in three words: *appropriate, compatible,* and *consistent.* They try to make their behavior appropriate to the demands of the situation, so that it will be neither an over- nor an underreaction. They endeavor to make their behavior compatible with the task, and with organizational and group realities. This requires a careful analysis of the significant variables before taking action. Finally, leaders strive to be consistent with their personalities and convictions. They may, because it is required, play this or that role for a time. There must, however, be some degree of congruity between values and behavior, management style and leadership strategies. Otherwise, leaders will be perceived as erratic at best, capricious at worst.

Clue Sense

To ensure that their behavior is as appropriate, compatible, and consistent as possible, leaders have three principal guides: *clue sense, cue sense,* and *negotiation sense.* Clue sense is skill in picking up those signals that every organization sends out to the observant. These signals enable the manager to tune in to behavior that is considered valued, rewarded, tolerated, ignored, unacceptable, or intolerable. Without clue sense, which sociologists call sensing ability, theory will amount to naught. In Jennings's terms, clue sense enables leaders to weave their way through the organizational maze getting a maximum of cheese, a minimum of shocks. It is an essential skill if managers are to work smoothly within the parameters of the firm. This matter is more fully discussed in Chapters 4 and 5.

Cue Sense

Cue sense involves the ability to pick up the signals that significant individuals and groups send the manager. Few managers have power to act unilaterally. They need sponsors, supporters, and authorizers of their proposed behavior. Without the cooperation of superiors, peers, and key subordinates, managers will encounter more failure than success. Team building most often refers to subordinates. It is far more important for leaders to build alliances of the proper sort with their associates and upper management levels. These are the people who, more than any others, can negate the manager's best-intentioned efforts.

A lower-level manager was sent to a two-week program about the Managerial Grid®. The program was an exceptional success as far as he was concerned. He returned to the job enthused and eager to experiment with his newly gained learning experiences. Unfortunately, he was completely frustrated. The company had not sent his boss to the same program. All too humanly, the boss perceived the new ideas as a criticism and a threat!

Negotiation Sense

Navigational skills is a descriptive term that has little meaning unless specified in terms of identifiable strategies. If leaders are to be effective, they must seek to bring about win-win relationships with superiors, peers, and subordinates whenever possible. There are four basic strategies available:

Collaborative strategies are used to bring about mutually beneficial cooperation.

Accommodative strategies are useful when the realities of a given situation do not allow for collaborative strategies.

Defensive strategies should be relied on when things do not go as planned, at least temporarily, and the leader is striving to remedy the situation while preserving a win-win orientation.

Assertive strategies are employed when the leader is convinced, or the situation demands, that a more forceful approach should be applied to a problem, decision, or course of action.

These strategies are discussed in detail in Chapter 8.

A Definition of Leadership

There are as many definitions of leadership as there are definers. A simple one states that it is the ability to gain consensus and commitment to common objectives, beyond organizational requirements, which are attained with the experience of contribution and satisfaction on the part of the work group. Thus, manager-leaders strive to surpass corporate expectations. Certain key terms require clarification.

Ability to gain: Leadership is an influence process that enables managers to get their people to do willingly what must be done, do well what ought to be done. But this influence process is rarely unilateral. If you influence your people, they in turn also influence you. In fact, on occasion they may influence your behavior more than you influence theirs.

Consensus and commitment: Lenin once said that 100 organized men, committed to an objective, would conquer 1,000. John Hancock is reported to have stated that he would prefer a decision that was only 50 percent technically correct and that the group would embrace with 90 percent enthusiasm, than a decision that was 90 percent technically correct and that the group would embrace with only 50 percent enthusiasm. These are the reasons why the leader, whenever possible, strives for consensus and commitment rather than the tyranny of the majority of one vote.

To common objectives: This distinguishes leadership from manipulation. The goals of the leader and the subordinates need not be, and rarely can be, identical. But there must be some common objectives if they are to work together. Samuel Gompers, a founder of the American labor movement, stressed this more than 60 years ago.

> The interests of the employer and the employee are in no sense identical. Do not confuse that point. They have not an identity of interest, but they have cooperation of interest—that same cooperation of interest which exists between a manufacturer and his best customer.[11]

Which are attained: Supported by authority, rules, and regulations, according to Koontz, O'Donnell, and Weihrich, you can get people to work at 60 to 65 percent of capacity—just enough to satisfy minimum job requirements. Leadership is a *multiplier factor* that deals with the other 35 to 40 percent. Its aim is to produce results that surpass the ordinary expectations of the organization. A mere administrator can achieve average results. The leader gets superior results from average people.

Experience of contribution and satisfaction: This involves much more than the mere feeling of contribution, success, and satisfaction. Unless your people genuinely *experience* more success than failure, the situation is bleak. Employees must also be stimulated by the quality of your leadership behavior. While the boss, head man, or figurehead is concerned solely for his or her own need satisfaction, the leader makes it possible for the troops to meet some of their significant needs. Thus, leaders are enablers or facilitators.

a knowledge base for leadership: why not learn from the research?

The Voice of Experience

In leadership, as in all skills, experience without a conceptual foundation is as useless as theory without practical application.

The Best Leaders

For several years, I have asked managers at all levels to describe the characteristics of the most effective manager they have ever known. From presidents to supervisors, they tend to cite similar clusters of behaviors. A sample of their comments is presented below.

"He taught me to be critical of my own work, something I'm trying to do with my own people."

"She inspired confidence by having respect for and confidence in us. Often she thought that I was better than I thought I was."

"He not only accepted new ideas, he went out of his way to encourage them."

"She had a short fuse. But if your evidence was good, she'd let you try something new and give you credit."

"He was the most professional person I've ever worked for. He knew the business backwards and forwards."

"He insisted on high standards of performance but helped us reach them."

"She gave us as much freedom as we could handle."

"He was a good communicator. He kept us updated on things that were important to us."

"She was so well organized that almost by osmosis you learned how to organize your work."

"He made us feel important and he convinced us that our work was important."

The Worst Leaders

The obverse side of this exercise is interesting. A sample of the remarks made follows.

"She was demeaning. You rarely left her office without feeling worse about yourself and angry with her."

"He motivated through fear. As a result, all he got was malicious obedience, the absolute minimum that had to be done."

"She was petty. She nitpicked about things that were trivial."

"He was a politician. He used everyone for his own purposes."

"He was indecisive. He'd never make a decision if he could avoid doing so."

"He was an idea rapist. Any good idea you gave him became his when he brought it to his boss."

"She had a wonderful division of labor. When things went

well, she took all the credit. When they went wrong, you got all the blame."

"He spoke with a forked tongue. He'd tell you one story and a different one to someone else."

"She was unapproachable. She was always too busy to listen to you or give you advice."

These 19 statements give the flavor of the managers' reactions. Certain observations can be made.

1. The memories are charged with feelings. Excellent leaders and terrible leaders always get an emotional reaction.
2. The reactions tend to cluster around two issues: the managerial skills and professionalism of the person and his or her helpfulness and supportiveness.
3. Groups do not mention unusual strengths or weaknesses. Generally, they recall simple behaviors that were motivating or alienating.
4. All groups agree that the worst managers could have improved, gradually substituting constructive for destructive behaviors. Such change would have required no superhuman effort.
5. Under questioning, all groups agree that the best leaders were aware of their impact on others, were open to feedback, knew what they had going for them, and worked hard to curb their negative tendencies. Few or none of these traits were typical of the worst leaders. Despite the unscientific nature of this evidence, the experiences of these managers offer realistic guidelines for the improvement of your leadership behavior.

The Voice of Research

Management research comes in two forms: *boring,* when it produces picayune findings irrelevant to managers' work life; and *beneficial,* when it provides behavioral guidelines for the leader. This section summarizes some of the more significant research in a simple but not simplistic manner to help you apply it to your situation.

Two Dimensions Are All You Need: Behavioral Approaches

In the 1950s, studies were done at the University of Michigan and Ohio State University.[1] Both sets of studies, using different terms, came up with two major dimensions: task achievement orientation and employee satisfaction orientation. The task-oriented manager emphasized organization of the work, definition of each subordinate's role and input, and evaluation of performance. The employee-oriented manager was friendly and supportive and was concerned with the welfare of the work group. Since the two dimensions were assumed to be independent, a supervisor could be rated high on both, low on both, or high on one and low on the other. The ideal condition, it was assumed, was to be rated high on both factors.

Although the evidence was at times conflicting, it was found that task-oriented managers (who initiated structure and were production-centered) often got high productivity, at least for the short term. More importantly, they were rated highly by their superiors—no minor item if managers wish to advance their careers. The hidden costs of such productivity, however, included turnover, absenteeism, and poor morale; in combination, these can represent a substantial dollar loss. Highly humanistic (consideration- and employee-centered) managers usually secured both high productivity and high job satisfaction.

The fact that many later approaches have built on these early studies is a tribute to their contribution. They do, however, raise certain questions. First, focusing on only two variables, to the neglect of other factors, was perhaps too strict a use of Occam's razor. Secondly, little is said in these studies about the personalities and group dynamics of the work groups. And finally, the assumption that a manager can be rated high on both dimensions may contradict personality theory, at least so far as some managers are concerned. Even so, it is interesting how compatible the reactions of the managers already considered are with the findings of these early studies.

Three-Dimensions Are Better Than Two: Personality Approach

Zaleznik emphasizes the personality of the leader.[2] Each of us is both beneficiary and victim of our own psychological history. No one can shrug off his or her psychological development as a snake sheds its skin. Thus, Zaleznik describes three types of managers, each of whom is geared to a certain pattern of behavior. *Person-oriented* leaders prefer activities of a *maintenance* type. Naturally friendly and approachable, these leaders are at home working with people. Their behavior is focused on internally generated organizational problems, its homeostatic purpose being to keep the firm on an even keel so that it can operate smoothly and harmoniously. In contrast, the *task-oriented* managers are more likely to engage in *proactive* behavior. Their fortes are achievement, change, innovation, excellence, competition, and the attainment of challenging objectives. They may step on toes and bruise feelings at times, but this does not perturb them as long as goals are attained.

One manager in a large corporation was called "Wonder Woman" by her envious peers. She was bright, tough-minded, and driving, yet still feminine. When reminded by her boss that she was hard on her people, she pointed out that her subordinates not only had the finest record in the division but also had the best promotion rate. She then asked, not so innocently, "Would you have me behave in such a way as to lower these accomplishments?" Interestingly, she was later done in by her associates despite her achievements.

The third type, the *fusion-oriented* manager, relates best to activities of the *mediative* sort, those that call for marshaling the resources of the company to cope with the demands made on it by the environment. It would appear that these managers have the best of all worlds, but not necessarily. Although able to work energetically, while taking people into account, they may be overly conventional and reactive.

Zaleznik goes on to point out that managers and leaders tend to be different types of people, with differing attitudes toward their goals, careers, relations with others, and themselves. Managers maintain a steady, stable, efficient operation. Leaders create new ideas and approaches for change and innovation. This concept is interesting but perhaps overly dichotomous. One can be a managerial leader. The roles are distinct, not necessarily separate.

Four Dimensions Are Better Than Three: Contingency Approach

The key idea for Fiedler is *favorableness of the situation.*[3] This is the result of three major factors: (1) *leader-member relations*—the respect and trust the manager has earned, (2) *task structure*—the extent to which the work is programmed, and (3) *position power*—the reward-punishment resources of the leader. A lesser consideration is the *homogeneity* of the work group—similarity of outlook and background both within the group and between it and the leader. The ideal situation is one where a trusted, respected leader interacts with a homogeneous work group in an operation that is governed by standard procedures and for which he or she has great position power. Many manufacturing and office operations are in this category. The least favorable situation is one where the leader is disliked by a heterogeneous group, manages a task that is ill-defined, and has little reward-punishment power on which to rely.

Fiedler's approach has many advantages. First, it allows for a range of behaviors, while destroying some common stereotypes about leadership. For instance, in both highly favorable and highly unfavorable situations it is advisable for the manager to be directive, but for different reasons. Highly respected leaders *can* be directive because their groups expect to be told what to do and are ready to follow orders. No fledging resident expects a noted surgeon to consult with him or her as to what should be done next. On the other hand, rebuffed leaders *must* be controlling: they have no other recourse. Managers in the intermediate range of favorableness, being neither greatly accepted nor rejected, should be consultative, perhaps even permissive. For instance, if you were brought in to head up a new venture, you might be well advised to get all the suggestions you could from your people. Once specific plans, strategies, and programs were formulated, however, you should shift to a much more directive mode.

Organizationally, too, Fiedler's findings have much in their favor. Any firm has five alternatives. (1) It can select only those managers whose leadership style is compatible with that esteemed by the firm. This entails the loss of many good people. (2) It can try to get managers to change their personalities, a fatuous endeavor at best. (3) It can place people in situations best suited to their natural leadership style. Although this can be done at times, on a grand scale it could be highly disruptive. (4) It can train managers to alter their styles—a useful undertaking but one that is usually costly, time-consuming, and difficult. There is also the danger of "regression to the familiar," that after training, managers will revert to the old habits with which they are comfortable. (5) It can engineer the job to fit the person, working with the four variables so as to get the best fit possible. According to Fiedler, this last approach is often the most realistic. In essence, Fiedler's research supports an old saying, "If you cannot change the person, then change the person's position."

Five Dimensions Are Best of All: Path-Goal Approach

This is the latest theory to come over the horizon. It is important for the simple reason that it is the only one emphasizing leadership *from the followers' viewpoint* and how the leader should behave in light of their perceptions and feelings. It hinges on three major concepts.[4]

1. *Valence.* People are reasonably logical. They will perform well only if by so doing they obtain valued rewards. Hence, the incentives and rewards that the leader provides must be

attractive to them. (This is discussed further in Chapter 10.)

2. *Expectancy.* People, being fairly smart, "play the odds." They make subjective probability estimates regarding their ability to perform as required and the likelihood that they will receive their valued outcomes if they perform well.

3. *Instrumentality.* The rewards for high performance are not ends in themselves. People perceive such rewards as a pay increase or a promotion as a means to attaining more important objectives—a better life-style or a better education for their children. Thus, first-level outcomes are instrumental in achieving second-level goals.

The role of the manager is the fourth dimension in this theory. The leader engages in four types of behavior, depending on the situation. *Instrumental* behavior includes organizing the work flow, making sure that subordinates know what is expected of them and how they will be evaluated. All must understand that the attainment of their desired outcomes is contingent on appropriate performance. (This is also called initiating structure.) *Supportive* behavior, also called consideration, involves building a warm, helpful climate, removing roadblocks to performance, and facilitating subordinate efforts to perform and achieve. *Participative* behavior includes consulting with subordinates, keeping them informed, providing feedback, and using group approaches to problem solving and decision making when appropriate. And *achievement-oriented* behavior involves setting challenging and meaningful objectives, while having confidence in subordinates' ability to attain them.

Finally, *subordinates and situations* are the fifth dimension. If there are many roads to Rome, there are also many paths to employee performance and satisfaction. Highly structured tasks, machine-paced and characterized by repetition, sameness, and potential boredom, call for friendly, interactive, socially supportive behavior—praise, interaction, friendliness, even tension-reducing banter. On the other hand, tasks that are ambiguous or high-risk in nature call for a more directive approach. Moreover, subordinates who have a high need for autonomy and/or are very competent will resent close, controlling behavior. Those who are less skilled or lacking in self-assurance may appreciate it, provided it is perceived as helpful, guiding, and supportive. The implications of these approaches are more fully explained in Chapters 9 and 10.

Some Attempted Syntheses

Several researchers have attempted to bring these factors together in ways that make sense. A few of their theories are listed in the paragraphs that follow.

Life-Cycle Approach

Hersey and Blanchard employ the familiar dimensions of concern for task (productivity) and concern for relationships (people) as the basis of their theory.[5] Task-oriented behavior does not mean being harsh, cold, or unfriendly. It refers to the leader's focus and input. Similarly, people-oriented behavior does not mean becoming "one of the boys." It refers to psychological support, facilitating behavior, and "strokes." The central idea in this approach is the *task-relevant maturity* of the group. There are two kinds of maturity. *Job maturity* connotes competence, achievement motivation, and willingness to assume responsibility. *Psychological maturity* connotes self-respect, self-confidence, and self-esteem.

In a sense, the leader's actions are the dependent variable, and the maturity of the group is the independent variable. The attitudes and behavior of subordinates cue the manager in on how he or she should interact with them. It is an application of the old saying that one learns to lead by following: the manager must follow the cues of the work group. For instance, with new employees, or those who are antagonistic or lethargic, the leader should focus on getting the job done (high task orientation, low relationship orientation). As the new employees learn to do the job, or as uncooperative employees change their attitudes, the leader can move to giving more emotional support (still relatively high task emphasis but high relationship orientation). As the troops mature even more, the leader can lessen the emphasis on task and invest more effort in getting them involved. Finally, as subordinates become very mature, the manager can lessen both task concern and concern for relationships. With increasing employee maturity, the leader shifts from being directive (telling), to emphasizing relationships (selling), to using a consultative approach (participating), to letting people run their own show (delegating).

The advantage of this model is threefold. First, the work group *owns the problem*. If workers want to be consulted or to participate in decision making, all they need do is demonstrate sufficient maturity, and the manager will let them. Secondly, this model enables the leader to change his or her behavior as subordinate maturity increases or decreases, which will always happen as long as people are not machines. And finally, the model impels the executive to deal with reality, rather than try to impose his or her self-centered ideas on it.

The Vroom and Yetton Approach

Instead of concentrating on such factors as productivity and satisfaction, Vroom and Yetton focus on how to get decisions made and implemented.[6] Logistically, they start with seven questions regarding the problem: (1) Does it have a quality requirement? (2) Is it structured? (3) Do I have enough information? (4) Is subordinate acceptance important? (5) If I make the decision, am I reasonably certain that subordinates will accept it? (6) Do subordinates share organizational goals in solving the problem? (7) Is there likely to be conflict regarding preferred solutions?

Using these criteria, managers have three strategies available. The *autocratic* strategy involves either solving problems themselves using whatever information is at hand, or obtaining specific data from their people before making the decision themselves. The *consultative* strategy involves either sharing the problem with relevant individuals and getting their suggestions and ideas before making the decision, or using a consultative mode in a group setting. Finally, the *group process* involves acting as a catalyst so that the group reaches consensus. Two conditions, in addition to the seven listed earlier, are significant. If *time* is of the essence, then a more autocratic approach may be best. This would be true of emergency situations and those that require time-effectiveness in terms of man-hours devoted to the process. If *development of subordinates* is the critical issue, then a more participative approach may be in order. As Vroom and Yetton state, "He [the manager] is neither universally autocratic nor universally participative but utilizes either approach in response to the demands of the situation *as he perceives* them."

A Revised Viewpoint: Tannenbaum and Schmidt

In a classic 1958 article, updated in 1973, Tannenbaum and Schmidt present a spectrum of alternative behaviors open to the manager depending on four variables. *Forces in the manager* include his or her value system, leadership preference, feeling of security in uncertain situations, and confidence in his or her people. *Forces in the work group* include their competence, readiness to assume responsibility, expectations, tolerance of ambiguity, interest in the problem, feeling that it is important, and degree of identification with organizational goals. *Forces in the situation* include the nature of the problem, time pressures, climate, the philosophy, traditions, and mores of the firm, and group effectiveness. And *priorities among objectives* are another variable: is the manager chiefly interested in improving the quality of the decision-making process? developing teamwork? increasing motivation and morale? helping subordinate growth? or facilitating subordinate acceptance of change? [7]

Stressing the interdependence of these factors, these authorities offer the following strategies for the leader.

1. Managers make the decisions and people accept them.
2. Managers must sell their decisions to get people to accept them.
3. They present tentative decisions subject to change and respond to questions.
4. They present the problems, consult with subordinates, and then decide.
5. They set limits, then allow the work group to decide.

6. They and their subordinates jointly decide within organizational constraints.

Obviously, the continuum ranges from direction to collaboration to subordinate autonomy. This model provides a range of behaviors on which you can rely.

What You Can Do to Improve Your Leadership

There is no magic formula for effective leadership, but you can take several positive steps to improve your behavior.

Be Simple but Not Simplistic. Leadership behavior takes place in the midst of an amazing number of force fields, including the following:

Organizational. These include the firm's philosophy, traditions, mores, climate, and ways of operating.

Technical. The types of tasks in a large company are numerous, each making its own demands and imposing its own discipline.

Work units. Groups vary widely with respect to their identity with organizational goals, attitudes toward the organization, pressures to conform, norms of behavior, reward-punishment systems, cohesiveness, and homogeneity.

Individual. Each subordinate has his or her unique pattern of needs, wants, aspirations, motivations, strengths, weaknesses, and goals.

Managerial. Every leader heads a team, is linked with peers, and reports to superiors. Each has his or her own idea of effectiveness, proper interaction, and acceptable behavior.

Moreover, the psychological history of managers, their philosophies of life and management, and their leadership style preferences steer their perceptions and actions. So resist the temptation to seek a quick leadership injection.

Develop Your Clue Sense. Diagnosis precedes understanding, and insight precedes action. In a relaxed manner, analyze the force fields that impinge on you, so that you will have an appreciation of the realities with which you must wrestle. This requires concentrated effort rather than great talent.

Develop Your Cue Sense. Power and influence take different forms and are unevenly distributed throughout any organization. Be sensitive to the signals that powerful groups and individuals send you. Build the right kind of alliances with key power figures, whether they are decision makers, recommenders, influencers, or implementers. If coordination and collaboration are to be meaningful, you must navigate within the system. This is not nasty politics but intelligent statesmanship.

Use the Known Research. Different work groups react positively to different mixes of structure and consideration. The task maturity of your work force is critical in selecting the appropriate behavior, and so are the chemistry between you and it, the power you possess, and the nature of the task. Finally, your subordinates will not extend themselves unless they perceive cooperating with you as an efficient path to immediate satisfactions and the attainment of rewards they value.

Define Your Input. You must meet the expectations of your superiors, or else your career will be nil. You must work harmoniously with your peers, or else they will frustrate you. You must initiate structure for your people, or else they will resent the resultant chaos. You must facilitate their progress, or else they will give only half-hearted effort. You must create a supportive climate, or else they will become disheartened.

Experiment. Habit often makes us blind to a better way. The research has provided you with a broad spectrum of possible behaviors: directive, achievement-oriented, supportive, consultative, participative, delegative, permissive, and group-process-oriented. Since we all tend to regress to the comfortable, it is necessary to experiment prudently with types of behavior that are not natural to you. Subordinate feedback will tell you which behaviors are best for which situations, in *your* organization, in *your* unit, with *your* task accountabilities, with *your* work force. Human beings do not learn by trial and error. They learn by experimentation and discovery. Those who will not experiment will not learn.

Make the Most of What You Have. Evolve strategies to capitalize more fully on your assets. Recognize those limitations that can be changed, and formulate strategies for remedying them. Stop pining for what can never be and learn to live calmly with those weaknessess that cannot be altered.

Make Your Impact. Leaders are not mere responders to circumstances, nor are they merely reactive to force fields. They make things happen, bring about changes for the better, and contribute critically needed input. Although it is foolish to equate managerial leadership with that which is appropriate to an NFL football game, there is always an *inspirational* element in true leadership. People must be convinced that their jobs are significant. Your task is threefold. You must set a climate that thunders loudly that the work we do is important. You must set a positive tone that helps employees identify with the mission and goals of the organization, division, or department. And you must model in your own behavior, as far as this is possible, the respect you have for each employee and the regard you have for his or her contribution. When leadership loses its inspirational element, it degenerates into lifeless administration.

Ask the Right Questions. Answer for yourself such questions as the following:

— In leading my people, what precisely am I trying to achieve for the short term? for the long term?
— What strategies have I relied on in the past? What results, positive or negative, have they produced? What changes should I make?
— Why do my subordinates work at all? Why do they work in this organization? in this department? What are they seeking from their work? from me? from one another? Remember that no two people make the same demands, or have the same expectations, regarding their jobs.
— What are they learning from the way I manage them? What kinds of human beings are they becoming?

— If I were to leave the organization, what would be the reactions and feelings of my superiors? associates? employees?

Answers to these questions require sober reflection and willingness to change your behavior where improvements should be made.

Be Patient with Yourself. Behavior is changed slowly and with effort; attitudes change even more slowly. If it is essential to be persistent, it is no less necessary to be patient with progress. In this sense, by the yard, it's hard; by the inch, it's a cinch!

A reasonable question at this juncture is, *"How* do I do all this?"* The best answers are worked out by you. However, the remaining chapters will try to facilitate your efforts.

a smorgasbord of leaders: where do you fit in?

A Formal View of the Manager's Job

Management is the scientific art of attaining intended organizational objectives by working effectively with and through the human and material resources of the firm. Thus, management as a process is a sine qua non in any organization, be it a corporation, church, prison, or hospital.

The job of managers is first to determine what is to be done and second to see that it gets done, whether they go about these tasks in a democratic, autocratic, or other fashion. Their responsibility is to ensure that needed corporate inputs are provided to achieve overall goals while coordinating these inputs with those of other departments in order to facilitate the work of the whole organization. Beyond this, the manager's role is that of a change agent, introducing innovations that will enhance the performance and promote the improvement of the work group, changes that would not occur in his or her absence. If they would take place without the manager, then he or she is merely an overseer with a high-sounding title and is probably overpaid.

A standardized litany of managers' ritual responsibilities can easily be formulated.

1. They *plan*, for if the thinkers do not think ahead, the doers will have nothing to do that is worth their time and energy. Managers try to anticipate the future so as to control it if possible, to capitalize on the opportunities that the future always offers the thoughtful and denies the unthinking, or at the very least to avoid becoming its victim.

2. They *organize* the manpower, money, machines, methods, and materials of the firm into well-integrated units so that objectives may be attained with a maximum of efficiency and a minimum of wasted effort.

3. They *staff* not merely to get today's job done but, more importantly, to ensure that the human resources of the company will develop so as to enable it to enjoy increasing prosperity.

4. They *direct* by allocating authority, by determining necessary functions, by assigning personnel to specific tasks, by allowing key people the autonomy to perform and achieve, by setting criteria for acceptable output, and by exacting accountability for results according to those criteria.

5. They *coordinate* the work of individuals and groups so that they operate as a unified whole.

6. They *gain cooperation* from and among their people by arranging conditions so that they can achieve organizational ends while satisfying some of their job-related needs, by giving an example, and by creating a climate of cooperation and mutual assistance.

7. They *control* the efforts of their subordinates by maintaining a feedback system that provides valid data early enough in the game to allow corrective action and reward or punishment of performance on the basis of justice rather than of politics or charity.

8. They *review* and evaluate the work of their people informally and formally not merely to satisfy the requirements of the firm but also to help subordinates become more productive and more valuable to the organization.

9. They *lead* their people so as to stimulate them to do willingly what must be done and do well what might otherwise be done in a barely acceptable manner.

10. They *budget* the four major assets they have going for

them—time, thought, talent, and behavior—to make certain that both they and the firm secure the best possible return on investment, with the corporation getting at least a fair and adequate return on its dollar.

An Informal View of the Manager's Job

Whereas no one would find much to criticize in these ten commandments of the manager's job, they suffer from over-simplification. They are too neat and tidy. As all managers know and all business school graduates are destined to discover to their dismay, rules never seem to work out as formulated. They concentrate on what managers should do rather than on what they actually do, often perforce, in that zoo we call a company or department. They give a platonic description of the ideal firm under ideal conditions in which the executives are masters of their fate and captains of their souls.

The evident truth is that managers spend as much time and energy reacting as acting, and perhaps more. They are involved and embedded in an amazing variety of relationships, few of which they can directy or solely control. A more realistic description of the day-to-day job of managers, as Sayles has pointed out, might read as follows:

1. They *work to implement* their personal career plans, using the firm as a vehicle for so doing while seeking to meet its requirements.

2. They *endeavor to be sensitive* to the expressed (or more often implied) expectations of their immediate superiors. They seek to tune in on new pressures, new developments, and new requirements that may subtly or sharply alter how they go about their work.

3. They *negotiate* continuously with peers in other departments with whom their own departments are interdependent to get the total job done effectively.

4. They *cultivate* good relations with staff and service groups whose attitudes and actions can make their jobs easier or harder, for they realize that at times support groups have the ear of the throne.

5. They *respond* to the requests, demands, and requirements of significant individuals and groups in their occupational life space so as to retain these people's goodwill or at least not alienate them. They must be flexible in adjusting to an astounding variety of personalities, cliques and in-groups, parochial loyalties, expertise, and eccentricities.

6. They *oversee* the flow of work into, within, and out of their departments to ensure that it proceeds with a minimum of interruption or static that may draw unwanted attention from superiors.

7. They *are alert* to the work output, needs, desires, and morale of their subordinates, interacting with them, yet maintaining a managerial position.

8. They *represent* subordinates and their views in dealing with superiors and other departments.

9. They *try to retain control* over their own lives while accommodating themselves to the legitimate demands of the organization. They must establish a valid order of priorities, balancing out what is rightly due to their firms, their families, and themselves.

10. They *attempt to cope* adequately with their own tensions so as to receive a fair share of psychic as well as economic income from their work.

11. They *strive to attain* valued organizational rewards, which they use instrumentally to secure more important off-the-job goals.

The Realities of the Manager's Life Space

Managers, as described in at least some textbooks, are like the abominable snowman—often depicted but rarely encountered. The ideal state is one in which they define their tasks, budget their time, control their activities, and reflect on the future while attending to the present. The research data yield a somewhat different picture. Mintzberg studied a small group of CEOs, while Peters investigated the decision-making processes in two dozen corporations in the United States and Western Europe. Their findings are generally compatible and include the following points.

1. Mintzberg concluded that managers work at an unrelenting pace. Brevity, variety, interruption, discontinuity, and fragmentation characterize the day's activities. This seems to be true at all levels. Guest found that foremen averaged 583 incidents a day. Stewart, in a four-week study of 160 managers, found that they averaged only nine periods of at least one-half hour without interruption. Mintzberg's subjects completed half of their activities in less than nine minutes.[1]

2. The CEOs averaged 36 written and 16 verbal contacts each day, almost every one of which dealt with a separate issue.

3. They spent from one-third to one-half of contact time with subordinates, most often in responding to requests, giving or receiving information, or making strategy. Only one verbal contact out of 14 was held on a scheduled basis; the other 13 were of an ad hoc variety. Of an average of nine pieces of outgoing mail each day, only one was initiated by the CEO; the other eight were responsive in nature.

4. The CEOs had catch-up days, crisis days, heavily scheduled days, normal days, and few free days.

5. Peters found that top-level managers rarely got a look at a proposal when the options were still wide open.[2] Instead of being presented with a wide range of alternatives, they usually were confronted with what amounted to a single choice of the yes-no variety. Moreover, they spent considerable time fighting fires. The organizational filtering process tended to shield them from really bad news other than that of a numerical nature. Finally, they rarely gave public commitment to a choice until its wisdom was no longer seriously questioned and it was organizationally agreeable. Because of this they sometimes seemed to vacillate for months or even years.

The picture of the manager, then, is that of a person with a job that is largely unstructured and open-ended. The consequential gets intermingled with the trivial, so that superficiality is an occupational hazard. Managers live by making things happen within deadlines. Things often get done not by order of importance but because of dire necessity. People continually compete for their time, attention, and energy. They are not so much masters of their fate as action-oriented originators, information-processing and -disseminating machines, adaptive strategists, and flexible, fast-moving responders to the pressures of the position and the requests of organizational claimants. Despite all this, however, they get results that add surplus and value to the organization and its constituencies.

Successful versus Effective Leaders

Bass has made a needed distinction among three types of leadership behavior. *Attempted leadership* is any effort the manager makes to influence superiors, associates, or subordinates. *Successful leadership* is the ability to get others to behave as the manager intended. The job gets done and the manager's needs are satisfied, but those of the other people are ignored. Finally, in *effective leadership* people perform in accordance with the manager's intention and find this a path to the satisfaction of their needs. Clearly one can be successful through coercion, dominance, threats, manipulation, fear, trickery, or persuasion. It is equally clear that successful leadership yields only short-term results and requires "snoopervision" rather than supervision. Thus, success has to do only with getting the job done, whereas effectiveness adds the concept of satisfaction on the part of those who do the job.

Leaders Who Are Merely Successful

Let's face it, research data are helpful but often tedious and difficult to understand. On the other hand, more colorful descriptions of managers are interesting because they have a flesh-and-blood aura about them. Because it is easier for managers to identify with real-life leaders, it might be well to examine the strengths and the weaknesses of those executives who are merely successful vis-à-vis those who are effective. The observations are drawn largely, but hardly exclusively, from such authorities as Jennings, McMurry, Downes, Fromm, Zaleznik, Reddin, and Maccoby.[3] Figure 1 sum-

Figure 1. **Leaders who are merely successful.**

Executive	Motto	Characteristics	Typical Behavior
Bureaucrat	"We go by the book."	Rational, formal, impersonal, politely proper, disciplined. May be slow-moving and/or jealous of his or her function, rights, and prerogatives. Well versed in the organizational "rocks and shoals."	Follows the letter of the law. Stickler for rules and procedures. Task-oriented, less concerned with people. Logical strategist but may be politically astute and/or a nit-picker.
Zealot	"We do things my way, in spite of the organization."	A loner. Impatient, outspoken, overly independent, extremely competent. Jumps the traces, a nuisance to the bureaucrats. Insensitive to the feelings of others. Modest political skills. Fair but demanding.	Devoted to the good of the organization, *as he or she sees it.* Excessively task-oriented but has little concern for people. Aggressive and domineering. Is insistent but fiercely supports all who are on his or her side.
Machiavellian	"We depersonalize and use you."	Self-oriented, shrewd, devious, calculating, amoral, manipulative. Excellent insight into people's weaknesses. Extremely opportunistic. Flexible, ranges from seeming collaboration to pitiless aggression. Cold but can be charming.	Treats people as things to be exploited and outwitted. Cooperates only when it is to his or her advantage. Personal considerations do not enter into thinking. Must win at any price and in any way possible.
Missionary	"We love one another."	Much too concerned with people and what they think of him or her. Subjective in orientation. Likable but tries too hard to be liked. Excellent interpersonal skills but does not win respect. Insists that conflict and friction be smoothed over.	A soft manager who prizes harmony above all else. Low task orientation. Gets emotionally involved. Acts on a personal basis. Tends to do what is popular or will make him or her liked. Inclined to ignore harder organizational requirements.

Type	Motto	Description	
Climber	"I vault over anyone I can."	Striving, driving, energetic, self-oriented. Often smooth and polished but always aggressive. Usually opportunistic, always plotting next move or maneuver. No loyalty to the organization or to anyone in it. Often quite competent. Constantly fronts self.	High political skills. Excellent at maneuvering into the limelight. Predatory toward weaker managers. Welcomes and initiates self-propelling change. May have high task orientation but for self-serving purposes, not for the good of the firm. Adroit with people but has no interest in them.
Exploiter	"When I bark, they jump."	Arrogant, insistent, abusive. Demeaning, coercive, vindictive, domineering. Often quite competent. Rigid, prejudiced, given to snap judgments. Exploits others' weaknesses.	Exerts constrictive and personal controls. Flogs anyone who is vulnerable. Uses pressure and fear to get things done. Demands subservience. High task orientation. Sees people as minions.
Temporizer	"We bend to the strongest pressure."	Procrastinating, compromising, vacillating. Earns contempt. Feels a helpless sense of being put upon. Survival instincts may be superior. May be politically aware.	Low task orientation, low people concern. Reacts to the strongest immediate pressure. Reactive, not active. Behavior varies with pressures.
Glad-Hander	"We sell the sizzle, not the steak."	Ebullient, superficial, effusive, deceptively friendly, extroverted. Excellent interpersonal skills. Lacks depth, minimally competent. May be an excellent politician. Survival instincts superior. Talkative, humorous, lacks substance.	Sells himself or herself very well. Low or modest task orientation. Unconcerned with people but excellent in dealing with them. Gets by on "personality." Always seeks to impress and to improve his or her position. May use people but rarely threatens them.

marizes the characteristics and typical behavior of successful managers. A brief description of each is in order.

The Bureaucrat

Those who are quick to criticize bureaucracy often forget three things. First, bureaucracy was a quantum leap forward from the whimsical and capricious management style of the old entrepreneurial owner. Second, increasing size and complexity inevitably bring bureaucratic tendencies. Finally, Weber, who made the landmark study of bureaucracy, foresaw with dismay its almost predestined deficiencies. Be that as it may, the bureaucrat's self-image is that of a rational, well-trained person who operates within a well-defined structure, according to well-established policies, procedures, and rules. However, as Thompson has pointed out, there may be anxiety accompanied by a desire to overcontrol, resistance to change, exaggerated aloofness, insistence on the rights of office, over-concern with minor details, and fear of the new and creative.[4] Although individual eccentricity is discouraged, bureaucrats may engage in politicking and jockeying for position far more than the average manager. Accordingly, these conservative standpatters may be difficult to deal with.

The Zealot

Every organization needs at least one zealot, but organizations with many show evidence of masochistic tendencies. Evangelistic in their insistence that their unit be the best, zealots have an apostolic fervor for their pet projects. Zealots are likely to be organizational loners, listening to the beat of their own drummers. As a result, they attract a relatively small group of like-minded but weaker key subordinates whose loyalty may be more provincial than organizational. Not surprisingly, the zealot's team tends to perceive other organizational units as friends or enemies. Zealots are often at odds with higher authority because of their proclivity for ignoring standard operating procedures and sandpapering the sensibilities of others. Although they make dreadful top administrators, their single-mindedness makes them excellent heads of special ventures that must be pushed through under strict time, cost, or pressure constraints. They are also efficient in revitalizing apathetic departments and in getting radical changes accomplished quickly and well.

The Machiavellian

Although the research on the Machiavellian is considerable, little is said of this character in management books. Since you will certainly have to contend with one of them somewhere along the way, you should understand some of their outstanding characteristics.[5]

They concentrate on winning as much as they can in zero-sum games by using power, not rational, strategies. Always exploitive, they can still be quite cooperative, even ethical, when it is to their advantage.

They have little faith in human nature. They think of people as basically gullible targets, to be manipulated to the extent that circumstances allow. They are suspicious of the motives of others.

They are tough negotiators. They test limits, have high demands, and yield only when forced to do so. Even when they present a facade of being reasonable, they have contempt for those who accommodate or compromise.

They read people well without being readable themselves. Their social and interpersonal skills are of a high order. They are more verbal than others, especially when it comes to beating around the bush. They control their behavior better than most people, lie more plausibly, are impervious to the influence of others, and often "look innocent," as though they had nothing to conceal.

They are cool, pragmatic calculators, concentrating on what works. They can shift roles according to the requirements of the situation. Their behavior is based on maximizing the payoff, not on human considerations.

Small wonder that the research shows that the Machiavellian usually triumphs in dealing with people who are more agreeable and reasonable!

The Missionary

At the opposite pole from the Machiavellian is the missionary who conducts a soul-saving clinic on company premises. Overly involved with their people, missionaries seek peace, harmony, and intimacy at all costs. Likable, they try too hard to be accepted. Their superior interpersonal skills may fail to gain them respect. Friction is smoothed over but not resolved. As a result, they may do what is popular or procrastinate in the hope that things will work themselves out. They are likely to be unduly understanding of the subordinate's viewpoint, especially if he or she is dependent, to the neglect of the organization's legitimate requirements.

The Climber

The climber is both similar to, and different from, the Machiavellian. Competent, politically astute, smooth, and perhaps charming, these self-propelled individuals are always plotting their next maneuvers. Lacking loyalty to the organization, their superiors, or their associates, except when it is to their benefit, they strive to move up the ladder, masking their aggression under a facade of cooperation. They welcome any change if it is self-enhancing. Emotionally shallow and rootless, they market themselves, front themselves, and maneuver themselves into the limelight. For them, careerism *is* success!

The Exploiter

The exploiter comes in two forms: abuser or protector. Abusers are autocrats who may possess great competence. But they are arrogant, vindictive, and rigid. They govern by intimidation and motivate through fear. They require not so much obedience as obeisance. They are martinets who think of subordinates as minions, immediately disposable should they affront their boss's delicate ego.

Protectors are paternalistic managers who think of themselves as the benevolent father (or mother) figure of a happy company family. Supportive and considerate, they are also quite possessive and emotionally smothering. They bind their people with silken threads of personal loyalty, sometimes at the expense of the best interests of the organization. Since father knows best, new ideas are heard but not heeded, and disagreement is oiled over without being resolved. The protector controls by conditional love. So long as his or her work group behaves as prescribed, the protector supports and shields it. Let it attempt to be independent, and his or her reaction is likely to be quite negative.

The Temporizer

To temporize is often an effective and wise strategy. However, to be a temporizer whose outstanding characteristics are vacillation, procrastination, and indecision is to make a mockery of both management and leadership. Everyone has encountered temporizers somewhere along the way, so little need be said, except to note that their survival instincts may be superior and their political skills above average. After all, even the weakest of managers need survival tactics.

The Glad-Hander

This type of leader makes a superb first impression. He or she is superficially friendly, socially skilled, likable, and outgoing. The problem is that behind this engaging facade there is little substance. Soon one realizes that glad-handers deal only in win-lose relationships, using people for their own purposes. They are much like rainbows—attractive, colorful, and enjoyable, but all this is merely cosmetic and lacks depth.

Leaders Who Are Effective

Figure 2 summarizes the characteristics and behaviors of those leaders who generally are not only successful but effective. A word about each may make the matter clear.

The Entrepreneur

Extremely competent, entrepreneurs are best suited either to launching a new organization or to turning around one that has come on bad times. They do not so much meet competition as devour it. Their risk-taking potential is exceeded only by their achievement drive; thus, they are likely to be workaholics and enjoy every minute of it. Forceful, driving builders, they are willing to meet any challenge, pay any price for personal and organizational success. They are originators and innovators who are almost always highly individualistic, firm-minded, and strong-willed—sometimes too much so. If they are demanding, they can also be quite supportive at times. If they inspire fear, they also earn respect. Unfortunately, entrepreneurs are not team builders: they tend to *be* the team. As a result, they rarely develop strong understudies. As long as they are in the saddle things go well. The chances are, however, that they will leave weakened organizations for the simple reason that they subconsciously feel infallible and eternal.

The Corporateur

Corporateurs possess the spirit of the entrepreneur and the skills necessary to run a large organization. Dominant but not domineering, polished but not phony, assertive but rarely aggressive, they are professional managers. Their achievement orientation is high. They relate well to subordinates without becoming emotionally involved with them. They are directive but not overcontrolling, giving their people ample autonomy within strict boundaries. They feel comfortable with a consultative approach, less so with one that is participative. The climate set by corporateurs is tough-minded yet supportive. They reward achievers generously, while prodding laggards implacably. This is easy for them because they treat their key subordinates in a cordial but impersonal manner.

The Developer

Excellent teachers, coaches, and counselors, developers make their impact by helping employees realize their potential. Their motto seems to be, "Help each subordinate grow, and high productivity is ensured." As a result, the work environment is warm and friendly. Unfortunately, at times human considerations may have a higher priority than less pleasant organizational requirements. Developers are liked and respected by the work group. In fact, the personal loyalty that they engender may occasionally interfere with the optimum attainment of the firm's goals. Be that as it may, anyone who has at some time had a developer for a boss has fond memories.

The Craftsman

According to Maccoby, craftsmen are generally found at the middle or lower levels of a firm, in some technical function.[6] Their motivation stems principally from the work itself and the drive to do something as well as it can be done. Their self-esteem derives from their excellent knowledge, skills, and self-reliance. Life is interesting when they are solving difficult problems and developing new projects. However, they are not completely comfortable with the currents and eddies of corporate complexities. Lacking hunger for power, they compete with challenges rather than with peers. Self-contained and independent, their political skills are of a lower order. Thus, they make no great demands on the company if they are given challenging work to perform and freedom to do it as they see fit. Again, anyone who has at one time reported to a craftsman has pleasant reminiscences.

Figure 2. **Leaders who are effective.**

Executive	Motto	Characteristics	Typical Behavior
Entrepreneur	"We do it my way. Only risk-taking achievers need apply."	Extremely competent, forceful, individualistic, egocentric, dominant, self-confident. Extraordinary achievement drive. Innovative, very firm-minded and strong-willed. Something of a loner. Not only listens to his or her own drummer but composes his or her own music. Can be very loyal, protective, and generous to team.	Unable to work well in a subordinate position for very long. Must be prime mover and binds small team to him or her with great loyalty. Offers challenges, opportunities to succeed, and great returns on risks taken. Does not develop subordinates. Is not open to ideas that differ from his or her own. Gets involved in all aspects of the organization. Exercises very tight control. Motivates by example, rewards, and fear.
Corporateur	"I call the shots, but we all work together on my team."	Dominant but not domineering. Quite directive but gives people considerable freedom. Consultative but not really participative. Sizes up people well but relates to them on a surface level. Cordial to people but keeps them at arm's length.	Concerned about the good of the organization. Wins respect. High task orientation. Polished and professional manager. Makes people feel needed. Delegates and consults but keeps effective control. Supportive but not emotionally involved with subordinates.
Developer	"People are our most important resource."	Trustful of subordinates. Intent on helping them actualize their potential. Excellent human relations skills. Wins personal loyalty, builds a supportive and achieving climate. Fine coach and counselor.	Very high people orientation. Although productivity is superior, at times people considerations may take precedence. People feel needed. Delegates and consults but keeps effective control. Supportive and emotionally involved with subordinates.

Craftsman	"We do important work as perfectly as we can."	Amiable, conservative, extremely conscientious. Principled, very knowledgeable and skilled, self-reliant. Highly task-oriented. Proud of competence. Work- and family-oriented. Self-contented, honest, straightforward, perfectionistic, independent, analytical, mild-mannered.	Likes to innovate, build, and tinker with quality products. Not overly concerned with status or politics. Motivated by a desire for excellence. Self-demanding but supportive of subordinates. Competes with projects, not people. Restive with organizational red tape. Likes to solve problems alone or in a small group.
Integrator	"We build consensus and commitment."	Egalitarian, supportive, participative. Excellent interpersonal skills. Superior people insight. A team builder, catalyst, adept at unifying different inputs. A subtle leader, prefers group decision making.	Shares the leadership. Thinks in terms of associates rather than subordinates. Gives great freedom and authority. Welcomes the ideas of others. Geared to win-win interaction. Acts as a synergistic catalyst.
Gamesman	"We win together, but I must win more than you."	Fast-moving, flexible, upwardly mobile. Very knowledgeable and skilled. Autonomous, risk-taking, assertive, and intent on winning but not petty or vindictive. Innovative. Takes no great pleasure in another's loss or defeat. Opportunistic but not unethical, not depressed by defeat.	Wants to be respected as a strategist who builds a winning team. Enjoys the game of winning within the organization's rules. Enjoys competition, jockeying, and maneuvering. Sharp, skilled, unbiased, and tough manager who challenges and rewards contribution. Impersonally eliminates the weak and nonachievers.

The Integrator

All the previously discussed forms of leadership connote some element of dependence on the part of the followers, however subtle it may be. In collegial management, the leader is *first among his or her peers.* The upper echelons of complex organizations, for example, are populated with experts, each of whom is proud of his or her specialty. If followers rely on the company, it relies on them. If they need the leader, he or she needs them. The danger is that centrifugal forces will overcome centripetal ones: specialization can diminish commitment to common objectives. The solution is exemplified in the concept of the president's office or the presidents' office. The primary task of the leader in this situation is to build a team commitment to organizational success among these strong-willed executives. Integrators create an egalitarian climate in which ideas are frankly expressed and rigorously critiqued. Productive confrontation is encouraged. Clash of viewpoints is taken for granted. Leadership is shared and exercised by the executive who possesses the needed knowledge or experience. Thus, the integrators' role is catalytic, their goal synergism.

The Gamesman

According to Maccoby, gamesmen are fast-moving, flexible, bright, and eager to take risks and to compete. They have a compulsive drive to win, not for power, status, or money, but for the sheer exhilaration of victory. They want to be where the action is, to keep their options open, to build and manage a winning team. These mercurial individuals have a curious mix of positive and negative traits. Unbigoted, they welcome to the team anyone who can contribute to victory. People are judged almost exclusively in terms of what they can do for the team. But gamesmen are contemptuous of the weak and replace the incompetent impersonally. There is little empathy for or sensitivity to the feelings of others in gamesmen, although they are supportive of subordinates' efforts. Terms like generosity, loyalty, and empathy, in their view, get in the way of achievement. They are opportunistic but not unethical, individualistic but cooperative, innovative but willing to abide by the rules of the game, dominating but not destructive, tough but fair, emotionally detached from subordinates but helpful to them. Gamesmen are admirably suited to the needs of the modern corporation, especially in the knowledge industries, where a rapid rate of change in strategies, markets, and technology is commonplace. However, the gamesman may ultimately pay a heavy psychological price for success. After all, life is more than a game, and no game can go on unendingly.

What Does It Mean To You?

There are no pure types in leadership. Every manager is like a symphony that has a major theme, one or more minor themes, interpolations on themes, and variations on themes. None of the executives just described is inflexibly consistent. Each manager, even the worst, engages in behavior that at times varies from his or her characteristic approach. Yet there remains a *dominant behavior pattern.* The same applies to you. You might like to reflect on *your* principal leadership behaviors and those you resort to as alternative strategies. By considering these leaders, you may discover yourself!

keys to clue sense: how well do you understand your organization?

The Life Cycle of Your Organization

Organizations are born, grow, flourish, weaken, and ultimately pass on. Few last unendingly; none remain unchanged. The adaptive prosper; the rigid disappear. As a leader, you must be aware of the life stage of your company and appreciate how compatible your leadership style is with that stage. Figure 3 summarizes the various life phases of any firm.

Birth. This is an exciting time when the founder or founders seize opportunity by the throat and satisfy some unmet customer or societal need. Faith, risk taking, and dedication of the few characterize this stage. The leadership is directive, forceful, fast-moving, opportunistic, and informal. Only venturesome people motivated by challenges need apply. This is a wonderful time to be with an organization!

Childhood. This stage is dangerous, since most failures occur within three years after birth. Moreover, 90 percent of small business failures are due to managerial incompetence and inexperience, according to the Bank of America. Finally, one out of every two new business establishments fails within

Figure 3. **Life cycle of an organization.**

Life Stage	Birth	Childhood	Adolescence	Early Maturity	Vigorous Maturity	Ripe Maturity	Senescence	Renewal
Primary objective	Survival	Short-term profit	Accelerated growth	Systematic growth	Balanced growth	Uniqueness, image	Maintenance	Revitalization
Leader type	Innovator	Opportunist	Consultant	Participant	Corporateur	Statesman	Administrator	Mover and shaker
Organizational character	Struggling	Achieving	Changing	Expanding, diversifying	Systems-oriented	Mature, self-satisfied	Status quo—oriented	Change-oriented
Organizational self-image	Self-centered	Local	Sectional	National	Multinational	Cosmopolitan	Complacent	Self-critical
Energy focus	The new and novel	Competing	Conquering	Coordinating	Integrating, controlling	Adjusting	Continuing existence	Renewing, developing
Central problem	Market entry	Existence	Market share	Multifaceted growth	Centralization and autonomy	Balancing divergent interests	Stability	Rejuvenation
Type of planning	Visionary	Catch-as-catch-can	Simple: sales, budgets	Formal: orderly, specialized	Sophisticated: a way of life	Social, political	Extrapolative	Creative
Management mode	One person	Small in-group	Delegated	Decentralized	Centralized	Collegial	Tradition-bound	Striving, driving
Organizational model	Maximization of profit	Optimization of profit	Planned profit	Good citizenship	Social responsibility	Social institution	Bureaucracy	Imitation of the Phoenix

its first two years, and four out of five small business firms collapse during the first five years of existence.[1] Short-term success is the goal during this period. Healthy existence and growth, rather than mere survival, are the objectives. All run at top speed to keep pace with increasing prosperity. Things are still run by the forceful captain and his or her original crew.

Adolescence. During this period of transition, spurts of growth, struggle for uniqueness, and strengthening of the muscles are intermingled with angularity, awkwardness, and less than optimum coordination. Simple planning, budgeting, and forecasting are now done. More orderly procedures gradually replace the venturesome quest for success. Specialists are hired, causing some friction with the old hands. The founder or founders must act like managers, rather than entrepreneurs systematically planning, coordinating, directing, and controlling the future of the firm.

Early Maturity. Expansion, differentiation, and perhaps diversification are the hallmarks of this period. Profit centers are commonplace. Many accepted management techniques are now utilized: formal planning, management by objectives, position descriptions, delegation, standards of performance, appraisals, and training and development activities. However, the beginnings of bureaucratic tendencies are evident, and there is power seeking and politicking as individuals jockey for more favorable positions. A certain element of provincialism infiltrates departments, but all this seems a small price to pay for accelerating success.

Vigorous Maturity. With a corporateur at the helm, the organization's aim at this state is balanced growth. Structure, coordination, stability, and control must be weighed against innovation, improvement, and decentralization. The concept of profit centers is accepted. New products, markets, and technologies must be managed, and management skills are much more polished. A "tomorrow, the world" climate pervades the organization as growth accelerates even more swiftly than during earlier stages.

Ripe Maturity. Under competent but hardly outstanding management, the organization practically runs itself. But a sense of urgency is wanting, and an undesirable complacency is setting in. Although the profit picture is acceptable, the rate of growth slows. Territorial imperatives are commonplace. The organization may be distracted from its primary purpose by societal considerations. It has arrived and is respected. Even so, weaknesses are all too evident. These symptoms are probably being ignored by those in charge.

Senescence. This stage would never occur if the corporation were sensitive to the need for revitalizing itself. In line with the Peter Principle, storekeepers rather than tigerish executives are promoted. More aggressive competitors nibble, perhaps gnaw, at the organization's market share. Politics, power seeking, bureaucratic entanglements, ineffective motivational systems, encumbering control systems, and an opaqueness to new ideas all combine to produce a condition of hardening of the arteries. As Drucker notes, it is very hard to stop doing the unproductive. Then, all of a sudden, things seem to come apart, as happened with the City of New York, the railroads, and Chrysler. The firm is forced either to adopt stringent strategies to revive itself or to collapse in the fierce embrace of an acquiring corporation. It now finds itself back where it started: in a struggle to survive.

Renewal. It is possible for organizations to rise from their ashes like the Phoenix. This can be done either by a new team of executives charged with the mission of regenerating the anemic firm, or through a planned program of internal organizational development.

You and the Life Stage of Your Organization

Managers can usually do little to modify the life stage of their organizations, divisions, or departments. They can, however, decide whether this is the best place for them or whether they should seek their future in another company. They can determine what their units need and strive to meet these needs. They can capitalize on the positive trends in the company and do what they can to counteract negative trends. They can try to make their leadership behavior compatible with the corporate life stage. (Behavior that is ideal at the adolescent stage may be self-defeating at the ripe maturity stage.) Finally, they can come to grips with the realities that confront them and adapt their strategies to these realities, avoiding the temptation to impose on them either mere theory of their own pet preferences.

The Many Systems That Can Help or Hinder You

Knowledge of the life stage of your organization gives valuable background data. In addition to this knowledge, other clues are needed to guide your behavior. Every company, division, or department represents a series of interconnected systems, each with its peculiar influence. Understanding these systems is a must for the leader.

Figure 4 lists many of the systems that impinge on your work environment as well as the behavior patterns that are often intrinsic to them. Forms for evaluating these systems are given in Chapter 5.

The Administrative System

There are at least six kinds of organizations. Some are innovative and risk-taking, while others strive merely to avoid failure. Some are concerned primarily with maintaining the status quo, while still others are ultraconservative and tradition-bound. Some firms focus on improvement and management by objectives. And some are erratic and impulsive. Each of these kinds of organizations has quite a different administrative system and a radically different value orientation. As a result, the interaction pattern between units, the pecking order, the tightness of controls, the urgency of improving on past performance, the risk-taking parameters that are acceptable, the concern for status, the interest in creativity, and the authority and power granted the managers will all vary markedly. Accordingly, such factors can be either a helpful resource or a dragging impediment to your efforts to lead. Study the administrative system of your organization to ensure that your behavior is as compatible with it as possible.

Figure 4. **Organizational systems and behavior patterns.**

Type of System	Principal Behavior Pattern
Administrative	The organizers manage the organized. Hierarchy, objectives, policies, procedures, rules, specializations, and accountabilities are well known.
Authority	Some people have great clout, while others have little. Some magnify the amount they have, others use it to the hilt, and still others use it minimally.
Power	Key individuals have different kinds of power, for different reasons, to varying degrees. Most seek to protect and augment the kind and amount they possess.
Political	People maneuver for positions of prominence, ethically or unethically, according to the unwritten rules of the game.
Status	Privileges and prerogatives are distributed unevenly to individuals and groups. Some people are unimpressed by the badges of office, while others are hypersensitive about them.
Influence	Different people have the ear of those with authority for various reasons, and most seek to influence key people.
Motivational	Managers seek to energize subordinates to achieve corporate objectives, and employees seek to attain their own personal goals.
Communication	This is the bloodstream of the organization. People use it to advance their viewpoints, and at times act as blood clots.
Compensation	Employees endeavor to obtain as much as possible, regardless of their performance. Managers seek to recompense performance fairly.
Reward and Punishment	People strive to advance their own careers, while securing as many organizational "goodies" as possible. Some are richly rewarded, while others are passed over.
Technical	People are esteemed for their ability to contribute to or manage technology, skill, and knowledge.
Interaction	People and units may work harmoniously or at cross purposes.
Social	People unite to attain personal satisfactions regardless of organizational requirements.

The Authority System

In the ideal organization, authority would be distributed in as rational a manner as possible. Things rarely work out this way, however. Sometimes "the tail wags the dog" as one department has far more authority than it should, while another has less. Some units push their authority to the limit while others use it only minimally. Also, certain people may magnify their authority at the expense of others. For instance, a staff person with functional authority may utilize it to the detriment of the line managers. It is prudent, therefore, to become thoroughly familiar not only with the manner in which authority is distributed in your organization but also with the manner in which people use, misuse, underuse, or abuse it.

The Power System

Authority is granted, but power is grasped. Power has five aspects. It connotes the ability (1) to make others dependent on you for the attainment of desired outcomes; (2) to determine the flow of events; (3) to make a strong impact on others, be they superiors, peers, or subordinates; (4) to keep as many of your options open as possible; and (5) to impose your will on others despite their resistance. It is obvious from all this that power is far more important than mere authority. It should therefore be considered in some detail.

In 1958, French and Raven discussed five bases of power, and the authorities have not added much to their classifications since then.[2]

Reward and Coercive Power. This refers to the rewards and punishments that the manager can administer. These two sources of power can be potent leadership tools if used appropriately.

Legitimate Power. This is the power that accrues to a manager by virtue of holding a given position. It entitles him or her to require compliance to reasonable commands while obligating employees to perform as expected.

Expert Power. A person can influence others simply by possessing the knowledge, skill, or talent that is needed to cope with an organizational situation.

Referent Power. Admired, respected leaders have personal power with their people. Subordinates do as requested largely because they identify with the manager, perhaps even behave as he or she does.

Certain observations are in order regarding the power system.

1. Power can take many forms. Power *over* is dominance or coerciveness that can be brought to bear on a given situation. Power *with* is a more subtle influence that can be exerted because subordinates accept and like the leader. Power *to do* is the power of an individual or group to make and implement decisions. Power *to influence* is the power of recommenders: those who do not have the last say, but who have impact on those who do. Power *to help* is the power of individuals or groups who, for whatever reason, can facilitate the efforts of someone else. Power *to hinder* is used by the implementers of a decision, who may not be able to participate in the decision-making process but can often hinder efforts to carry out the decision. And power *to frustrate* is the power to negate someone else's best efforts, often by the simple process of withholding the make-or-break input that would spell success.

2. In all relationships there is a balance of power. Leaders' subordinates are dependent on them. Leaders, in turn, are dependent on subordinates for productivity. In fact, the work group may have more power over its members than the manager does. Even the weak are able to exert some degree of power.

3. Most managers are attracted to power. If you lack a power drive, you will not go very far in management. However, too high a need for power is likely to be damaging.

4. How power is used is more significant than the need for power itself. As McClelland as pointed out, power has two faces: *personalized,* which is exploitive, self-aggrandizing, and demeaning to others in a win-lose relationship; and *socialized,* which is utilized for the benefit of the group in a win-win interaction.[3]

The Political System

Politics is as indigenous to organizations as is the pursuit of power. Every company is an arena in which hopes are born and ambitions perish. Side by side are in-groups and out-groups, friendships and animosities, temporary coalitions and lasting alliances, collaboration and conflict, winners on a fast track and derailed losers. Moreover, a division or department is a field on which jealousy and altruism, statesmanship and self-centered advocacy, honesty and duplicity, straight dealing and egotistical maneuvering, ethical and reprehensible behavior are played out simultaneously. Because of all this, it is not surprising that at times the formal organization is overshadowed by informal politics.

When he left for a business trip to the Middle East, Robert Sarnoff was *numero uno* of RCA. When he returned, he had been ousted. His father had built the business, but the Board wanted nothing to do with the son. Years later, he commented, "If I had been more political and less trusting, it wouldn't have happened. I stayed away from politics, and that was naive. I've now learned to be more alert about the things that are going on around me."

Organizations consist of pyramids and people. The shape of the former and the nature of the latter mean that there will always be some form of jockeying to improve positions and to advance careers. It is not for the leader to judge or criticize the political picture, but rather to gain an understanding of its dynamics and mechanics. Without a keen insight into the quality, extent, and unwritten rules for politicking in the firm, you are destined to bump your head much more than you have to.

Usually the political game is played according to well-known codes of conduct, but it sometimes degenerates into internecine warfare. In either case, you must have coping strategies.

The Status System

The sensitivity of others to their status appears comical, but any affront to our own is intolerable. Such is human nature. Yet status is necessary in any organization, for it goes along with titles and ranks. From the organization's viewpoint it represents both an incentive and a form of earned recognition. For individual employees it signifies the trappings of office to which they are entitled, the manner in which they should be treated, the behavior that is appropriate to their position, and their perch on the organizational totem pole. Status is no trivial matter, and it can create many problems. Status fluctuations, status anxiety, status jealousy, status incongruity, and status loss have caused many a manager much emotional damage. Ignorance of the status system of your organization may cause you to step on people's toes and to affront their sensibilities. With respect to status, Newton's law should read, "To every negative action there is an exaggerated retaliatory reaction."

The Influence System

Not everyone with a key title is necessarily a key person. Some exert great influence on the thinking, attitudes, and behavior of significant people, while others exert little. The sources of influence can range from the possession of needed expertise, to having sponsors in high places, to knowing "where the bodies are buried." If you drew up an influence chart of your organization, executive secretaries and other less authoritative individuals would rank considerably higher than many lower and middle managers. The administrative, authority, and status systems are easy to analyze because they are public. The power, political, and influence systems are difficult to understand because they are never written in detail and because those who are deft at using them generally keep a low profile. People who boast or make a great display of their power, political skills, or influence are more often than not like the Wizard of Oz.

The Motivational System

Some organizations motivate people principally through fear, others through a paternalistic concern for their welfare, and others through rewards and punishments. Where one strives mightily to help employees satisfy their needs, a second redesigns jobs and institutes job enrichment programs to make work more meaningful and motivating. A third may rely on challenges, freedom to perform, achievement, and career progress. Most companies combine these and other strategies, emphasizing certain motivational techniques while placing less stress on others. You should understand the major motivational approaches approved and utilized in your organization so that you can capitalize on what works and experiment with different techniques that will produce even better results.

The Communication System

Interpersonal communication is really a simple matter, involving the following questions: Who speaks to whom and with what effect? Who ignores whom? Who keeps whom informed and updated? Who keeps whom in the dark, if possible? Who listens to whom and for what reasons? What networks are used to get the word around? What types of information are exchanged freely? What types are jealously guarded or shared only with a few intimates? Who are reliable information sources? What barriers tend to block or distort communication? In one department communication may be free-flowing and authentic, whereas in another it may be formal, even pedantic. In a third, it may be sporadic and rumor-laden. In still a fourth, it may be imperious and aggressive. You must gain some insight into the way the word gets around your organization before you are in a position to lead.

The Compensation System

At first glance, this might not seem very important. However, you will lead differently in a firm that rewards task accomplishment and improvement on past performance than in one that rewards most people equally regardless of their contribution. If the compensation system is fair, you have a great resource at your command. But if it is basically unfair or unduly influenced by favoritism, then your leadership efforts will be hampered.

The Reward and Punishment System

Related to the motivational and the compensation systems is the reward and punishment system. It is easier to lead in an organization that recognizes superior performance than in one that rewards cronyism, the old school tie, seniority, or a talent for making no waves. Promotions should be based primarily on past performance, present contribution, and future potential. There are also many types of rewards besides promotions. Freedom to perform, increased responsibility, a consultative and participative mode of management, delegation, and building career paths—all are potent resources for your leadership effectiveness. If your organization imposes needless constraints on your ability to reward or punish, you are handicapped.

The Technical System

A manufacturing production line requires a different leadership approach than does the typical research and development department. Companies with high technology and knowledge are not the same as those whose technology is simple, stable, repetitive, and routine. The leadership requirements in Digital and McDonald's, for example, are quite different.

The Interaction System

Within a given department, or between organizational units, the pattern of interaction may be supportive and friendly or aggressive and suspicious. It may be informal and relaxed or impersonal and proper. It may be either constructively competitive or destructively competitive. It may be supportive and collaborative or accusing and complaining. The attitude within or between departments may be win-win or win-lose. Finally, the interaction may be cooperative or a never-ending game of one-upmanship. Since it is hardly possible for you to lead without interacting with other organizational units and key individuals, it is essential that you know clearly the types of interaction that characterize your company, division, or department.

The Social System

People do not merely make an economic contract with the organization. More important, they make both a psychological and a sociological contract with it. They expect the organization not merely to help them satisfy their important work-related needs but also to be an environment in which they can gain acceptance, respect, friendship, and the liking of others. Hence, regardless of what management may wish to happen, you can rest assured that employees will devise their own strategies for meeting their personal aspirations and wants. To call this system the informal organization is to cloud its reason for being and to minimize its importance. It is, rather, the way in which people live and work together to attain their personal objectives while satisfying the demands of the organization.

Working within these systems, and coping with them, takes a high order of skill. Leaders are rarely the masters of their fate as these forces impinge on them.

In the following chapter, detailed forms are presented to help you analyze the specific characteristics of your company, division, or department.

analyzing your organization: how keen is your insight?

What Makes Your Organization Distinctive?

Every organization is like *all other* organizations in some ways, like *some other* organizations in some ways, and like *no other* organization in some ways. This adaptation of C. Kluckhohn's insightful statement reminds us that to speak theoretically about leadership is self-indulgent. Leadership is geared to action, and action should be based on an accurate diagnosis of your company, division, or department. You need a systematic procedure for identifying the elements that make your organization unique.

Managers in RCA, Exxon, ITT, Stanford University, the U.S. Navy, Du Pont, Chase Manhattan, and the CIA are both similar and different. They are affected by their organizations, and their organizations are affected by them. Leaders must take into account the force fields that can facilitate or frustrate their efforts to lead.

This chapter helps you put your clue sense to practical use. It consists of a series of checklists that can be applied to your organization, however large or small. Not every possible area or detail is covered, but when you have filled in the forms provided you should derive three benefits. You will confirm what you already know, identify the forces that you now understand only incompletely, and pinpoint those with which you should be familiar but are not. If, however, you skip through the checklists in a casual manner, little will be gained. It might be wise first to think about the specific topic covered by a given form, then complete it, and finally reflect on how the items you have checked should affect your present and future behavior.

For the sake of clarity, the checklists are classified under three major categories: analyzing the background forces, analyzing the interacting forces, and analyzing the organizational transactions.

Analyzing the Background Forces

Anyone who has ever entertained children by making shadow figures with his or her hands realizes that the screen is at least as important as the finger manipulation: it gives meaning to the shapes formed. It is the same with organizations. No manager is a free agent. All must be aware of, try to control, respond to, and wrestle with a network of background forces that are largely beyond their control. Pope John appreciated this when he commented, "Even as Pope, I cannot do what I would really like to do." The purpose of Figures 5 through 10 is to sharpen your understanding of the subtle influences that shape and guide your actions. The figures examine the climate, value orientation, self-image, leadership style, thrust, and tempo of your organization.[1]

The Climate

"Climate" is an elusive term that almost defies definition even though everyone knows experientially what it is. Climate comprises the philosophy, purposes, values, life-styles, traditions, manners, norms, attitudes, and spirit that permeate the organization and make it different from all others. Ethereal as it seems, your company's climate is one of its most basic assets or liabilities, and a clear comprehension of it is a sine qua non for leadership. Figure 5 helps you analyze your organization's climate.

Figure 5. **The climate of my organization.**

Climate	Within My Unit	Within Related Units	Organization as a Whole
No-nonsense and businesslike.	————	————	————
Conflict-ridden.	————	————	————
Warm, friendly, and relaxed.	————	————	————
Secretive and suspicious.	————	————	————
Mutually respectful.	————	————	————
Helpful and supportive.	————	————	————
Mutually aggressive.	————	————	————
Open to new ideas and approaches.	————	————	————
Nonsupportive and uncooperative.	————	————	————
Aloof and distant.	————	————	————

Other:

1. ———————————— 3. ————————————

2. ———————————— 4. ————————————

The Value Orientation

Basic to the climate that permeates the organization, of course, are the values that determine acceptable and unacceptable behavior. Figure 6 helps you delineate some of these factors.

The Self-Image

With organizations, as with human beings, self-perceptions are important. Organizations have attitudes about themselves and reactions to themselves. They often react not to reality but to what they perceive as reality and to the images they have of

Figure 6. **The value orientation of my organization.**

Value	Within My Unit	Within Related Units	Organization as a Whole
Help others as much as you can.	_____	_____	_____
Don't help others if you can avoid it.	_____	_____	_____
Do a good job.	_____	_____	_____
Do as little as you must.	_____	_____	_____
Cooperate with others.	_____	_____	_____
Outmaneuver others if you can.	_____	_____	_____
Treat others ethically.	_____	_____	_____
Undercut others if you can.	_____	_____	_____
Strive to improve on past performance.	_____	_____	_____
Be content with acceptable performance.	_____	_____	_____
Identify with organizational goals.	_____	_____	_____
Concentrate on personal or provincial unit goals.	_____	_____	_____
Be concerned about people's needs.	_____	_____	_____
Be concerned about number one only.	_____	_____	_____

Other:

1. _____   3. _____

2. _____   4. _____

Figure 7. **The self-image of my organization.**

Self-Concept	Within My Unit	Within Related Units	Organization as a Whole
Competent and self-assured.	————	————	————
Self-satisfied and complacent.	————	————	————
Opportunistic and resourceful.	————	————	————
Good and getting better.	————	————	————
Poor and getting worse.	————	————	————
Listless and apathetic.	————	————	————
Ultraconservative and cautious.	————	————	————
Arrogant and superior.	————	————	————
Rigid and inflexible.	————	————	————
Hypersensitive and defensive.	————	————	————
Risk-taking and innovative.	————	————	————

Other:

1. _____ 3. _____

2. _____ 4. _____

themselves. For this reason, knowing the self-image of your company is a necessary step in functional leadership. Figure 7 shows some aspects of the organizational self-image.

The Leadership Style

Climate, value orientation, and self-image stem primarily from the leadership style of those who control a corporation's destiny, so it would be wise to appraise your organization's leadership pattern carefully. Figure 8 helps you do this.

Figure 8. **The leadership style in my organization.**

Leadership Style	Within My Unit	Within Related Units	Organization as a Whole
Consultative and participative.	_____	_____	_____
Oriented toward joint problem solving.	_____	_____	_____
Directive and controlling.	_____	_____	_____
Bureaucratic.	_____	_____	_____
Primarily task-oriented.	_____	_____	_____
Primarily people-oriented.	_____	_____	_____
Partly task-oriented, partly people-oriented.	_____	_____	_____
Autocratic and exploitive.	_____	_____	_____
Autocratic and paternalistic.	_____	_____	_____
Supportive and facilitating.	_____	_____	_____
Demanding but fair.	_____	_____	_____
Innovative and improvement-oriented.	_____	_____	_____
Focusing primarily on short-term perspective.	_____	_____	_____
Focusing on both short- and long-term perspective.	_____	_____	_____

Other:

1. _____   3. _____

2. _____   4. _____

Figure 9. **The thrust of my organization.**

Direction	Within My Unit	Within Related Units	Organization as a Whole
Growing according to plan.	————	————	————
Growing only when the economy grows.	————	————	————
Holding its own but not really growing.	————	————	————
Growing in spurts, erratically.	————	————	————
Struggling to stay in position.	————	————	————
Slowly declining.	————	————	————
Emphasizing profitability.	————	————	————
Emphasizing cost control.	————	————	————
Emphasizing innovation.	————	————	————
Emphasizing technology.	————	————	————
Emphasizing human resources.	————	————	————
Emphasizing management competence.	————	————	————
Emphasizing centralization and tight controls.	————	————	————
Emphasizing team building.	————	————	————
Earnestly seeking to improve.	————	————	————
Relying on outdated management techniques.	————	————	————
Emotionally tied to past concepts and procedures.	————	————	————

Other:

1. ————————————   3. ————————————

2. ————————————   4. ————————————

The Thrust

Some companies are being born, some are growing, others are in their prime, still others are declining, and a few are dying. The direction in which your firm is headed is critical, for it spells out the dimensions of the desired future toward which it is striking. Figure 9 helps you analyze your organization's thrust.

The Tempo

The pace at which you move as a leader must be consistent with that of your organization and unit. Moving too rapidly courts rebuffs. Moving too slowly means missed opportunities. To assess your organization's tempo, see Figure 10.

Figure 10. **The tempo of my organization.**

Tempo	Within My Unit	Within Related Units	Organization as a Whole
Fast-paced and brisk.	_____	_____	_____
Deliberate and planned.	_____	_____	_____
Slow-moving and lethargic.	_____	_____	_____
Impulsive and erratic.	_____	_____	_____
Diffident and tentative.	_____	_____	_____
Crisis-dominated.	_____	_____	_____
Frantic and counterproductive.	_____	_____	_____

Other:

1. _____   3. _____

2. _____   4. _____

Analyzing the Interacting Forces

If it is necessary to be familiar with the background factors that have impact on the manager, it is far more important to understand the day-to-day dynamics of your organization. These dynamics include the patterns of power, politics, status, friendship, and friction. This section helps you dissect these interacting forces.

Figure 11. **The power pattern of my organization.**

Kind of Power	Power Wielder	Source of Power	How Exercised
Power to decide.	_____	_____	_____
Power to do.	_____	_____	_____
Power to recommend.	_____	_____	_____
Power to reward.	_____	_____	_____
Power to punish.	_____	_____	_____
Power to hinder.	_____	_____	_____
Power to procrastinate.	_____	_____	_____
Position power.	_____	_____	_____
Expert power.	_____	_____	_____
Personal (social) power.	_____	_____	_____
Power to distribute power.	_____	_____	_____

Other:

1. _____ 3. _____

2. _____ 4. _____

The Power Pattern

Power, as was said earlier, comes in all kinds and is wielded by different people regardless of their authority and titles. People who should exercise great power according to organization charts and position descriptions may exert little. Others, who may not even be on a chart, cast a long shadow. Figure 11 lists different kinds of power that people may have.

Figure 12. **The political pattern of my organization.**

Nature of Politicking	Within My Unit	Within Related Units	Organization as a Whole
Discouraged, not rewarded.	————	————	————
Accepted according to known rules.	————	————	————
Limited to a few climbers.	————	————	————
Played by nearly everyone to an extent.	————	————	————
A major means for getting ahead.	————	————	————
Cliques compete for greater power.	————	————	————
Gentlemanly jockeying permitted.	————	————	————
Slightly unethical behavior tolerated.	————	————	————
Basically unethical strategies allowed.	————	————	————
Machiavellian maneuvering permitted.	————	————	————
An indoor sport. Protect yourself at all times.	————	————	————
Behind-the-back character assassination fairly common.	————	————	————

Other:

1. ———————————————   3. ———————————————

2. ———————————————   4. ———————————————

The Political Pattern

It is silly to ignore politics. The politically naive invite their own disillusionment. It is not the prevalence of politics but the quality of the maneuvering that is significant. Figure 12 helps you analyze your organization's political pattern.

The Status Pattern

As was said earlier, status sensitivity is the butt of humorous cartoons and anecdotes. In real life, however, status is neces-

Figure 13. **The status pattern of my organization.**

Status Importance	Within My Unit	Within Related Units	Organi- zation as a Whole
Minimized, and considered unimportant.	_____	_____	_____
Taken for granted in an informal, relaxed way.	_____	_____	_____
Governed by strict protocol.	_____	_____	_____
Taken seriously and considered important.	_____	_____	_____
Emphasis on status symbols and perks.	_____	_____	_____
Strenuous striving and status seeking.	_____	_____	_____
Great status sensitivity. Emphasis on territorial rights.	_____	_____	_____

Other:

1. _____   3. _____

2. _____   4. _____

Figure 14. **The friendship-friction pattern of my organization.**

Roots of Friendship	Within My Unit	Within Related Units	Between Units
Like each other.	_____	_____	_____
Agree on most things.	_____	_____	_____
Team up to prevail.	_____	_____	_____
Need each other.	_____	_____	_____
Help each other.	_____	_____	_____
Protect each other.	_____	_____	_____
Cover for each other.	_____	_____	_____
Exchange confidential information.	_____	_____	_____
Are social confidants.	_____	_____	_____
Have similar areas of expertise.	_____	_____	_____
Have similar ethnic or cultural backgrounds.	_____	_____	_____
Have similar interests or hobbies.	_____	_____	_____
Have similar objectives.	_____	_____	_____

Other:

1. _____   3. _____

2. _____   4. _____

sary and can be a source of many problems. To understand
how your organization deals with status, see Figure 13.

The Friendship-Friction Pattern

In the social system, friendships and animosities are bound
to develop. Friendships may have simple or complex roots,

Figure 14. **The friendship-friction pattern (continued).**

Roots of Friction	Within My Unit	Within Related Units	Between Units
Disagree on most matters.	____	____	____
Are suspicious of each other.	____	____	____
Have conflicting goals.	____	____	____
Dislike each other.	____	____	____
Vie for greater power.	____	____	____
Rub each other the wrong way.	____	____	____
Have different areas of expertise.	____	____	____
Are jealous of each other.	____	____	____
Frustrate each other if possible.	____	____	____
Resent each other.	____	____	____
Have different ethnic or cultural backgrounds.	____	____	____

Other:

1. _____   3. _____

2. _____   4. _____

ranging from compatibility of personalities or working closely together, to unity in resisting higher authority or a desire to satisfy affiliation needs. The roots of antagonism are no less varied. If you do not want to be shot down in the cross fire between conflicting people, you would be well advised to study the friendship-friction picture. Figure 14 helps you do this.

Analyzing the Organizational Transactions

Organizational transactions take at least three major forms: interpersonal communication, individual and group interaction, and the roles that people adopt. The better you understand the workings of these systems, the better off you will be. (Group interaction will be discussed in Chapter 11.)

The Communication Pattern

Interpersonal communication should be a company's source of nourishment, providing the corporate organism with a constant supply of nutriments in the form of ideas, information, data, feelings, and opinions. Unfortunately, the arterial network is sometimes so anemic that the corporate organs become malnourished. For this reason a clear concept of the effectiveness of the communication flow is essential for leadership. Figure 15 helps you understand your organization's communication pattern.

The Individual Interaction Pattern

The less people interact with their fellows, the less human they become. Superiors, associates, and subordinates are involved in countless interactions each day. As with communication, the quantity is not as important as the quality. People who interact can be either time wasters, troublemakers, or constructive helpers, and you would be wise to know the difference. Figure 16 shows different kinds of interaction patterns.

The Role Adoption Pattern

Every leader plays many roles. Some are imposed by the organization in the form of duties, pressures, and accountabilities; others stem from the leader's view of the role that should be exercised. It is useful to be aware of the roles

Figure 15. **The communication pattern of my organization.**

Quality of Communication	Within My Unit	Within Related Units	Between Units
Open, direct, and candid.	————	————	————
Selective among friends.	————	————	————
Formal, proper, and polite.	————	————	————
Imperious and demanding.	————	————	————
Mutually aggressive.	————	————	————
Critical and accusing.	————	————	————
Primarily via the grapevine and often inaccurate.	————	————	————
Helpful and constructive.	————	————	————
Misleading and manipulative.	————	————	————
Self-enhancing and self-fronting.	————	————	————
Defensive and suspicious.	————	————	————
Upwardly blocked or filtered.	————	————	————
Upwardly free-flowing.	————	————	————
Laterally inadequate.	————	————	————
Laterally open and honest.	————	————	————
Downwardly blocked or filtered.	————	————	————
Downwardly direct and authentic.	————	————	————

Other:

1. ————————————   3. ————————————

2. ————————————   4. ————————————

Figure 16. **The interaction pattern of my organization.**

Quality of Interaction	Within My Unit	Within Related Units	Between Units
Supportive and facilitating.	_____	_____	_____
Formal and at arm's length.	_____	_____	_____
Informal and offhand.	_____	_____	_____
Constructively competitive.	_____	_____	_____
Destructively competitive.	_____	_____	_____
Self-oriented or self-insistent.	_____	_____	_____
Rife with cliques and factions.	_____	_____	_____
Antagonistic and hostile.	_____	_____	_____
Team-oriented.	_____	_____	_____
Oriented toward dominance and power seeking.	_____	_____	_____
Conducive to ignoring each other if possible.	_____	_____	_____
Conducive to working independently.	_____	_____	_____
Geared to working at cross-purposes.	_____	_____	_____
Not conducive to constructive disagreement.	_____	_____	_____
Geared to managing clashing ideas well.	_____	_____	_____
Largely for social purposes.	_____	_____	_____
Geared to one-upmanship.	_____	_____	_____

Other:

1. _____ 3. _____

2. _____ 4. _____

habitually adopted both by yourself and by other key individuals. Figure 17 shows some common roles. You may want to make a list of specific names of people who fill these roles in your organization.

Figure 17. **The role pattern of my organization.**

Role Adopted	By Me	By Key People in My Unit	By Key People in Related Units
Information provider.	_____	_____	_____
Truth twister.	_____	_____	_____
Idea generator.	_____	_____	_____
Task achiever.	_____	_____	_____
People influencer.	_____	_____	_____
Constructive critic.	_____	_____	_____
Tension reducer.	_____	_____	_____
Obstructionist.	_____	_____	_____
Rumormonger.	_____	_____	_____
Reliable helper.	_____	_____	_____
Adviser or counselor.	_____	_____	_____
Petty nitpicker.	_____	_____	_____
Shrewd strategist.	_____	_____	_____
Pleader for personal interests.	_____	_____	_____

Other:

1. _____   3. _____

2. _____   4. _____

Summary

If you have filled in the checklists in this chapter thoughtfully and seriously, you should have a rather insightful grasp of the inner dynamics of your organization, or at least of your department or unit. One of the most important skills of leaders is to have their radar antennae revolving constantly so that they can scan the environment and detect the forces that are likely to help or hinder their leadership efforts.

understanding human behavior: how sharp is your cue sense?

Why Is It So Difficult to Understand Another Person?

John D. Rockefeller once commented that he would pay more for the ability to handle people than for any other executive talent. Maximizing ROI—return on individuals—is one of your most challenging and difficult tasks. There are at least four reasons why it is not easy to understand another individual.

Trained Incapacities. Managers tend to perceive others through the prism of their own expertise. We are proud of our own specialty and get much of our ego strength from it. How natural then to use it, however subtly, as spectacles for perceiving others. To the economist, people are surplus-oriented animals logically intent on maximizing their monetary power, status, and prestige. To the psychologist, people are behaving animals who may act rationally or irrationally depending on the situation. The tunnel vision of our specialty, whether it is engineering, finance, marketing, or systems analysis, limits our view of others and blinds us to full comprehension.

Impatience. Most managers are pressured and busy. They are usually neither philosophers nor scientists, so it is tempting to use an easy strategy for analyzing superiors, peers, and subordinates. Yielding to this temptation, however, is foolhardy and makes you an easy mark for the charlatan. If people are unique regarding such a simple thing as facial features, how complex they must be in the fullness of their personalities!

Forcing People into Categories. Classification is the basis of all science. Without categories, data remain jumbled and unintelligible. There is a temptation, though, to force the individual to fit the category rather than using the classification system to gain insight into the person. It should be obvious that no one can really understand another person through the use of two, three, or even four categories. Such an approach results in merely labeling people and in responding to the labels rather than to the people's uniqueness.

Simplistic Thinking. "Find his hot button" and "Find out what makes her tick" are acceptable phrases if they are rooted in the hard work required to come to grips with another person's individual differences. Too often, however, they are used as though the person were an elevator or a clock. Dominant or submissive, extroverted or introverted are helpful dimensions if each is thought of as a continuum. But it is highly unfair to size up an individual on the basis of a few, often highly idiosyncratic, criteria.

The Simple Complexity of Human Nature

Getting to know an individual is no easy matter for the simple reason that at least five different "persons" are ever alive and active within the same human being.

The Animal Person. Intent on survival, the animal person wants what it wants when it wants it. It explores, experiments, and experiences under the domination of its impulses, drives, basic needs, and feelings.

The Social Person. Realizing that people who live unto themselves alone are not fully human, the social person seeks acceptance, relatedness, belonging, recognition, reputation, status, power, friendship, and love.

The Psychological Person. In its quest for self-esteem, inner harmony, and uniqueness, the psychological person yearns for security, activity, variety, change, growth, achievement, creativity, and independence.

The Ideal Person. To have true meaning and worth, life must be examined. The ideal person searches for values, convictions, and ideals that serve as sure behavioral guides and consistent criteria for evaluating actions. Unfortunately, these guidelines are sometimes distorted into neurotically tyrannical inquisitors of what we do.

The Rational Person. Left uncontrolled, the four facets of human nature just described will cause chaos. It is the rational person that uses ideas, knowledge, learning, insight, reasoning skills, judgment, prudence, and hopefully some wisdom to integrate these disparate elements into some form of order, unity, balance, and coherence.

Fortunately, the situation is not *that* perplexing. All people have the same basic nature and needs. In a given culture or subculture, they are likely to have similar expectations, aspirations, wants, and objectives which differ quantitatively, not qualitatively. People can be compared to rugs in which the threads are identical but the patterns differ. Put another way, every person is a fraction: 1/9, 2/9, 4/9, 5/9, and so on. The denominator represents the common humanity that we all share; the numerators, our individual differences. Any group of people contains a complex combination of constants and variables, of similarities and differences. You must live with this not merely at the intellectual level, where it does little good, but at the behavioral level, where it is all-important.

The Requirements for Understanding Others

The essentials for understanding another person include the proper attitude, clear notions about the perceptual process, familiarity with certain human relations principles, and a systematic analytical procedure.

The Proper Attitude

The blunt truth is that some managers spend more time on coffee breaks than they do on the planned analysis of their people. As in all other things, attitude is crucial, because behavior follows attitude. Unless you are persuaded that return on individuals and return on interaction are of primary importance, you will not accomplish much. Here is an experiment you can perform. Over the next week, observe how much time managers spend judging, evaluating, criticizing, or perhaps complaining about their subordinates as compared with how much they invest in trying to understand them. Then draw your own conclusions regarding the importance of a constructive attitude.

The Puzzle of Perception

Behavior depends on perceptions as a door depends on its hinges. Yet it is surprising how little time is devoted to this process in management books. Nothing is so successful in making fact fiction, and fiction fact, as perception. Accordingly, it is essential that you have clear ideas regarding just what happens when one person perceives another.

Images, Not People, Interact. As Figure 18 indicates, people may affect each other, but images interact. Note the strong subjective element in all these images: perceptions are rarely objective. Any serious clash between, or among, these images means that perceptions will be twisted and misunderstood by the other party. Isn't this the problem of paternalistic managers who see their people as needing protective leadership, when the subordinates feel self-confident and competent? Here is a second experiment you can conduct over the next week. Watch how often disagreements and antagonism are caused not by substance but by misinterpreted or conflicting images.

Perceptions Are Forced on Us. We are compelled to perceive what we need and want to see, what we are accustomed to seeing, what we expect to see, what makes sense to us, and what fits in neatly with our preconceived notions. For exam-

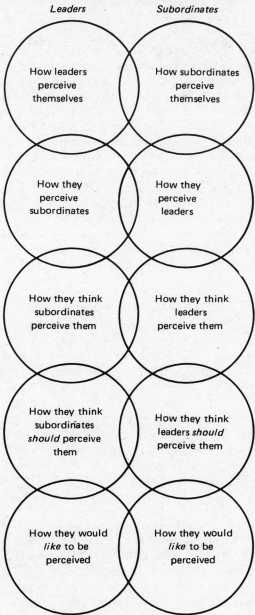

Figure 18. **The images that interact.**

ple, if a newly appointed woman manager perceives that the higher-ups are eager for her to succeed, she will see criticism from them as helpful. If another feels that promotion is unlikely, the same criticism will be resented as an "I gotcha" tactic.

A Way of Seeing Is Also a Way of Not Seeing. In any human transaction there are just too many stimuli to take in. By a *law of parsimony,* we focus on those that seem to be the most important. Unless we are careful, perception can become a form of monocular vision as we concentrate on some kinds of input to the neglect of others that may be more significant. This is made worse by the fact that first impressions, which are strong and lasting, serve a filtering and steering function. They allow facile entrance to confirmatory stimuli, while distorting contradictory ones. This, of course, is the basis of the well-known principle of self-fulfilling prophecy. An example should make this clear. If a manager misinterprets a subordinate's assertive efforts to improve the operation as undue pushiness, the manager will be sure to notice any later behavior that seems to confirm this initial reaction.

Perception Can Be Projection. Projection takes two forms: blaming others when we are really the ones at fault, and seeing in others the negative traits we possess. For example, managers may criticize their subordinates for a job poorly done when they themselves did not plan well or communicate precisely what they wanted done in the first place. Or exploitive people may justify their behavior on the grounds that everyone does it: "Do unto others before they do unto you."

There Is No Such Thing as Open-Mindedness. Nothing would seem more logical than that the first applicants for a job would have the best chance of being hired. On the contrary, Robert Half, an executive recruiter, has found that in his experience only 17.6 percent of early applicants are hired, whereas 55.8 percent of those interviewed last are hired! [1] Perhaps the first applicants are forgotten, or the pressure to hire *someone,* or sheer weariness with the whole process, exerts more influence than objective, rational data. We all have our personalized rules for perceiving. No two people see the same phenomenon in an identical manner, and thus what the leader considers to be critically important may be seen by the troops as being only of marginal significance. Finally, we are not blank pages when we perceive. We bring to the process all our past experiences, habits, preferences, and aversions.

You and Your Perceptions

What leaders need is not a litany of principles but practical suggestions to improve their ability to perceive others accurately.

Observe Carefully. Perception is a skill that can be learned. It starts with an attitude of vacuuming your mind, to the extent that you can, of preconceptions, biases, preferences, and so on. It continues with sorting out the relevant from the irrelevant cues. Make sure that first impressions provide data, not conclusions. Use impressions as hypotheses that will later be confirmed, adjusted, or radically changed with further input.

Don't Jump to Conclusions. Take a sheet of paper for each significant superior, associate, or subordinate and draw a line down the center. In the left column, write down your impressions, perceptions, and judgments of the person. In the right column, note the bases for these reactions. You may be surprised to find that you are sometimes taking strong positions on inadequate information. In the cases where the data are valid, positively or negatively, keep the sheets and add additional data as they occur. People do change, and your perceptions should change with them. In short, be open-minded to new data, not closed-minded.

Break Habit. Habit makes us blind. Now and then, particularly with people who rub you the wrong way, objectify the relationships and deliberately try to perceive the people from a different perspective than you have used in the past. At best, this approach will help you see more of their attractive characteristics. At worst, it will prevent you from being emotionally seduced by traits that get under your fingernails. If this seems naive to you, here are two questions you can answer for yourself. How many people right now make a persistent effort to understand you within your frame of reference? How do you feel and react when they go out of their way to do so?

Avoid the Four Pitfalls of Perception. The halo effect, stereotyping, perceptual defense, and projection are dangerous traps. The *halo* effect occurs when we allow a general impression of a person, positive or negative, to color our evaluation of specific traits. This happens because of a natural tendency to expect trait linkage: we expect certain characteristics to go together. (A quiet and reserved individual may easily be judged unambitious.) *Stereotyping* takes place when we attribute to an individual a characteristic that is rightly or wrongly associated with a group of which he or she is a member. (He went to Harvard, so he must be bright.) *Perceptual defense* involves ignoring, distorting, denying, or isolating an event that does not fit in with our past experience or is a threat to it. (Heavy smokers often ignore the overwhelming evidence of the dangers of smoking.) *Projection,* as was already explained, involves blaming others for our mistakes or seeing our negative traits in others.

Growing in Self-Perception. Most of us cause many of our own problems, but being human, we tend to blame them on others. Periodically ask yourself such questions as the following:

— What is there about the way I perceive others that gets me into difficulty?
— What is there about the way I act that attracts people to me? that alienates them?
— When was the last time I saw my own behavior as it appears in the eyes of others?
— How often do I listen to my own voice as it sounds in the ears of others?
— When did I last observe my own interaction with others as they perceive it?
— What changes in my ways of perceiving people and behaving toward them are likely to improve our relationships?

Honest answers to these simple questions can help you become more sensitive to your view of others.

Some Principles of Human Interaction

Principles are guides to thought and action. Accordingly, it might be well to review a few basic ideas about human interaction.

1. All people exist as the center of their own world of experience, as Carl Rogers and others have stated. They react to the reality that they perceive and experience.

2. People have a basic drive to maintain, enhance, and actualize themselves. People change to gain increased satisfactions and to avoid decreased satisfactions.

3. People who live differently tend to think and act differently because they perceive reality differently.

4. All behavior, regardless of how illogical or bizarre it appears to the uninvolved observer, makes sense to the person and is perceived to be goal-directed and need-satisfying at the moment.

5. The only circumstances that people really understand are those they have experienced. The only courses of action they truly comprehend are those they have helped formulate in some way.

6. The language of feelings and emotions is at times far more compelling than that of the intellect.

7. True cooperation is possible only if a mutual-influence system prevails, if a climate exists that rewards cooperation, and if people are helped to appreciate the benefits of collaboration.

8. The methods of attaining cooperation may be more important than the decision, course of action, or problem solution itself.

9. Feelings and attitudes change very slowly. They are not changed by telling, urging, or teaching. They change when people convince themselves of the advantages of the new attitudes.

10. The best vantage point for understanding the perceptions, attitudes, and behavior of another is from the internal frame of reference of that person.

11. Empathy means *thinking with* people, not for or about them; *feeling with* people, not becoming emotionally involved; *moving with* people, not rushing ahead or lagging

behind; *working with* people, not doing things for them; *accepting* people, not judging or evaluating them; and seeing situations from other people's viewpoints, not merely from your own.

If you reflect on these principles you will see that would-be leaders who try, within the limits of their personalities and situations, to implement these principles in their day-to-day behavior will gain acceptance and loyalty from subordinates much more easily. How would you react to managers who did their best to apply these principles in interacting with you? Are your superiors, associates, and employees so terribly different from you? Once more, draw your own conclusions.

An Analytical Procedure

This section presents and explains a system for analyzing any person. Certain cautions are in order. First, you are not to play junior psychiatrist. Amateur psychiatry is like amateur brain surgery: no one survives. Second, it is not the *many trivial* traits that you are interested in, but rather the *vital few* that will help you understand the individual's uniqueness. Finally, as was said earlier, do not force the person to fit the classification. Instead, use the checklists to follow the person according to the behavioral cues he or she sends you. This means that for some of the items you may have to put down DK (don't know).

Profiling the Person's Thinking Pattern

It is surprising how much emphasis is devoted to people's psychological nature and how little is devoted to their cognitive side. Although there are many things you would like to know, five are significant: speed of comprehension, intellectual preference, cognitive complexity, cognitive orientation, and cognitive movement. Figure 19 helps you analyze these factors.

Profiling the Person's Psychological Pattern

For your purposes, a person's psychological structure is composed of two major elements: the need pattern and the cluster of personality traits that typify him or her. Figures 20 and 21 help you to gain insight into these two important realities. Again, certain caveats are necessary. For example, a person is synergistic and is more than the mere sum of personality characteristics. It is the clustering of traits that is important, not merely their presence or absence. Also, the same traits may be expressed in quite different kinds of behavior. (Aggression in one individual may be naked and overt, whereas in another it may be masked and expressed in a polished manner.)

It is not sufficient to know only a person's dominant needs; you must also get a clear idea of how his or her personality traits are grouped. Figure 21 facilitates your efforts to do this.

Profiling the Person's Value Pattern

A person's most important attribute is neither cognitive capacity nor psychological make-up, but rather his or her value system. This is the nucleus that holds the person together and gives meaning to his or her life. A value connotes at least three things. It is an ideal or conviction concerning what should be done or left undone. It is a standard by which we judge our own behavior and that of others. Finally, it is a criterion for evaluating the relative importance of situations and people. Everybody has a different mix of the following values.

Political Values. These may be conservative, liberal, libertarian, middle-of-the-road, eclectic, or independent.

Economic Values. A person may defend capitalism-with-a-conscience, support free enterprise, advocate business-government cooperation, or be a proponent of socialism and the welfare state.

Class Values. People may have views that are lower-upper class, upper-middle class, middle-middle class, lower-middle class, or upper-lower class.

Figure 19. **Analyzing a person's intellectual pattern.**

	Above Average	Average	Below Average
Speed of Comprehension (Select one)			
Wax-wax: quick to learn, quick to forget.	___	___	___
Wax-marble: quick to learn, slow to forget.	___	___	___
Marble-marble: slow to learn, slow to forget.	___	___	___
Marble-wax: slow to learn, quick to forget.	___	___	___
Intellectual Preference (Rate all)			
Abstractions: prefers ideas and theories.	___	___	___
Concrete situations: prefers practical problems.	___	___	___
Social situations: prefers to deal with people.	___	___	___
Cognitive Complexity (Select one)			
Simplistic: black-white, either-or type of thinking.	___	___	___
Orderly: logical and concise.	___	___	___
Complex: delves deeply into ramifications.	___	___	___
Cognitive Orientation (Rate all)			
Language: comfortable with words.	___	___	___

	Above Average	Average	Below Average
Numbers: comfortable with numbers.	_____	_____	_____
People: comfortable with people.	_____	_____	_____
Ideas: comfortable with theories and abstractions.	_____	_____	_____
Cognitive Movement (Select as applicable) Slow and plodding: a patient thinker.	_____	_____	_____
Fast-paced: a rapid thinker.	_____	_____	_____
Analytical: a logical, orderly thinker.	_____	_____	_____
Unconventional: an unusual thinker with far-out ideas.	_____	_____	_____
Subjective: an emotional thinker.	_____	_____	_____
Imaginative: a creative and innovative thinker.	_____	_____	_____
Thoughtful and reflective: a deep thinker.	_____	_____	_____
Evaluative: a thinker who sizes up situations accurately.	_____	_____	_____

Societal Values. People may want the government to legislate rights and actively intervene in solving social problems, or they may favor limiting the government's role to that of impartial arbitrator.

Ethical Values. Some people are sensitive to moral standards, some stick to the letter of the law, and some feel free to get away with whatever they can.

Esthetic Values. People may love the fine arts, letters, and crafts, or may be quite uninterested in them.

Philosophical Values. Some people respond to philosophi-

Figure 20. **Analyzing a person's need pattern.**

Need for	High	Average	Low
Power			
Dominance over others			
Affiliation			
Control of situations			
Achievement			
Attention			
Increased competence			
Ego-building responses			
Aggression			
Deference to others			
Status and prestige			
Independence			
Recognition			
Sense of adequacy			
Sense of self-esteem			
Dependence			
Success orientation			
Failure avoidance			
Risk taking			
Closeness with others			
Social distance from others			
Hostility			
Interaction with others			

Figure 21. **Profiling a person's personality pattern.**

Is generally	1	2	3	4	5	
Open and authentic	—	—	—	—	—	Secretive
Emotionally mature	—	—	—	—	—	Lacking in self-control
Self-sufficient	—	—	—	—	—	Dependent
Cooperative	—	—	—	—	—	Exploitive
Objective about self	—	—	—	—	—	Self-deceptive
Cautious	—	—	—	—	—	Venturesome
Considerate	—	—	—	—	—	Self-centered
Conservative	—	—	—	—	—	Liberal
Friendly	—	—	—	—	—	Antagonistic
Energetic	—	—	—	—	—	Passive
Even-tempered	—	—	—	—	—	Moody and changeable
Gregarious	—	—	—	—	—	Introverted
Conventional	—	—	—	—	—	Unconventional
Self-assured	—	—	—	—	—	Timid
Predictable	—	—	—	—	—	Erratic
Positive-minded	—	—	—	—	—	Negative
Cooperative	—	—	—	—	—	Aggressive
Independent-minded	—	—	—	—	—	Conforming
Future-oriented	—	—	—	—	—	Past-oriented
Spontaneous	—	—	—	—	—	Reserved
Inner-directed	—	—	—	—	—	Other-directed

cal issues and questions while others are interested only in the practical, the pragmatic, and the mundane.

How Well Do You Understand Yourself?

It is a waste of time to understand someone else if you do not take some pains to understand yourself. You should complete Figures 19–21 not only for other people but especially for yourself! Answering the following questions as honestly as you can will also help you understand yourself better.

1. What are my assumptions and attitudes toward those with whom I interact? How constructive are they?
2. What are my expectations of others? Are they realistic?
3. What are my preferences and aversions in dealing with others? my blind spots? my biases? my tender nerves?
4. What are my strong points? my weaknesses? What is there about my behavior that wins respect? that alienates people?
5. What satisfactions do I seek in my relationships with others? Are they the right ones for building lasting relationships?
6. What manner do I project in my dealings with others? Is it constructive and stimulating?
7. What kind of reputation do I have with my superiors, peers, and subordinates? Is it the kind I would like to have?
8. What do people generally like about me and my behavior? dislike?
9. What do I like about myself? dislike?
10. What tends to get me into trouble in dealing with others?
11. What interpersonal strategies do I habitually use? Are these likely to build a collaborative relationship?

If you have answered these questions as candidly as possible, the next step is to formulate tactics for capitalizing more fully on your positive traits while doing the best you can to remedy your negative ones.

selecting the right leadership behavior: what combination is right for you?

The Remote Determinants of Leadership Behavior

The manager is influenced by a broad aggregate of forces that must be taken into account. Some are unobtrusive but basic, others obvious and immediate. The culture, the model of mankind, the ideology, the societal structure, the political philosophy, the political dichotomy, and the government are some of the remote determinants of management behavior.

The Culture

The Romans built 70,000 miles of the best roads in existence. They had only two requirements: enough slaves and enough whips! Those days are past, although now and then one encounters a returned Roman in organizations. Managers in Italy, Russia, Japan, Canada, and Argentina are both similar and different, because culture affects management style. Moreover, you cannot lead in precisely the same manner in

New England, the Deep South, the Far West, and the Midwest. Sectional nuances and subcultural mores call for somewhat different behaviors.

The Model of Mankind

May heaven protect us from managers who become philosophers! The only thing worse is philosophers who become managers. On the other hand, how leaders think of their fellow humans affects how they behave toward them. Although Adolf Hitler and Albert Schweitzer had roots in quite similar cultures, one major difference between them was the conviction of each regarding the sacredness of humanity. G. K. Chesterton once remarked that if he were to run a boarding house, he would be more interested in the philosophies of the residents than in their incomes. If residents had the right philosophy, Chesterton would be sure of getting the rent. If they had the wrong philosophy, he might never be paid no matter how much money they earned. Perhaps one reason why IBM has been so successful over the years is that its management has a sensitive regard for the integrity of the individual employee.

Do you believe that your subordinates are essentially good? More evil than good? More good than evil? Infinitely perfectible? Bound by heredity and environment? Capable of being programmed in a predictable manner? Defined but capable of learning, growth, and self-fulfillment? Self-determining and accountable for their behavior? Honest answers to these questions, singly and in combination, are far more important ingredients of effective leadership than techniques are.

The Ideology

"Ethos" is a favorite buzzword in top-management development programs. It is that complex of values, attitudes, and perspectives that permeates a society and gives it a distinctive coloring. Some managers yearn for a return of the puritan ethos with its emphasis on self-reliance, independence, individualism, competition, and survival of the fittest.

Unfortunately, the puritan ethos too often denied our common humanity. A more communitarian ethos now prevails, with a reasonable emphasis on the social responsibility and obligations of the corporation. As the trustee of society's resources, the corporation must consider the impact of decisions on its constituencies. A secondary ethos involves "doing your own thing" in a much more leisure-oriented culture that asks hedonistically, "What's in it for me?"

The Societal Structure

If culture is what people do, then society is how people organize themselves. Hierarchy, status, social classes, behavioral norms, rights, taboos, and regard for individuality are defined by society. Some societies are closed, others open; some are tightly restrictive, others almost too permissive; some are highly industrialized, others but newly developing; some are past-oriented, others future-oriented. It is interesting that if you substitute the word "corporate" for "societal," much of what has been said remains true. Complex organizations are like Renaissance states, becoming more self-contained and self-reliant as they become more transnational. How well do you understand the workings of your corporate societal structure?

The Political Philosophy

The four fundamental beliefs in any political philosophy have to do with the consent of the governed, the guarantees of human rights, equality, and freedom. Clearly democracy and socialism have a high regard for the first two. Fascism and communism ignore them except when it is expedient to profess them. What about equality and freedom? Rokeach [1] found fascism to be low on both dimensions and socialism to be high on both. Clearly democracy, of which socialism is but one type, is high on both. Communism is high on equality but low on freedom. Capitalism, he concluded, is high on the freedom dimension but low on the equality dimension. Small wonder that at times the citizens of a democracy are at loggerheads with large corporations.

The Political Dichotomy

H. L. Mencken once stated that if a politician running for office were to discover a large group of cannibals in his district, all eligible voters and all happily engaged in their favorite pastime, his attitudes toward cannibalism would undergo a radical change. Since the birth of America, two theories of the proper role of government have waxed and waned with changing conditions. The first espouses the view of Jefferson that government is best when it governs least and is least intrusive. Opposed to this is the Jacksonian concern for the common person: the ill-housed, the ill-educated, the ill-hospitalized, the ill-represented. In pendulum fashion, the voice of the people swings back and forth with the midpoint as its center of gravity. Liberalism and conservatism are the extremes between which public opinion oscillates to the benefit or detriment of the private enterprise system. The election of Jimmy Carter followed by that of Ronald Reagan is an excellent illustration.

The Government

Government is the way people rule themselves. There are two governments: the one elected by the citizens that passes the laws, and the one elected by nobody that regulates the day-to-day affairs of organizations. The paperwork for one car year at General Motors would stack up as high as a 15-story building. U.S. Steel must wrestle with some 5,600 regulations emanating from no less than 27 agencies. The regulators are busy people! Moreover, they may be opposed to business, in favor of the marketplace, or simply itching to produce a defect-free society regardless of the cost. The average of 150,000 laws passed each year by governments at all levels, coupled with the average of ten pages of regulations for each, means that your leadership efforts will be constrained by legal and regulatory realities.

The Immediate Determinants of Leadership Behavior

The immediate forces that tell the leader how to behave in a given situation include the technology, the organization, the task, the work group, the leader's superiors, the leader's peers, and the leader's resources.

The Technology

The impact that technology has on organizational structure, roles, and interaction among people is well known. Studies done by Lawrence and Lorsch have revealed that a high degree of specialization, rigid structure, tight coordination, and little freedom and authority at the lower levels are appropriate in firms characterized by little innovation or change, such as those that mass-produce containers. The situation is quite different, they found, in companies characterized by innovative, fast-changing technology. Here managers prefer greater independence and have greater tolerance of ambiguity. Interestingly, the two different ways of running things fit the personalities and expectations both of managers and the work force!

Functional areas, such as research, sales, and production, have different orientations toward structure, time, interaction with others, and the environment. Leaders must take into account the technology that typifies their division or department, because behaviors that are fine for leading design engineers or systems analysts may be quite ineffective for supervising workers in a bottling plant.

The Organization

As discussed in Chapter 5, each organization has its own unique climate, value orientation, self-image, leadership style, thrust, and tempo. It also has its own unique patterns of power, politics, status, friendship and friction, communication, interaction, and role adoption. All these factors should help you determine what management style is appropriate for you.

The Task

The discipline and logic that are essential in manufacturing and accounting would be ludicrous in sales or advertising. Moreover, matrix management makes different demands on the leader than does a programmed operation. Each type of task imposes its peculiar role demands and requirements, and each also has its own level of expertise, status, and technical knowledge.

The Work Group

The manager is appointed by higher authority. The leader is accepted by the work group. Every group—hostile, apathetic, cohesive, proud, cooperative, conscientious, or conflict-ridden—has its own particular expectations of the leader. The nature and influence of the work group are considered in detail in Chapter 11.

The Leader's Superiors

Regardless of theory, most managers operate in ways that are rather similar to those of their superiors. There are two reasons for this. First, companies are not likely to promote anyone who departs too far from the esteemed mode of managing. Second, potential managers who find the accepted mode intolerable are likely to seek their futures in another organization. Although leaders are responsible for their own behavior, it is their superiors who are accountable for it. Many decisions cannot be made without the support and/or authorization of superiors. In addition, superiors often have better access to higher-ups than the leader does.

How can you secure the continued backing of your superiors?

1. Complement their weaknesses with your strengths. Become an essential subordinate.
2. Anticipate their needs.
3. Learn their real expectations, sometimes in spite of what they have told you.

4. Go out of your way to make them look better and make their jobs easier.
5. Get to know their true priorities, at times in spite of what they have said.
6. Take time out now and then to see their problems and pressures—*through their eyes*.
7. Volunteer to take some of the burden off their shoulders.
8. Study them to understand what catches their minds, stimulates their hearts, and turns their stomachs.
9. Grow in and through your own job, and enrich it. Do not wait until superiors do it for you.
10. Serve as a buffer for them, absorbing some of the shocks when you can prudently do so.
11. Reveal yourself to them. Make sure they know your strengths, your abilities, and your willingness to take on more responsibilities.
12. When you honestly can, speak well of them to others.
13. Keep them informed of your contributions, achievements, aspirations, and plans.
14. Work with them, not for them. Be loyal, even if this means disagreeing tactfully at times.
15. Avoid crying on their shoulders, stepping on their toes, twisting their arms, breaking their hearts, or shocking them with unpleasant surprises.

The Leader's Peers

If superiors are authorizers and supporters, associates are helpers or hinderers. In any organization, managers receive work from one group, make their input, and then move the work on to another group. Evidently, your peers can make your life easier or more miserable. Everything just said about building good relationships with superiors applies equally to working smoothly with associates.

The Leader's Resources

Leadership is where opportunity and preparation meet. St. Paul is wrong in this respect: the leader cannot be all things to all people. The manager's unique pattern of talents, skills, attitudes, experiences, and motivations determines what he or she does with deftness and ease; with some effort; and with difficulty and intensive effort. It also determines what the manager does not do. Some leaders take naturally to counseling subordinates; others feel uncomfortable in this relationship. To be tough and tenacious is a piece of cake for some, but requires effort for others. Thus do not expect the impossible of yourself.

Determinants, Not Determiners

The fourteen important factors discussed so far in this chapter are often either ignored or minimized in leadership books. Managers must be attuned to them if their behavior is to be reality-oriented. Yet although these forces must be taken into account, they are not forms of predestination that absolutely determine what managers do. They are clues that signal which actions are likely to be effective, which ineffective. They are guidelines that enable managers to lead not only effectively but smoothly and fluidly.

Fitting the Behavior to the Situation

Figures 22 and 23 present a spectrum of unproductive and productive leadership patterns. The unproductive approaches range from merely ineffectual to downright destructive. The figures also give, in a comparative manner, the types of behavior that usually accompany each style.

Unproductive Leadership Patterns

Domineering managers are fools. Not only do they arouse resentment on the part of subordinates, but merely by being domineering they expend an enormous amount of energy, time, and attention. One study of the slave labor factories in

World War II Germany found that it would have been cheaper and more effective to substitute the guards for the workers because so many guards were required to control workers who were intent on sabotage. *Pseudodemocratic* leaders are equally foolish, but in the opposite direction. They waste personal resources without getting the work done effectively. Being *accommodative* is sometimes necessary, but when it becomes a prevailing pattern it degenerates into compromise, expediency, and nonintervention. *Paternalism* is basically emotional manipulation that keeps people dependent and tied with silken threads of personal loyalty, at times to the harm of the organization. Finally, a *bureaucratic* approach is self-defeating because it assumes that people are emotionless robots rather than thinking, feeling human beings.

Productive Leadership Patterns

Although *directive* leaders are often confused with exploiters, their virtues usually outweigh their deficiencies. They get the job done well, they win respect, they often inspire pride, and they reward achievers and get after foot-shufflers. More often than not, they are polished autocrats, skilled at getting people involved and astutely interacting with them, while at the same time keeping a certain social distance to avoid becoming emotionally involved with them.

In an ideal world, the *collaborative* pattern would be best. Here delegation and a consultative mode of management are natural. Communication is free-flowing and authentic. Participation in decision making is the norm. Unfortunately, in an imperfect world, it is not always possible to operate in this manner, despite what some books urge.

A *collegial* approach, which is as old as the Romans, works well when an executive group is composed of highly competent specialists whom the leader needs as much as they need him or her. The role of the leader is that of catalyst, integrator, team builder, mediator, and arbitrator. The expertise, acknowledged competence, and pride of the individual members of the group take care of problems of motivation and achievement.

Figure 22. **Unproductive leadership patterns.**

Variable	Domineering	Pseudo-Democratic	Accommodative	Paternalistic	Bureaucratic
Basis of leadership	Coercive power	Popularity with the group	Talent for avoiding waves	Personal loyalty of subordinates	Position power
Customary behavior	Arrogant	Hand holding	Undemanding	Protective	Ritualistic
Leadership climate	Despotic	Ultrapermissive	Retiring	Avuncular	Protocol-conscious
Leader's role	Driver	Group sustainer	Figurehead	Shepherd	Overseer
Subordinates' role	Obey the boss	Adjust to the group	Go their own way	Please papa	Follow the rules
Achievement orientation	Do as told	Avoid conflict	Compromise	Demand filial responsiveness	Foster consistent mediocrity
Decision process	Dictatorial imposition	Group think	Expedience	Benevolent imposition	Adherence to official policies
Leader-subordinate relationship	Hostile	Mutually ego building	Mutually indifferent	Parent-child	Politely formal
Control method	Threats and punishments	Group tyranny	Noninterference	Conditional love	Application of bureaucratic regulations
Subordinates' reaction	Resentment and sabotage	Other-directedness	Contempt for the leader	Anything for the Old Man	Apathy
Conflict resolution method	Suppression	Denial of conflict	Agreement to disagree	Oiling over of conflict	Legalistic appeals system
Communications	Downward and insistent	Free flowing but not authentic	Intermittent and tension-releasing	Downward and reassuring	Downward and impersonal
Motivation process	Force and flogging	Fear of alienating the group	Inconsistent incentives	Emotional manipulation	Official rewards and punishments
Morale indicator	Subservience	Group contentment	Absence of trouble	Compliance with leader's wishes	Lack of grievances
Subordinate needs met	Survival and avoidance	Affiliation	Pseudo-independence	Dependence	Security

Figure 23. **Productive leadership patterns.**

Variable	Directive	Collaborative	Collegial
Basis of leadership	Competence and force of personality	Acceptance by group	Recognition by peers
Customary behavior	Task-oriented	Consultative	Catalytic
Leadership climate	Exacting but fair	Supportive	Egalitarian
Leader's role	Energizer and compeller	Team builder	Integrater
Subordinates' role	Perform as expected	Contribute to group goals	Share the leadership
Achievement orientation	Shape up or ship out	Cooperate to achieve objectives	Work for team success
Decision process	Adjudication by the leader	Consensual decision making	Acceptance of competent judgment
Leader-subordinate relationship	Psychologically distant	Psychologically close	Mutually respectful
Control method	Close supervision	General supervision	Self-supervision
Subordinates' reaction	Pride in group; respect for and annoyance with leader	Involvement in group success	Personal responsibility for team success
Conflict resolution method	Solution by leader	Integration of views	Productive confrontation
Communications	Downward and directive	Free flowing and relevant	Authentic and multidirectional
Motivation process	Challenge and reward or clobber	Participation	Self-motivation
Morale indicator	Efficiency: taut ship	Attainment of group goals	Improvement and innovation
Subordinate needs met	Pride, competence, and growth	Affiliation and ego satisfaction	Ego and self-actualization

Leadership Behaviors, Not Behavior

A good leader will adapt his or her behavior to the mandates of the situation. Below are given 15 situations, together with the behaviors that are likely to be effective in dealing with them. Obviously, these behaviors cannot be mechanically fitted to each situation—you may have to combine several to meet a specific situation—but they will give you a clear idea of the range of behaviors available to the leader.

The Situation	*The Appropriate Behavior*
1. The work group encounters an emergency situation for which no standard procedures exist.	Act quickly and decisively, and announce your decision to the troops with the expectation that they will follow your instructions without question or hesitation.
2. The work group is new and minimally competent, lacking confidence in its ability to do well.	Treat employees as though you were convinced of their ability to perform well. Be directive. Make sure that each person knows what is expected, and supervise closely. Train and coach as time permits. Be supportive, patient, and available.
3. A decision or change has been imposed from above. The group is competent and has goodwill.	Announce and explain the reasons for the decision or change, pointing out the advantages, if any. Discuss with the group the best way to implement the decision or change. Get the group's help in identifying obstacles and ways to cope with them.
4. The work group is discouraged because of a series of defeats and setbacks. It is competent and has goodwill.	Conduct a group discussion of the reasons for past failures and how to avoid them in the future. Show your confidence in the group's ability to do well. Be alert for signs of discouragement,

The Situation	*The Appropriate Behavior*
	and move to counteract them. Give positive reinforcement of any improvement made.
5. The work group's attitudes are resentful or hostile.	Analyze the reasons for the attitudes. Be directive and controlling at the outset, and supervise closely. Spell out the rules of the game, making certain that everyone knows what is expected and what behavior will be rewarded or punished. Make it clear that sabotage will not be tolerated. Reward any positive change in attitude. If prudent, have a constructive group confrontation, helping the group to analyze its own attitudes and the harmful results that will occur.
6. The work group is competent but lethargic and apathetic. Productivity is lower than it should be.	Analyze the reasons for the apathy. Clarify objectives, expectations, and standards of performance. Monitor work closely at first. Make sure everyone knows the reward and punishment system you will employ. Model in your own behavior the importance and contribution of the work, and reinforce any improvement.
7. The work group is competent and well disposed. A problem has arisen that is starting to hurt production. The work group is capable of handling it.	Let the group members know that the problem must be resolved. Let them resolve the problem, while you set the limits of a permissible solution. Support their efforts with your continuing interest, but do not intrude. Let them know that you are available if they feel a need for your assistance. Intervene if

The Situation	The Appropriate Behavior
	the group cannot or will not solve the problem.
8. You have been brought in from another unit to head your group. There is some resentment on the part of two subordinates who had hoped to get the promotion.	Establish your credibility by doing the job as well as possible. If the resentment continues, have a constructive confrontation with each subordinate privately. Speak well to key authority figures of the positive achievements of the work group. Spike their guns by either appointing them devil's advocates or getting their criticisms of any important action in advance and privately. Reward any positive attitude change. Do not think of them as enemies.
9. You have been appointed from another unit to succeed a manager who has been promoted. The work group is not resentful but has a wait-and-see attitude. The group is competent.	If possible, speak with your predecessor and get his ideas. Do the job as well as you can to win respect. Analyze the previous manager's methods, evaluating his or her successes and failures. Move in smoothly, making as few changes as necessary. Learn the strengths and weaknesses of the group and of each individual. Make it clear how you intend to operate and why. Be available and interact without becoming "one of the boys." Encourage the work group's ideas, and implement the good ones.
10. The group resists a change in policy imposed by higher authority. Group members are competent to implement it.	Explain the reasons and beneficial results of the change, if any. Let group members ventilate their feelings about the change. Make it clear that no sabotage will be permitted. Ask their help

The Situation	*The Appropriate Behavior*
	in making the change work, and make sure they know how to implement the change. Supervise work closely at the outset, but be as supportive and helpful as possible. Reward success immediately.
11. You have made a decision, but it is important that the work group accept it. Group members are competent and have reasonable goodwill.	Explain to the group members the reasons for the decision. Let them express their questions, doubts, and objections, and answer these as best you can. If their criticisms or suggestions are valid, modify your decision. Seek their help in making the decision work. Then implement the decision.
12. You and the work group are confronted with a new situation that neither you nor they know exactly how to handle.	Explain the situation, if necessary. Present your ideas on how the situation *might* be handled. Invite members of the group to present their ideas. Discuss and evaluate all ideas, getting the best combination possible, and get the group involved in implementing the best approach. Monitor the implementation closely, being supportive and available.
13. The work group is full of conflict and is breaking down into warring camps. Group members are competent and respect you.	Show clearly that you will not allow the friction to hurt production. Call the leaders of the cliques together privately and explain that you will give them a certain time span to come up with a plan to reduce the friction. Warn them that if they fail to do so you will take unilateral action to resolve the matter. Try to act

The Situation	*The Appropriate Behavior*
	as a mediator to bring the parties together. Make it clear that no undercutting will be tolerated. If possible, assign representatives from each group a task with joint accountability for success or failure. Reward increased cooperation.
14. The work group must cope with a radical change in the method of doing the job. Group members lack confidence and are uneasy, but are competent enough to cope with the change. They trust you and respect you.	Explain the reasons for the change and its advantages. Spell out just how the change will be implemented, taking time to answer doubts and questions. Make sure all employees know what is required of them and how each person relates to the others. Treat them as though you were sure of their ability to perform as expected, and get the show on the road. Monitor work closely at first, being supportive and available if they need advice or help. Reward each success promptly.
15. The work group was not doing very well but has recently begun to improve.	Recognize and reinforce any progress made. Let key higher-ups know of the improvement. Reinforce the need for further improvement, stressing the rewards for doing so. Be supportive, and interact in an encouraging manner. Coach and train, if needed.

win-win leadership strategies: how effective are your negotiation skills?

Leadership and Negotiation

Management involves continuous negotiations with key people and groups.[1] Every department would prefer to do things its way, and each manager would prefer to do his or her own thing. Yet both are components of an interdependent input-throughput-output system in which coordination is essential. To be effective, then, leaders must become adept at interacting smoothly with those who can help or hinder them. Crucially important as personality traits and situations are, all the talk about them really misses the point. Effectiveness stems essentially from the negotiation skills of the leader. How strange that few management or leadership guides stress this obvious fact! And small wonder that the negotiation skills of the typical manager are not of a very high order. As Karrass has pointed out, if a 5,000-year-old Babylonian were to sit at a negotiating table today, his methods would not be very different from those most managers use.

The Nature of Win-Win Negotiations

Negotiation is the art of interacting with a person or group with different views in order to produce mutually beneficial agreement. Self-interest is always front and center, but it should not blind either party to the interests of the other. Thus, negotiation is not *a zero-sum game,* in which people strive to outwit each other in order to get the best deal they can at the expense of their opponent. It is not *persuasion,* in which the persuader triumphs over the persuaded. Nor is it *compromise,* which disappoints both sides because each is forced to yield on important issues to arrive at a pseudoagreement.

On the contrary, true negotiation is rooted in four strengths: (1) an *attitude* that prompts the negotiator to work for those solutions that will benefit both sides, although rarely in a 50–50 manner; (2) a *perceptual set* that views the other person as a potential partner rather than an adversary; (3) a *climate* that stimulates both parties to realize that they are more likely to attain their objectives if they work together than if they battle one another; and (4) *strategies* that facilitate the process of securing mutual advantages.

The Win-Win Strategies

This section summarizes the four principal cooperative strategies and the tactics relevant to each.

The Collaborative Strategy

A collaborative strategy is appropriate when you are dealing with reasonable people who have basic goodwill, even though they may hold very strong views.

Float a Trial Balloon. The purpose of this tactic is to ferret out the other individual's ideas, feelings, and reactions without committing yourself to a fixed position. Although it may take many forms, two of the most common are: "What if we were to ...?" and "Suppose that working together we could ...?" The aim of such nondirective leads is to keep your options open. If the other person shoots down the balloon, nothing has been lost. But if the reaction is positive, you have taken a giant step toward becoming partners.

Be a Problem Preventer. Far too much has been written about solving problems and far too little about preventing them. Don't we all appreciate people who take the time to help us avoid difficulty? For instance, someone in accounting might say to a sales manager, "Some of the salespeople have been inflating their expense accounts a bit. So far it's not that serious, but it could easily get out of hand. Why don't we work out a system that will give your people the freedom they require and yet conform to company policies and procedures before it gets both of us into trouble?" The same idea, of course, applies to opportunities. "We are planning to make some small changes in our work flow. I've been thinking we might be able to do so in a way that would make life a little easier for your people. I thought you might like to discuss it." It generally takes less thought and energy to make a friend than it does to make an enemy.

Help Make Lemonade. This imperfect world is full of problems, despite our best efforts to avoid them. When people face a disruptive problem at work, the natural tendency is to criticize, blame, or perhaps sympathize with them. Unfortunately, none of these reactions address the difficulty. Negotiation may be stalled simply because the employees are so distracted by the problem that their attention is elsewhere, or the difficulty may be that they agree to a solution but see no way of implementing it. Few people will resist sincere efforts to understand their situation and to help extricate them from a tiresome problem. The approach may be as simple as recognizing the other person's position. "You sure have a tiger by the tail there, don't you?" Or you might sometimes volunteer to be of direct assistance. "Perhaps if we put our heads together we can work this thing out."

Get a Foot in the Door. "I realize that if we do all these things at once, it'll cause a lot of trouble for you people. That would be unfair. Which might we do that would cause you the least difficulty?" Even though you plan to "do all these things," the fact that you demonstrate concern for the other person's situation often reduces the opposition that would be forthcoming if you were to try to attain your objectives in one fell swoop.

Deal with Clean Hands. Dealing with clean hands does not mean being totally candid; it means using as much frankness as is appropriate to the situation. Complete truth telling is frequently an act of hostility or inconsiderateness. Partners level with each other, but they do not burden each other with truths too heavy to bear. "We're perfectly willing to go along if you make these changes, but we will need two additional people if we are to keep our end of the bargain." Or, "Frankly, we cannot go that far. We just don't have the necessary resources. But could we work together on a modification that will be satisfactory to us both?" A spirit of willingness often begets reasonableness.

Keep in Touch. Disagreements sometimes occur because the parties ignore each other or isolate themselves, building up adversary attitudes because of severed communication. Wise negotiators, like good farmers, prepare the soil of negotiation by interacting positively *before* contention arises. Keeping in touch serves not only as a bridge but also as an early warning system. It can take many forms: keeping others informed, showing an interest in what they are doing, exchanging ideas, or even keeping casual social contacts. The time spent in such activities can pay handsome dividends when the negotiator must wrestle with a sensitive issue. The idea is to undermine fixed positions before the concrete of stubbornness has set.

Front for the Other Person. One of the best executives I ever met once said, "When things went well I tried to give my people a *little* more of the credit than they deserved. When things went wacky, I took a *little* more of the blame than was really mine." Letting other people shine may be as simple as speaking well of them to significant others, sharing the leadership, giving credit for contributions, or allowing them to bask in the limelight to some degree. The basic notion is that partners have a common stake in success. When things go well, there is enough satisfaction for all concerned.

Supplement Limitations. The Johari window, discussed further in Chapter 12, demonstrates clearly that there are four categories of knowledge in every negotiation: what both parties know, what A knows but B does not, what B knows but A does not, and what neither party knows. In negotiating there is always the temptation to manipulate or perhaps play games with the other person. In fact, this is the standard strategy of the Machiavellian. The problem with outmaneuvering, however, is that the other party has the same option.

Collaborators complement each other. It takes no talent to give the other person your ideas and skills, especially where you are stronger. Doing this to a prudent extent can stimulate the other person to respond in kind if he or she is interested in reaching an agreement.

The Accommodative Strategy

Although cooperative tactics are preferable, conditions often require that we accommodate our views to those of others. Accommodation, however, is not compromise. Your eyes do not compromise with a bright light. They adjust to it so that they can do their job.

Keep Sawing Wood. Many a salesperson has finally secured an order by the simple process of calling on a reluctant customer time and time again. Your boss may not have the same priorities as you; another department may not put what you consider important very high on its agenda; or the organization may move more slowly than you would prefer. In such circumstances, you have two choices. You can beat your head against the stone wall while wallowing in self-pity. Or, as occasion permits, you can tactfully stick to your position and gradually wear down the other person's resistance. Patient persistence is more than a virtue: it often gets the job done, as long as you are not perceived as a nag.

Leave Well Enough Alone. This is very difficult for the convinced, conscientious, or perfectionist person to do, but it is often the wisest course of action. A company once lost its executive vice president. For the better part of a year management searched in vain for a replacement. Curious, a consultant asked the president how things were going. "Rather well," was the reply. "What the vice presidents can't do, and I can't do, we do together." The consultant responded, "Perhaps there is no need to fill the slot at this time." Not every problem must be resolved. A shrewd negotiator can live with some.

Let Things Go Downhill. Timing is essential to successful negotiation, and there are situations that must get worse before any attempt to improve them has a chance of succeeding. Closed minds are not convinced by logic, especially the logic of another person. Events must be the persuader.

One president toyed for almost two years with the idea of installing a computer. His people made studies. Since his was a small firm, he spoke to sales representatives. But no decision was made. The vice president of finance was impatient to get on with the matter, because he felt that they were losing time and operating inefficiently. He was advised to let things go downhill a bit more before pressing for a decision, because the president was still hesitant. As things worsened, the president felt more pressure and finally made a decision that probably should have been made a year earlier.

Make an Exception. Everyone now and then makes unrealistic demands of another person. A manager may ask for special treatment, or a department may demand that your people extend themselves to make it look good. Although you have the right of refusal, there are occasions when it is wise to make an exception. The appreciation you can gain by doing so may help you later, when you need a favor yourself. It is critical, however, for the other party to understand that it *is* an exception, under no circumstances to become a matter of habit.

Change the Focus. In a nightclub it is difficult not to watch the performers for the simple reason that the spotlight is focused on them. Negotiations sometimes go sour because the two parties act as though they were in a cock fight, with their eyes riveted on a single combative issue. For example, few organizations or superiors take kindly to increases in personnel, but shifting the concentration to the value of the added personnel often places the costs in their proper perspective. This is precisely what every company does when it demands a premium price for its products or services. After all, every cost is relative to the benefits obtained.

Absorb the Sting. Turning the other cheek is for saints, not negotiators. But there are times when, within limits, it is an effective tactic. It allows others to ventilate their negative feelings and can provide a needed catharsis. Once the other people have gotten the emotion off their chests, they are often more open to constructive ways of reaching agreement.

A partner in charge of a large accounting firm was harshly criticized by the president of a client firm, in the presence of his subordinates, for something that was in no way his fault. He absorbed the sting at the moment, but later he visited the president privately and said, "I'm aware that you were under great pressure. But we both know that this was the first, and the last, time that such a thing will happen, right?" "I apologize," replied the president. "I got some bad news just before the group meeting and took it out on you."

Trim Your Objectives. To be thwarted and frustrated is a fact of managerial life. When this occurs, there is a temptation to intensify your efforts fruitlessly. To do so is to lose sight of the objective. A more mature response is to make whatever progress realities permit. After all, sailors do not fight a contrary wind, nor do they sit there helpless. They tack against it, navigating as best they can until the wind changes.

Give in Reluctantly. Victory too easily attained tastes less sweet. If there is no fun derived from the bargaining process, we might as well let a computer do it for us. However, you must be clear in your own mind about which items you are willing and unwilling to sacrifice. Moreover, if the other person misinterprets your willingness to accommodate as weakness, then more harm than good will result.

The Assertive Strategy

The best defense is often an effective offense. To preserve your self-respect, to gain the respect of the other person, and

to safeguard the relationship, it may be necessary to be assertive at times. This is especially true when coping with *exploiters,* who push aggressively to test limits; *seducers,* who try to
make you lose your cool; *pip-squeaks,* who nitpick insistently;
manipulators, who fancy themselves clever and perceive you
as less than bright; and *fearfuls,* who lack self-confidence and
need your self-assurance as a support. One caution: the discussion has to do with assertiveness, not aggressiveness.
There is a difference.

Start High. If you are dealing with exploiters, seducers,
pip-squeaks, or manipulators, you can start out by stating your
highest objectives firmly and boldly. This excellent tactic accomplishes two things. It shows people that you are neither
timorous nor dim-witted, and it reminds them that negotiation
can take place only between equals. You can always lower but
never raise your objectives, so you have nothing to lose. However, your demands should not be so high that they are perceived as a threat.

Act as a Devil's Advocate. The role of the devil's advocate is
to provide friendly, supportive loyal opposition. This role is
useful when people are about to act on the basis of emotion or
when they ignore the real problem, consciously or unconsciously. For instance, someone may be so frustrated that he
pushes for a solution that will be ineffectual. You might say,
"Of course, we could agree to this solution. But would either
of us really get what we want from it?" Or a self-insistent
person may demand that a solution be hers and meet her
needs, even though it is unfair to others. A reasonable response might be, "This is fine for you in this instance. But it's
very unfair to the rest of us. Suppose all of us acted just out of
self-interest without considering the rights of others. Might it
be that you'll get your way this one time only to set everyone
against you for the future?" In a sense, then, the devil's advocate forces the person to stop and think, or at least probe the
consequences of what he or she proposes to do.

Lay Your Cards on the Table. This is a more assertive tactic
than dealing with clean hands, and its strength lies in its
simplicity. Someone is pushing you to squeeze out every con-
cession possible. You have reached the limits of accommoda-

tion, so you might counter with, "I am willing to work with you in every reasonable way. However, there are certain things I can do and others that are just impossible. Let me briefly explain both sets."

Shorten the Time Dimension. Some lawyers pride themselves on their ability to delay, hinder, prolong, and procrastinate; and some negotiators try to wear you down in order to win concessions through fatigue. The only effective tactic here is to tighten up the time that you will remain in the negotiation. "I'm sorry, but we are making no progress after going over this again and again. If we cannot reach some kind of agreement within the next hour, I'll have to put the matter on the back burner. So why don't we buckle down and arrive at a solution we can both live with?"

Rely on the Record. Something has gone awry or you have blundered, and the boss or another department head is telling you off in no uncertain manner. To defuse the situation and to put the annoying mistake in perspective, you might say, "I'll admit that I blew it this time. I'll get right on it and straighten it out fast. On the other hand . . ." (now you present some of the excellent things you have done recently). Superiors have a human tendency to react to the pressures of the moment and see yesterday's failure more clearly than last month's success. This is why managers should keep a "hero file" of past successes.

Appeal to Higher Authority. You have been doing your best to work with a person, but he or she is obstinately resistant, for whatever reason. You might say, "Listen, we both understand each other's position, but we are getting nowhere. If we don't start making progress, we may have to buck this matter topside for a decision. Why don't we call in Bill and get his opinion?" If the person is stalling for self-centered reasons, this is likely to shake him or her up some. Naked intimidation stimulates aggression, apathy, or sabotage. A subtle, implied intimidation, however, has its place.

Wave a Red Flag. A watchman along a road signals caution by waving a red flag. You too can wave a red flag when the other person is refusing to reach a decision or agreement. Effective red flags are appeals to ethics, competitive pressure, customer goodwill, law, or the efficiency of operations. "I know you are opposed to this. Perhaps I'm not overjoyed with it either. But the fact is that the law requires us to comply with this regulation."

Simply Refuse. It well may be that the other person wants you to do something that goes against your ethical code or organizational policies and procedures. A clear but diplomatic statement that you cannot do what is requested is enough to settle the matter. It may prompt him or her to focus on other areas, where agreement is possible. At the very least, you will gain the respect of the other party.

The Defensive Strategy

You need defensive tactics to cope with a bad scene. People become irate, things go wrong at times, and failures are a part of life. When such unhappy events occur, you must have available tactics for defusing the situation, protecting yourself, and preserving the relationship.

Avoid a Showdown. Serious negotiation can sometimes become highly emotional. The danger is that issues may be smothered under egos in a win-lose confrontation that imperils the future of the relationship. A comment such as the following may serve to prevent both parties from saying things they will later regret: "Look, we're both getting pretty uptight about this. Why don't we get together tomorrow when we'll both be in a better frame of mind to discuss it?"

Draw a Line. When the other person seeks to demean you or treat you in an uncivil manner, it is not enough to absorb the sting. Here you must control your temper, no matter how much you would like to tell the person off. Then calmly and quietly make it clear that there are limits to your tolerance. This tactic may be necessary in dealing with naive managers who fatuously believe books that counsel them to come on like gangbusters and intimidate people whenever they can. It is also necessary when negotiating with folks who are overly concerned with "taking care of number one."

Be a Fabian. Fabius was a Roman general who defeated Hannibal by losing battles only to win the war as he wore the

Carthaginian army down. Sometimes the best course of action is to fall back as an army does at first under an initial heavy assault. Allowing people to win victories that are meaningful to them but not essential to you may enable you to get your agenda on the table. "Why don't we work it this way? We will help your people by readjusting our schedules slightly. We can even rearrange to some extent the number of people we will put on your job for a day or so, OK? Now let's discuss some of these other items."

Destroy a Straw Man. What you really want is a substantial salary increase. So you use your "hero file" of past achievements to persuade the boss to give you a promotion, even though you know that one or two of your peers not only have seniority but have performed a bit better than you. He explains why he cannot offer the promotion, giving his reasons. You gradually agree, asking for his guidance on how you can best prepare yourself the next time around. Assuring him that you will do your best to merit the promotion in the future, you might then say, "OK, I guess the promotion was overreaching a bit. On the other hand, in view of my contributions to the department, I feel that in justice I have earned the right to such-and-such a raise, don't you?" Having allowed the superior to destroy your promotional straw man, you have created a climate that makes it easier to attain your principal objective.

Offer an Unacceptable Alternative. The president of a medium-size company made it a habit to speak informally to the head of the union. When bad times necessitated a serious layoff of union people, he met with the union head privately and gave him the bad news. At first, the union head bristled. After the initial emotional outburst subsided, the president said, "Help me with our problem. Either we lay these people off for a short time or we will have to close down the plant, perhaps even think of relocating from New York to northern New Jersey. What will be best for all concerned?" After the union leader was convinced that the layoff was actually the best available alternative, negotiations were as smooth as silk.

Confess with a "But." Things go wrong or you commit a blunder. Resist the temptation to blame someone else, to defend yourself, or to plead for understanding. The best course of action is to admit what went wrong simply and very briefly. Then focus attention on how a repetition can be avoided. "I know we let your people down. But I've given it a lot of thought, and I think that I have a procedure for preventing this from happening again. Why don't we discuss it?" Confession is sometimes good for the souls of both the offended and offending parties.

Buy Time. We all occasionally encounter situations where the emotional climate is too turbulent for rational discussion, or those where we are caught by surprise, or where the other individual brings up an unanticipated issue or demand. Rather than trying to rely on instant inspiration, it's better to make some comment like, "This is an item that we should consider carefully. Mind if I check with my boss before we get into it?" Or, "This sounds like something that might work out, but I'm not sure it's within my authority. Let me check first and get right back to you. Then we can work it out."

Call in the "Heavies." There are situations in which you may find yourself outmaneuvered by other people. They may have more facts than you do; they may have greater authority or status; they may simply be brighter or faster thinkers; or they may have gotten you into an uncomfortable position. What do you do? Keep your cool and respond to the other person as follows: "You are bringing up some excellent points. However, I think that several heads may be better than two. Why don't I ask Judy and Mark to join us to get the benefit of their ideas?" The people you bring in, of course, will be your allies who are capable of supplementing your deficiencies in this situation with their authority, power, status, or expertise.

Application of the Strategies and Tactics

These 32 techniques are all geared to win-win interaction. There are other negotiation devices that you can use, but they are of a conquering, persuasive, manipulative, or tricky nature and tend to destroy cooperation.

In applying these techniques, be sure to remember that a

mere litany of tactics is of little help. You should experiment with these methods to discover which ones work best for you in the situations that confront you. Practice them until you can employ them smoothly. Also, enter each negotiation situation with a clear notion of your primary, secondary, and contingency tactics. If you follow these suggestions, your negotiation skills should improve markedly.

organizational approaches to motivation: do the jobs stimulate or stifle people?

The Stricture of the Structure

The fabled Greek giant Procrustes was wont to stretch or shrink his victims to fit his iron beds. This is precisely what some organizations are doing. A misinterpretation of scientific management prompts the higher echelons to determine the organization's structure, specify the work flow, and design the jobs with little or no concern for the people who will ultimately make the organization a success or failure. Then managers are expected to lead and motivate their subordinates in an environment that is unconcerned, depressing, perhaps even depersonalizing. This is unrealistic because employees are motivated largely by the organizational climate and the satisfactions derived from doing work well. When the structure is stultifying, it is difficult to lead. Thus, the first step in motivating employees is to look at the organizational context, not at the leaders or their people.

There are organizations and organizations. Figure 24 describes the various kinds, along with the role of the leader, his or her power base and influence methods, and the subordi-

Figure 24. **Types of organizations.**

Type of Organization	Leader's Role	Power Base	Influence Methods	Subordinate Needs Met
Paternalistic	Supportive Protector Subtle manipulator	Charisma Referent power Blind faith	Conditional love Emotional entanglement	Dependency Affiliation Identification Safety
Bureaucratic	Maintainer	Legitimate power Appeal to tradition	Policies Rules Procedures	Security Stability
Autocratic	Self-insistent dominator	Coercive power	Fear Conditional whimsy Flailing and flogging	Survival Power (for the few)
Authoritative	Executive director	Expert power Rational faith	Reward and punishment Supportiveness Management by results	Competence Growth Dependency Prestige
Consultative	Catalyst Supporter Facilitator	Referent power Rational faith	Consultation Joint analysis of problems and opportunities	Growth Social needs Contribution Interdependence
Innovative	Energizer Integrator	Expert power Rational agreement	Participation Joint determination	Growth Achievement Autonomy Creativity

Adapted from D. Hampton, C. Summer, and R. Webber, *Organizational Behavior and the Practice of Management*, 3rd ed. (Glenview, Ill.: Scott, Foresman, 1978), p. 60.

nate needs met by each organization. It is clear that an authoritative, consultative, or innovative company will greatly facilitate your leadership tasks. However, if you find yourself in a paternalistic, bureaucratic, or autocratic firm, you will have to work against many built-in restraints.

Constraints to Making Jobs More Satisfying

Some behavioral scientists thrust most of the blame for lack of employee motivation on the organization. This is hardly fair, because there are many realities over which the firm has little or no control.

Personal Factors

Emotional Maladjustment. Slightly more than half the adults in the United States show some symptoms of mental health problems. Employees who have marked difficulty adjusting to life in general are likely to have trouble adapting to the requirements of the job.

Unrealistic Aspirations. In a culture that stresses rising expectations, it is not surprising to find employees who have career expectations far beyond their talents. Until they acquire enough maturity and experience to accommodate to reality, there is little the organization can do.

Individual Differences. No two employees make identical demands on the same job or have the same priorities. The methods an organization can use to reconcile these differences are rather limited.

Disparate Job Objectives. Many workers like challenging jobs, but some are not overly concerned about self-fulfillment at work. Still others take an instrumental view of their work; they use the rewards received to obtain more important off-the-job goals.

Native Ability. The levels of education, intelligence, and skill of some workers make it difficult to grant them increased autonomy, authority, or responsibility.

Group Pressures. Union contracts or the antagonistic attitudes of union representatives may undermine corporate efforts to make work more satisfying. The fact is that few unions favor job enrichment programs. Every union wants the exclusive right to negotiate the nature and conditions of work. It is wary of *management-sponsored* enrichment programs because they are interpreted as intrusions on its jurisdiction, because they are seen as weakening the union's control over its membership, and because they may be perceived as a corporate strategy to divide and conquer. More significantly, as management treats its people as an important productive and innovative resource, and as employees derive greater rewards from what they do (Herzberg's satisfiers), they are likely to identify less with the union and become less dependent on it.

Organizational Factors

Technology. In many factories and offices, machines determine the work flow, logic, and discipline. Many workers are mere operatives or observers whose input to the end result is minimal. The production process is the key element, not the brains and skill of the operator, and few jobs require craftsmen.

Management Attitudes. Lower-level managers are sometimes opposed to allowing subordinates greater freedom and opportunities to use their skills. They perceive this as a threat to their status, their control, or even their position. Without managers' support, attempts to redesign jobs are likely to fail.

Compensation System. If they achieve and produce more, workers naturally expect increased compensation. Redesigned jobs may not be compatible with current wage and salary administration policies and practices.

Economic Condition of the Firm. Few cost/benefit studies have been made of the advantages and disadvantages of redesigning jobs. A financially pressed firm is not likely to invest scarce economic resources in an acitivity that does not yield immediate payoffs.

Size of the Organization. Large companies have huge sums of money invested in current production processes, which are often delicately interdependent. Tinkering with this or that unit, without considering its impact on the total system or subsystem, may be a risky endeavor.

The realistic leader does not clutch at the latest isolated bit of research or the most recent theory. Psychologists sometimes have much to offer management. However, few have ever managed anything. The good leader analyzes thoroughly the factors presented above instead of naively launching a program that looks good on paper but may be at odds with the realities of the shop floor or office.

Why People Dislike Their Jobs

Here are some of the most significant reasons why employees become dissatisfied with their jobs:[1]

Fractionalized Jobs. Specialization may help production efficiency and make sense to high management, but it prevents employees on the line from doing either an entire unit of work or even a meaningful segment of one.

Repetitive Work. Every job has some repetition built into it. But when a job involves spending hour after hour performing the same seemingly inconsequential bit of work, it is deadening.

Underutilization of Skills. Everyone has a brain and would like to use it. Every employee possesses skills, or at least the aptitude to acquire them. Unfortunately, many people work at jobs that permit them to employ only some of their skills and very little of their intelligence. This is a serious problem.

Lack of Freedom. Some jobs are programmed by others in such detail that there is little opportunity for the workers to make decisions or to act like self-determining adults.

Meaningless Work. Many workers see little or no relationship between the operations they perform and some significant end result. They have no opportunity to plan their work or to take responsibility for it.

Short Work Cycle. The time cycle for some workers at the GM Lordstown plant was only 36 seconds. Thus, some workers performed the identical small operation on a new car about 800 times in a single eight-hour shift!

Lack of Feedback. When employees get no feedback on how they are doing, they feel that their work is neither important nor appreciated.

Lack of Social Support. People are social animals who need opportunities to interact with others. Salespeople on the road sometimes have so much freedom that they feel lonely.

Making Jobs More Motivational

The first step in improving the quality of work life is to analyze the organizational forces noted above. Research has found that motivational jobs possess some combination of the following characteristics: (1) variety; (2) a longer time cycle; (3) social interaction; (4) accountability; (5) skill utilization; (6) reasonable autonomy; (7) feedback on performance; (8) contribution and participation; (9) recognition and rewards; (10) growth, learning, and achievement; (11) opportunities to use discretion, to plan, and to organize one's own work; and (12) freedom to contact organizational clients to get and give information that facilitates the work flow. Rarely is it possible to incorporate all these elements into a group of jobs, but some managers make little effort to build any of them into their subordinates' current positions.

Six major strategies that have been employed to improve the quality of work life in organizations. These are job enlargement, job rotation, job enrichment, autonomous work groups, quality circles, and participatory democracy.[2]

Job Enlargement

In this strategy, the worker performs additional operations of a similar type. This has the advantage of providing a longer work cycle, giving variety to work, and making it less boring. However, as Herzberg points out, it may be adding zero to zero since it connotes doing more of the same kind of work (*horizontal loading*) rather than increasing the qualitative challenges of the job in terms of planning, organizing, decision making, and so on.

Job Rotation

This approach moves the worker from job to job. Like job enlargement, it offers variety. It also increases a person's competence and provides a longer work cycle.

Job Enrichment

This strategy is defended by Herzberg as *the* way to improve the quality of work life. It is a process of changing the content of jobs so that they become more meaningful and motivational; stimulate workers' responsibility, contribution, competence, and growth; and become more productive and satisfying. The central core of this method is *vertical loading*, or adding qualitatively different motivational elements to a job that it lacked before. Such elements might be challenge, accountability, skill utilization, variety, or any of the other characteristics of motivational jobs listed earlier. In a word, the employee controls the job rather than being controlled by it.

Although there are many permutations and combinations, the basic steps toward job enrichment include the following: [3]

1. Select jobs that are worth enriching. These are jobs where worker motivation can improve production; where the relative costs of pay and fringe benefits are becoming unduly expensive; and where the costs invested in job enrichment will produce a rich return.

2. Use small group discussions, brainstorming, and other suitable techniques to draw up a pool of potential changes that will enrich the jobs.

3. Eliminate all proposed changes that are mere generalities (such as "getting people involved"), that are concerned primarily with pay and fringe benefits, or that cannot be operationally defined.

4. Ask such questions as these about each remaining item.
— Will it increase productivity and worker satisfaction?
— Will it build into the job increased worker planning, organizing, self-control, accountability, freedom, input, and knowledge of results?

— Will it contribute to employee growth and learning?
— Will it enable the worker to perform a meaningful unit of work, rather than an insignificant part?
— Can it be introduced without disrupting the ongoing work flow and without sabotage on the part of lower-level managers?

5. Select the proposed changes that give the best promise for increased productivity and satisfaction.

6. Try out the changes in a pilot study, under controlled conditions. Caution those in authority that productivity may fall somewhat before it improves, because of the change process. After a suitable time, take measures of important criteria such as production, costs, morale, and turnover. Make any necessary modifications.

7. Introduce the changes on a large scale, monitoring them as required.

Herzberg's job enrichment method is a considerable contribution to motivational theory. However, there are certain limitations to his approach. First, it ignores the influence of organizational force fields, including unions. (Union leaders are not panting to introduce job enrichment.) Second, it ignores the need to discover just what payoffs the employees are looking for from their work; programs are initiated by management and imposed on the work force. Finally, blue-collar workers and other lower-skilled employees are usually less interested in job enrichment than in pay and security.

A serious constraint on efforts to enrich jobs involves three givens: the sophisticated technologies that are utilized in many organizations, the huge capital investments that have already been committed to existing plants, and the complex, interrelated production systems that are already in place. Sometimes psychological practitioners, who often know very little about these areas, tend to ignore these formidable realities that cannot be changed easily or quickly.

Fein has reviewed many of the studies and is less thn impressed.[4] He finds the results biased because some of the jobs were poorly designed to begin with, or a few carefully selected people were involved, or the organization had a long history of concern for the welfare of the employees. Finally, it must be remembered that job enrichment is only one approach to redesigning jobs to make them more meaningful and contributing.

Autonomous Work Groups

More common in Europe than in the United States, this strategy stresses the design of sociotechnical systems in which the *production rationality* of the engineer is combined with the *individual rationality* of the psychologist and the *social rationality* of the sociologist. It is based on the concept that man is a "group animal" who prefers a balance of independence, dependence, and interdependence. Instead of being programmed by others, a work group is assigned a whole unit of work and allowed to plan for itself just how that work is to be accomplished. For instance, in the assembly of an engine, instead of each person doing the same activity over and over, a group of workers with related jobs may be given the freedom to decide that (1) each group of workers may follow the engine around the line, assembling the entire engine, or (2) each group may build a third of the engine, passing it along to another group.

The autonomous work group arrangement, where it is possible, has numerous advantages. It not only incorporates the advantages of job enlargement, rotation, and enrichment, but also takes into account the social character of work. Job enrichment may add to the *personal* meaningfulness of work, but autonomous work groups make the additional contribution of *social* meaningfulness. If you doubt this, observe how often a team victory is much more pleasant than an individual tour de force.

Quality Circles

More than 40 years ago, Phil Murray, president of the United Steel Workers, suggested to management that it would be well advised to solicit the contributions of the work force. He was politely ignored. Traditional management has always been largely a layer-cake matter: the few at the top did the thinking, and the many at the bottom did the doing. Astute executives, of course, realized that such polarization was arrant nonsense which was inimical to the best interests of both parties. Today, quality circles are the most popular technique for obtaining the input of the employees, increasing their sense of responsibility and self-control, and getting them to identify more enthusiastically with the objectives of the organization.

Quality circles, however, represent more a philosophy of managing than mere technique. According to Drucker, they required a radical readjustment of Japanese management's concept of its role, its attitudes toward workers, and its strategies for interacting with them.[5] Any organization that wants to increase productivity by implementing quality circles must be prepared to make similar major adjustments. Management must have an enduring commitment to the new philosophy if the movement is not to degenerate into a transient fad or mere cosmetic. Finally, cultural support for quality circles was essential in Japan. It will be no less necessary in other cultures and nations.

Participatory Democracy

Thomas Jefferson once wrote, "The mass of mankind has not been born with saddles on their back, nor a favored few booted and spurred, ready to ride them legitimately, by the grace of God." This philosophy is the cornerstone of participatory democracy, which is sometimes also called codetermination, workers' councils, or self-management. It takes different forms in various countries, such as Germany, Yugoslavia, Sweden, and Israel. Participatory democracy hinges on four convictions:

1. The privileges and burdens of democracy should not stop at the plant entrace.
2. The quality of work life should be enriched, not merely the job.

3. Power should be distributed throughout an organization and shared by the corporate citizens at all levels.
4. Employees should participate in decision making to a far greater extent than is often the case.

At one end of the continuum, employees are consulted about and participate in decisions that affect the work environment and process. Quite a number of companies have experimented with this approach, often with considerable success. At the opposite end of the continuum is direct democracy, where employees participate in all major aspects of the conduct of the organization. In the center are attempts at representative democracy in which representatives of the employees—not to be confused with union officials—join top management in making decisions and running the firm. The concept of greater participation is undoubtedly good, but there is no one satisfactory model. It is important to note that participatory democracy in its extreme form can be incompatible with the private enterprise system. One may question how "democratic" a private enterprise can become without degenerating into "mobocracy." If some degree of democracy is desirable, meritocracy is no less essential.

Why People Don't Do a Better Job

It is important for leaders to know something about the mechanics of redesigning jobs in order to help subordinates do their jobs as well as possible. Figure 25 presents 11 reasons why employees do not perform as well as they might, together with an appropriate course of action for coping with each.

The Nuances of the Job. A position description is a bloodless picture of a lifeless job. It does not include the human expectations of either superior or subordinate. Hence, you must communicate with your people day-in and day-out to clarify which activities you consider to be essential, important, and incidental, including your personal preferences and aversions. You should also help them to understand your situation and the

Figure 25. **Why people don't do a better job.**

The Cause	The Cure
Employees do not know	
The nuances of the job.	Dialogue with you to clarify what you consider to be essential, important, and routine, and in what order of importance the work should be done.
How to do it well.	Training, coupled with a development program for each key subordinate.
Where the job fits in.	Team-building activities.
The results expected.	A management by objectives philosophy, coupled with standards of performance.
Why they should do the job well.	Motivation, rewards, and incentives.
How much freedom they have.	Delegation.
Their successes and failures.	Feedback.
How to get help.	Coaching and counseling.
What they can contribute.	Consultation and participation.
What they should do better.	Performance appraisals.
Where success will get them.	Career pathing.

pressures that affect you. If you fail to do this, the whole relationship degenerates into a guessing game.

How to Do It Well. Every job has a learning curve. Your task is to shorten it as much as possible by *making* time to teach your subordinates. This can be done by holding private conferences and group meetings, and by noting the aspects of the job that are done less than well.

Where the Job Fits In. An organization does not need individual stellar performers as much as it needs coordinated and cooperative effort among people with related positions. Unless people feel that they are respected members of a group and know how their input facilitates the team's efforts, each job tends to become an end in itself.

The Results Expected. It is difficult to hit an unknown target. Specific, measurable goals should be set with each key subordinate. Unless goals are jointly arrived at, clearly understood, within the subordinate's control, attainable, fair, and accepted by the subordinate, goal setting becomes a mere paper exercise in which neither you nor your people have any faith.

Why They Should Do the Job Well. Left to his or her own devices, an employee can do a given job very well, reasonably well, acceptably, or just well enough to get by. The intervening variables that motivate the employee to excel are the incentives, satisfactions, and rewards that are contingent on superior performance. Each subordinate should know clearly the rewards and punishments that you intend to apply to performance.

How Much Freedom They Have. Too much freedom, especially in dealing with very unstructured situations, can do more harm than good. People can be so independent that they feel alone. On the other hand, too little freedom is cramping: a six-foot person cannot perform well in a four-foot job. Since different people perform more productively and comfortably with diverse degrees of freedom, your delegation should fit the burden to the back. Some people are tigers who enjoy being on their own. Others perform best when given reasonable autonomy, as long as they know that you are available in time of need. Still others require your close support.

Their Successes and Failures. Positive feedback is more motivational than negative feedback, but even the latter is preferable to no feedback at all. Unless there is a feedback loop between subordinate performance and superior approval and disapproval, subordinates miss the opportunity to gain satisfaction from their successes and never find out precisely where improvement is necessary.

How to Get Help. People have a habit of seeking advice from those with whom they feel comfortable, rather than from those most competent to offer assistance. Moreover, subordinates at times hesitate to ask the counsel of a superior for fear that he or she may think them less than bright. Others are reluctant to ask for help because they do not wish to bother the boss. Still others fear the possibility of being criticized. Thus, you must make the first move by convincing your people that, when it comes to help with their job-related problems, you have an open-door policy. Bear in mind, however, that there is a difference between an open door and a swinging door. If they are to come to you for counsel in time of need, they are not to barge in about every petty obstacle.

Coaching helps people become improved performers, and *counseling* facilitates their efforts to become improved human beings. Both are guided by the principles of learning and teaching. However, two cautions are necessary: do not go beyond the limits of your competence in either activity and make certain that the problems discussed are job-related. For serious personal difficulties, there are specialists to whom employees can be referred for guidance.

What They Can Contribute. A consultative style of management, group discussions, participation in group decision making, and similar activities all provide avenues for employees to get a hearing for their suggestions and innovative ideas. Your attitude must convince your people that you have a genuine interest in their opinions and views.

What They Should Do Better. The purpose of performance appraisals is not to dredge past failings, but to plan improvement on past performance. This means recognizing and rewarding past success, while attending to performance that has been less than acceptable. It also implies a sincere effort to help the person develop an improvement program that is realistic and attainable.

Where Success Will Get Them. Achievers are more interested in careers than they are in jobs. If people are to be motivated to excel over the long run, it is essential that at least some career planning be their reward. People soon weary of the game of the "carrot" of short-term incentives and the "club" of control, if something far more important and attractive is lacking: career implementation and success.

The Tip of the Iceberg

A host of powerful background factors helps or hinders your motivational efforts: the philosophy, climate, and personnel policies of the firm; the attitudes of higher management; the technology employed; the size and resources of the company; the manner in which jobs are designed and the work flow is managed. The personalities, expectations, and peer pressures of the work force are critical. Even more crucial is the need to analyze the eleven reasons why people do not do a better job, together with the recommended cures. On the other hand, a variety of strategies are available to you to make work more motivational: job rotation, enlargement, and enrichment; re-design of jobs; consultation; participation; autonomous work groups; and even quality circles. These potent background variables represent the hidden two-thirds of the motivational iceberg. Chapter 10 presents the major research findings and practical suggestions for motivating individuals and groups.

interaction approaches to motivation: do you move or motivate your people?

Psychological Malnutrition: The Greatest Problem

The vast majority of people go to a new job or promotion with a desire to perform well. When this enthusiasm is squeezed out of them, for whatever reason, the symptoms of malnutrition quickly appear—shoddy work, irresponsibility, apathy, and an "I'm just putting in my time" attitude. Unlike its physical counterpart, psychological malnutrition is internal and may ulcerate unnoticed. To motivate people, the leader must ensure that subordinates enjoy a balanced diet of need fulfillment and valued rewards from their work.

A simple formula, $P = C \times M \times S$, indicates the importance of motivation. P stands for productivity, profitability, proficiency, and performance. It is the vitamin that makes the organization healthy. C refers to the competence of the individual or group, while M refers to the motivation of the work group, and S denotes the satisfaction obtained from the work. Accordingly, motivation is the process of stimulating people to improve on past performance while obtaining increased psychic income from what they do. Motivation multiples human effort; demotivation divides human effort.

The Labyrinth of Motivation

If management theory is a jungle, motivation theory is a maze. The leader has a choice of using:

Need theory
Two-factor theory
Achievement theory
Affiliation theory
Equity theory
Social exchange theory
Cognitive dissonance theory

Incentive theory
Expectancy theory
Reinforcement theory
Power theory
Self-concept theory
Psychoanalytical theories
Behavior modification

Which theory, or combination, is the practicing manager to rely on? The matter becomes even more complicated when you realize that each theory is based on incomplete evidence, tends to ignore the others for the most part, has its own particular successes and failures, and is unable to encompass all the elements of the motivational process.

Instead of describing each approach in sausage-link fashion, it is more useful to adopt a systems approach. Figure 26 does this. Although hardly complete in every detail, it does depict the sequence and interaction of many of the factors that go into motivation. Each factor is described below.

The Individual

Each employee brings to the job a unique mosaic of talents, skills, experiences, habits, attitudes, and values. The stage of the person's life cycle is also important. Older people place greater emphasis on security and affiliation, whereas young eager beavers are likely to stress freedom, achievement, and advancement. The person's past success-failure history is critical: winners expect to do well and usually do, but losers an-

Figure 26. What actually takes place in motivation.

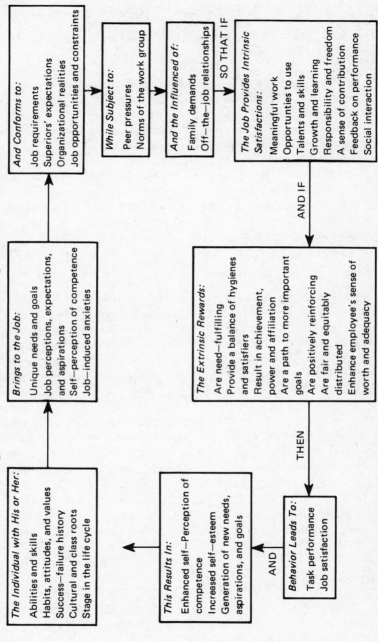

ticipate reverses and generally find them. Cultural and class roots make their subtle input as well.

A vice president of a small bank managed a supervisor who was not performing well. She was from an intensely labor-oriented family and resented having to work overtime now and then. She identified with the work group, having minimal concern for the bank's needs. Her absence rate equalled the average of her subordinates', even though there was often no legitimate reason for her absences. She had no desire to become a manager. In fact, it was not clear that she even wished to act like a supervisor. Although efforts might be made to motivate her, it would probably be better to think of her replacement.

Employee Expectations

To organizations, many jobs are identical. To the subordinate, his or hers is special. Each subordinate perceives the same position differently. Job expectations, aspirations, needs, and goals vary from person to person. Workers' differing self-perceptions of their competence induce differing degrees of anxiety about failing, succeeding, or advancing beyond the position.

Increasingly, both academics and businessmen are lamenting the state of business schools: the inability of newly minted MBAs to communicate, their overreliance on mathematical techniques, and what one disgruntled executive recruiter calls their "expectations of becoming chairman in four weeks." Someone who is arrogant, elitist, and tells management that they've been doing everything incorrectly for the past few years is unlikely to be hired.[1]

Requirements of the Job

If employees have their role perceptions, the organization defines its role prescriptions. Demotivation results when these two role sets are markedly out of sync. Apart from the job requirements, the employee must conform to the demands and expectations of superiors, some of which may be highly personalized. Moreover, each position has its own built-in constraints.

"Man, am I ever glad to be back out in the field," said one former district sales manager. "I was cooped up in an office. I attended more and more boring meetings. I shuffled paper. I had to check up on my people. I was loaded down with administrivia—keeping records, analyzing sales reports, keeping track of expenses, and on and on. It was nice in some ways being a manager, but I'm basically a salesman. I love to sell and I'm good at it."

Social Pressures

The group is the social world of the employee at work. The pressures that it can bring to bear are clearly illustrated in the following charming anecdote from Benjamin Franklin, written long before Kurt Lewin demonstrated the force of the informal group for good or ill.

Watts after some weeks desiring to have me in the composing room, I left the pressmen. A new sum for drink, five shillings, was demanded of me by the compositors. I thought it an imposition, as I had paid below. The master thought so too, and forbade my paying it. I stood out for two or three weeks, and had so many little pieces of private mischief done me, by mixing my sorts [letters in a font of type], transposing my pages, breaking my matter, if I were ever so little out of the rooms, and all being ascribed to the chapel [composing room] "ghost" that *I found myself obliged to pay the money; convinced of the folly of being on ill terms with those one lives with.* (Italics added.)[2]

Off-the-Job Influences

The phenomena of single parents, of marriages where both partners have independent careers and share care of the children, and the problems of transferring one manager when the spouse is unwilling to relocate all illustrate the influence that family responsibilities have on the subordinate. In a time when the work ethic has weakened, off-the-job pursuits may sometimes take precedence over the drive for career success.

A bright, very competent, extraverted young woman was offered a management position, only to turn it down. Management was surprised. Her explanation was, "I can do this supervisory job with almost no effort. It gives me time to think about my outside activities." She was very involved in community affairs and was planning to run for the local board of supervisors in the next election. Politics was her real "thing."

Some senior managers are becoming weary of the rat race. This is not the immature quest for a second adolescence that took place in the sixties and early seventies, when a few executives sought vainly to imitate the "me generation." It is a reaction to both forced retirement and a shift in values. These managers have proved what they set out to prove and now wish to serve the community. An illustration of this is the number of successful executives who have become deans and professors in business schools.

On-the-Job Rewards

Redesigning jobs to make them more intrinsically rewarding has already been discussed in Chapter 9. Equally important is providing extrinsic rewards that fulfill employee needs. Most managers are familiar with Maslow's hierarchy of needs. Alderfer has regrouped them into three categories: *existence,* which combines the physiological needs and the material aspects of the safety needs; *relatedness,* which includes the social needs and those esteem needs that stem from the regard of others; and *growth,* which accounts for the self-respect aspects of the esteem needs and self-actualization. Alderfer's classification is more useful to the manager and explains frustration far better than Maslow's.[3]

The existence, relatedness, and growth approach presents seven propositions that can be reduced to three. First, the *more* the needs at one level are satisfied, the *more* the person will desire those at the higher level. Second, the *less* the needs at a given level are satisfied, the *more* they will be desired. Finally, the *less* the higher-level needs are satisfied (the more they are frustrated), the *more* those at the next lower level will be desired. The first two propositions are self-evident. The third is interesting because it explains one form of reaction to frustration. For instance, if an employee desires mightily to be promoted but is thwarted, then he or she will back down and concentrate on satisfying as many lower-level needs as possible. This is precisely what the "rate buster" does. Alienated from and ignored by peers, the thwarted employee strives to make as much money as possible.

There is a caution here for the leader: because subordinates complain about salary or working conditions does not mean that this is the real problem. It well may be that they really want more support from the manager or a greater say in how things are done. There is an old Navy saying, "The storm signals are not the storms." Leaders should be aware that the verbalized communication is not always the real message. They should diagnose problems, not deal merely with symptoms.

A Balance of Hygienes and Satisfiers

Most managers are already familiar with Herzberg's two-factor theory, so a brief summary should suffice. The first of the two factors is the *hygienes*. They include such things as pay, fringe benefits, working conditions, supervision, peer relations, company policy, and hours of work. Since they cater to a person's survival needs, their absence causes dissatisfaction. They deal with the *context* of the job, rather than with the job itself, and are extrinsic in nature. The importance of the hygiene factors is well illustrated by the following incident. Years ago, a psychologist was interviewing a worker in a textile firm to discover her feelings toward the company. After some hesitation and no little embarrassment, she stated that there was only one toilet in the women's rest room, and its seat was cracked. "Every time I sit on it," she continued, "it *pinches* me, and I say, Goddamn _____ Mills!"[4] The absence of hygienes can sometimes cause intense dissatisfaction!

· The *satisfiers* are intrinsic, deal with the *content* of the job, and are the motivators. They include meaningful work, achievement, recognition, advancement, increased responsibility, and growth possibilities. Each set of factors is important. The hygienes make for a healthy environment, tranquilize dissatisfaction, and are a base on which the satisfiers build. But their motivational effect is slight for most employees. The satisfiers, on the other hand, are geared to growth and self-actualization on the job.[5]

The lesson for leaders is clear. They must provide, as best they can, the proper mix of these factors according to the individual differences of the subordinates. One great contribution of Herzberg is to remind organizations that too much emphasis is placed on the hygienes, important as they are; too little on the satisfiers. For one thing, the hygienes are both expensive and largely taken for granted by personnel. On the other hand, organizations can appeal to the higher needs of people by using job enrichment programs to permeate jobs with satisfiers, when this is possible. When subordinates achieve and become more effective, the increased performance justifies both the costs and any additional compensation that may be required.

Achievement, Power, and Affiliation

McClelland believes that achievement, power, and affiliation are *the* potent motivators.[6]

Achievement. People who are high on the achievement motive have the following characteristics:

1. They get a kick out of excelling.
2. They set realistic goals and take calculated risks; they do not believe in luck.
3. They assume personal responsibility for the outcomes.

4. They act like entrepreneurs, seeking out challenging tasks and engaging in more initiative behavior than most people.
5. They require quick concrete feedback on their performance.
6. They do not work primarily to obtain either money or power.

It is clear how one motivates achievers: give them work that makes them stretch; give them autonomy, feedback on success and failure, opportunities to grow, and challenges to keep their motivational motors running in high gear.

Power. Although some speak of the drive for power as though it were a character defect, the fact is that it is a strong motivator. For managers, it may well be *the* most puissant motivator, since it connotes the desire to make a strong impact on others and to influence them. McClelland, however, makes a needed distinction. As mentioned in Chapter 4, power has two faces: personalized and socialized. Too much personalized power is self-aggrandizing and demeaning to the followers, who are either manipulated as pawns or treated as serfs. Socialized power is used for the good of the followers, to formulate goals that benefit the group, to inspire them to rise above petty concerns for the good of all, to consult with them and work out the best ways to achieve the common objectives and, ultimately, to be evaluated by the followers. Thus, personalized power is either threatening or manipulative, whereas socialized power is catalytic.

Affiliation. Some people have a strong need to be accepted, to belong, and be liked by their associates. For them, the words of the song "People who need people are the luckiest people in the world" are truth. They seek out others and work hard to obtain their approval and approbation.

The Mix. No one is so rigid that he or she works for one of these motivators to the exclusion of the others. It is the relative mix of the three that is significant for the leader. The autocratic person is likely to be very high on personalized power, low or high on achievement, and low on affiliation. The achiever will be relatively low on affiliation, very high on achievement, and unconcerned with power of either type. The person with a high affiliation drive will, of course, be low on both power and achievement. And what about leaders? There is no one best mix. But a high achievement drive, coupled with a reasonably high need for socialized power and a moderate affiliation need, would be greatly in their favor. The real problem for leaders is that they must walk a tightrope. On the one hand, they must make their personal impact and be dominant. On the other, they must be sensitive to the needs of the followers and open to their input and influence. This balancing act is never an easy task.

A Path of More Important Goals

In Chapter 2 the path-goal theory of leadership was discussed. Its motivational equivalent is expectancy theory.[7] This theory involves the following assumptions:

1. Employees will perform well only if the potential rewards are attractive. (The degree of attractiveness of a reward is called its valence.) The more enticing the outcomes, the more intense will be their efforts to do a superior job.

2. People work for personal goals. They will perform well either to secure intrinsic satisfactions (*basic outcomes*) or to obtain extrinsic rewards (*first-level outcomes*)—a pay increase, promotion, recognition, greater autonomy, more challenging tasks, and so on. These extrinsic payoffs are rewards that the leader uses to motivate subordinates. But they are not ends in themselves. They serve as the means, or *instrumentality*, for attaining more important objectives (*second-level outcomes*) such as food, shelter, a better life-style, and a better education for the children. Two ideas are central: the motivating force of the valences associated with these two sets of outcomes, and the extent to which the subordinates are convinced that the first-level outcomes will lead to the second-level payoffs. This may range from +1 (always leads to the second-order goals) to 0 (no relationship between the first- and second-level outcomes). Thus, a salesperson may be convinced that if she surpasses her quota consistently, the handsome pay increases will enable her to buy a new car that she has her heart set on.

3.   People are odds-makers. They make a *subjective* probability estimate about their chances of being able to perform as
required (Expectancy I). This personal calculation can range
from 1 (complete belief) to 0 (complete lack of belief). One
foreman may be almost convinced that he can increase production by 10 percent (Expectancy I = .85). But another may
be persuaded that, because of outdated equipment, union opposition, or his own lack of management skills, there is little
chance that he will be able to increase productivity (Expectancy I = .30). Expectancy II connotes the subjective belief
that, if the person performs as required, the desired reward
will be forthcoming. The first foreman may be pretty sure that
if he raises production by 20 percent, he will get a promotion,
or at least an unusual salary increase (Expectancy II = .70),
whereas the second foreman might have a hunch that, even if
he were to increase production, the company would not reward him in any way (Expectancy II = .40).

This theory is more complex than most. Of what use is it?
First, it concentrates on what should be stressed: namely, the
*perceptions, expectations, and beliefs of the people to be
motivated.* Second, it reminds the manager that rewards are
effective only to the extent that the subordinates perceive
them to be attractive and useful for obtaining more important
goals. Third, since the forcefulness of the valences, expectan-
cies, and instrumentalities is *multiplicative,* it means that if
any of them is low, motivation will be decreased. Additionally,
this theory reminds the leader that rewards, intrinsic or extrinsic, are in the eye of the beholder. Far too often organizations
act as though they knew for certain without consulting employees which outcomes provide incentives for them.

The leader does not have a monopoly on the payoffs that are
prized by workers. Outside interests, pressures of the informal
group, or coercion by the union may offer countervailing rewards. Accordingly, leaders should analyze the variety of desired payoffs available to the person or group, ensuring that
those at their own disposal are more motivating than those
from competing sources. Finally, conflict may arise from conflicting performance payoffs. A salesman, for instance, may
dislike his job (intrinsic dissatisfaction) but stay with it be-

cause it allows him to make more money (extrinsic outcome) than he could elsewhere. Or a newly hired worker may take pride in doing the very best job possible (intrinsic satisfaction) only to find out that the quantity of her output may be unacceptable, and as a result she may not receive a desired raise (extrinsic outcome). It is ironic that organizations and managers may unwittingly create conditions that put the employee in a conflict situation.

Positive Reinforcement

In 1911, E. L. Thorndike introduced his *law of effect*. It stated that people's behavior is governed by its consequences. Behavior followed by pleasant outcomes tends to be repeated; that bringing unpleasant results tends to be avoided. B. F. Skinner has refined and developed this law with great effectiveness. All behaviorists are less interested in vague concepts such as needs, perceptions, and beliefs than they are in observing, changing, and controlling behavior. The major concepts include the following:

1.   Positive reinforcement is better than negative; negative is better than none at all; and punishment should be used with caution because it produces negative *side effects*. For instance, workers can be taught to arrive on time by rewarding them for doing so (*positive reinforcement*), or by informing them that continued lateness will affect their pay increases (*negative reinforcement*), or by bawling them out before their co-workers (*punishment*). The difficulty with punishment is that it may win a battle and lose the war. Bawling out may get short-term results but generate unanticipated consequences in terms of hostility toward the supervisor and overall lower production on the part of the work group (*side effects*).

2.   *Standards of performance* must be clearly defined. The types of behavior that will be rewarded must be measurable, clearly understood, and reasonable to the people affected. *Feedback* should be quick, specific, constructive, and preferably accompanied by efforts to help the employee improve if improvement is called for.

3.   The leader should reinforce any progress employees

make toward the appropriate behavior, rather than waiting for complete success. This is called rewarding *successive approximations*. In this way, behavior is *shaped,* and people are "led to learn" and motivated to continue the progress.

4. What do you do to get people to stop behaving inappropriately? In unusual cases, punishment may be necessary as a last resort. But most of the time, it is enough simply to stop rewarding undesired behavior either directly or indirectly. Unrewarded actions tend to disappear, or become *extinct,* for lack of nourishment. People are smart and find more rewarding ways of acting.[8]

It is important to note that behavior modification involves much more than the mechanical process of reinforcing or not reinforcing behavior. A careful study must be made both of the individualizing characteristics of the situation and of the people to be affected. Since leaders will get in return only the rewarded behavior, they must make certain that the right kinds of actions are reinforced. If they reward docility and obedience, they will get these reactions. If they reinforce initiative, suggestions, and improved ways of doing things, they will get these reactions instead. Improved fringe benefits, across-the-board pay increases, and better working conditions are not likely to have any direct or marked impact on productivity. Finally, as has been noted, the manager is not the only one in a position to reinforce subordinates. As Skinner points out, reinforcement of behavior is going on all the time, whether the organization or the manager realizes it or not. This approach is vulnerable to some genuine philosophical criticisms. Even so, it has had some marked, if limited, successes.

Equitable Distribution of Rewards

Justice always comes before charity. It is not surprising, therefore, that equity theory is important. Subordinates expect a fair return on their invested effort. Equity hinges on the rewards received, as *perceived* by the person; note that it is not the objective fairness that is significant. The following equation, based on Homans's social exchange approach, summarizes the basic concepts.[9]

$$\frac{\text{Rewards} + \text{satisfactions}}{\text{Investments} + \text{costs} + \text{contributions}} = \text{motivation}$$

Investments refer to the talents, skills, energy, and so on, that the employee puts into the job. Costs connote negatives, such as working in unpleasant conditions, overtime, heavy work loads, abiding by the rules of the organization, and the orders of the boss. Contributions denote the input toward organizational success made by the worker. As long as the numerator is greater than the denominator, subordinates will be motivated. If it is less, then people will be demotivated. If people are to be convinced of the fairness of the rewards received, a management by objectives and results approach is a must. Additionally, leaders must review their subordinates' work frequently, giving them feedback and helping them improve on past performance. Most important of all, however, is the need for the leader to communicate clearly with subordinates so that they will understand and accept the standards and rewards as he or she does. Otherwise, they will be working on different wavelengths to the disappointment of both.

It is also necessary that the rewards be distributed throughout the group in as evenhanded a manner as possible. Success is rarely absolute; it is relative to that of one's co-workers, judged by *social comparison.* If Pete gets a 20 percent pay increase, he may be motivated to do better. But if Mary, a co-worker who has done just as well as Pete, receives only 10 percent, she will be demotivated.

Enhancing the Employee's Sense of Adequacy and Worth

The implementation of a *self-concept* theory has much to offer the leader. People who anticipate success usually get it; those who expect to fail generally do. Leaders can do much to enhance their people's sense of adequacy and worth by giving them a strong vote of confidence, by being generous with earned praise and recognition, and by emphasizing their people's assets rather than their deficiencies. The opposite is also true, unfortunately. A major objective of the manager, then, is to facilitate his or her subordinates' efforts to success and to help them think better of themselves and their potential for improvement. Self-perceived competence is not fixed. It can be raised or lowered by the manner in which leaders interact with their people.

A young, new salesman for a small high-technology firm was thrown into a new territory with little training. The product was a high-ticket item so that decisions to buy were made by a committee and were long in coming. After two months of vigorous effort, he had no orders. The new salesman was discouraged as he walked down the hall. The president passed him, noticed that he was low, stopped for a moment, and asked, "How are things going?" "Terrible," responded the salesman. "I'm breaking my back, but there are no orders." "Don't worry," replied the president, "this is not like selling ash trays. It takes time and effort. We are convinced that you are a good salesman and will do very well. Just hang in there. You'll do just fine. If there is any way we can help, let us know."

This incident took less than five minutes. The results? The salesman made quota for that year and broke every sales record in the company for the next two years! Too many leaders forget the importance of the Pygmalion effect—the importance of a little encouragement. They should study *My Fair Lady* once a year to improve their perceptions of, and attitudes toward, their people.

The Results

When the job provides a reasonable combination of intrinsic satisfactions and extrinsic rewards, the task gets done in an excellent manner. Moreover, employees derive psychological nutrition from their work, perceive their abilities in an improved light, feel better about the organization, and raise not only their self-esteem but also their level of aspiration. Thus, the motivational process loop is completed.

Putting Motivational Theory into Practice

1. Remember that all behavior, even the most puzzling, is caused, goal-directed, need-satisfying, and justifiable at the time to the person who so behaves.

2. Adopt the frame of reference of the other person, since motivation is defined in the eye of the beholder, not yours.

3. With respect to two different people, keep the following points in mind. First, the same motive may get you quite different responses. (Praise may stimulate one but prompt another to become complacent.) Second, different motives may get the same response. (Autonomy may work well with this individual, but close supervision may work better with that.) Finally, a motive that is overused loses its efficacy. (Praise can go only so far; you cannot get a new suit with praise.)

4. Different people may have different ways of satisfying the same needs. One may get attention by constant complaining, another by becoming an achiever.

5. Motivating others is like playing the piano. First you read the sheet music—try to understand the person. Next you practice hitting the right keys—experiment with the various motivational techniques. Finally you develop your own style—learn which approaches are best for you, your situation, and your subordinates.

6. Remember that work has technical, economic, social, and psychological aspects to it. Each aspect has its own motivational potential on which you can rely in interacting with your employees.

7. Serve as a model as much as you can. People are motivated by example and behavior more than by words or techniques.

8. Use the research findings to help your people learn, achieve, and grow:
— Provide a balance of the hygienes and satisfiers.

— Try to make jobs meaningful and contributing.
— Give rewards whose valences and instrumentality provide incentives for the subordinates.
— Make rewards equitable and fairly distributed.
— Help, in whatever way you can, to enhance the person's self-perception of competence and his or her sense of adequacy and worth.
— Give feedback that is positively reinforcing, and make certain you are rewarding the right behavior.
— As circumstances permit, serve as a path that subordinates can use to attain *their* objectives and satisfy *their* needs.
— Interact with your people in a supportive way; the personal touch is invaluable.

9. Be realistic. You will not be able to motivate everyone; the chemistry will sometimes be wrong. But do not give up too easily. Be as patiently persistent as reality allows.

capitalizing on group resources: do you have a crowd or a team?

Individuals Achieve, but Groups Accomplish

Lenin once noted that 100 organized men, committed to an objective, would overcome 1,000 unorganized men. In the 1980 Olympics, the U.S. hockey team proved how correct Lenin was by defeating a far more skilled Russian outfit. The leader's task is similar to that of an orchestra conductor. Both must stimulate each individual to achieve better than he or she thought possible. Then comes the harder job: getting the individual achievers to support one another to produce a polished performance. The analogy limps, of course, because whereas the maestro is in full charge, managers are dealing with an open system and must therefore contend with a host of variables beyond their control.

The Nature of a Group

A group is neither an aggregate nor a crowd. Group members have an explicit psychological relationship to one another; it is the glue that unites them. The characteristics of a cohesive group include the following:

Common Purposes. There is a synergistic thrust toward attaining goals that are important to the group.

Shared Sentiments. The emotional state of the American people is far more important than the numbers that economists love to count. The values, feelings, attitudes, and interests of a group are a cement that gives it strength.

Participation Opportunities. Even joggers like to trot along with others. Satisfying interaction is a reward that the group provides.

Cohesiveness. In unity there is not only strength but exclusivity, a "we-ness" that nonmembers do not enjoy.

Structure. Organization, status, role assignments, and pecking orders vary from group to group.

Social Control. Every group has its own customs, rituals, behavioral norms (what *should* be done) and its own rules (what *must* be done). Hampton, Summer, and Webber give some interesting illustrations of the influence that others have on individual performance even among lower creatures.[1]

An ant, working alone, moves 232 gm of earth every six hours. Add another, and his production increases to 765 gm. Add a third and the output of the first ant rises to 778 gm. This occurs despite the fact that they seem in no way to coordinate their efforts. Apparently a "beneficial tension" (competitive attitude?) is produced by the mere presence of others. Now remove the second and third ants and the productivity of the original ant drops to 180 gm. Goldfish are different. One can master a maze in 35 minutes on the fourth trial. Put others in the tank and they will master it in 7 minutes! Apparently the first teaches the others. Cockroaches, however, are "dummies." One can learn a maze in 4 minutes on the tenth trial. Two, however, take 6 minutes, while three require 10 minutes!

From such small creatures the leader can learn. The group sometimes facilitates learning and production, but at other times the group approach is little more than a fatuous endeavor to attain wisdom by pooling ignorance.

What People Get from Groups

A person will remain in a relationship only if the costs are less than the returns on his or her invested effort. Accordingly, the manager should be well aware of the returns that groups often provide the members.

Need Satisfaction. Cohesive groups provide many satisfactions that the leader and the organization cannot or may not provide: belonging, acceptance, security, learning, loyalty, identity, recognition, status, exclusivity, aggression, defense, interaction, and so on.

Support. The group often protects the members from incursions from outsiders—management or members of another department or unit. The group is a natural vehicle of communication. It can teach and train the members, particularly new ones.

Social Validation and Definition. "What is a fair day's work? What should my attitude toward management be? How should I feel toward my fellow workers?" Questions like these are frequently answered by the group, which defines reality for the members.

Change. The group can have a great influence in changing the ideas or behavior of the members for better or worse. Few people so prize independence that they are willing to be considered deviates.

Stability. The group can be a safe haven where people can find security and permanence when they are uncertain or uptight. Most people will take risks with the support of the group that they might never take on their own.

In a sense, the work group is like a surgeon's scalpel. In the hands of the competent, it can be an effective force for good. In the hands of the incompetent, it can be destructive.

Types of Groups

There are all kinds of groups: task-oriented or social, formal or informal, cohesive or conflicted, supportive or antagonistic, interacting or counteracting, conservative or erratic. Rather than dissecting each type, it might be more to your benefit to consider the strategies you might employ to cope with different problems. How would you lead each of the following work groups?

1. *A resentful group.* You have been brought in from another part of the organization to head up the department, and the group had assumed that one of three people already in the department would get the promotion. Members of the group are not hostile, and their work has not fallen noticeably. But they do resent the fact that an outsider was given the promotion and placed in charge of them.

2. *A conflicted group.* At one time, the group consisted of all men with rather long tenure with the firm. Now minorities and women represent about 30 percent of the group. There is no union, and the group does office work. Most older workers resent both the women and the minorities. Most of the minorities are male and do not get along very well with the women either. The level of production has dropped about 10 percent over the last three months. Moreover, for the group to do a good job, a certain amount of teamwork and coordination of effort is necessary. Members of each faction complain about the others whenever they get a chance and cooperate only when they have to in order to get the work done.

3. *An apathetic group.* The group is discouraged and dependent, and the work it does is essential but not glamorous. There have been some setbacks lately: things went wrong largely for reasons beyond the control of the group. Group members lack confidence and self-assurance and are not greatly esteemed or respected by your superiors. In fact, two months ago, you were put in charge to put some "zip" into the group.

4. *A bureaucratic group.* Historically, the group was required to follow procedures and rules to the letter. They had to go by the book no matter what. However, there have been some important changes at the highest levels of the firm. The climate now encourages initiative, innovation, management by objectives, delegation, and disciplined freedom all the way down the line. But members of your group still cling to the old way of doing things. You have been put in charge to turn them

around, to bring their thinking and behavior in line with upper management's new philosophy.

5. *A complacent group.* The group does an acceptable job but hardly an outstanding one. In an effort to reduce the higher costs of doing business and to increase production, upper management has sent out the word that what was good enough in the past is no longer good enough. Even so, members of this particular group have shown no real effort to increase productivity or to reduce costs. They feel that management is trying to "get blood from a stone." You have been brought in to energize the group, to increase production, and to cut needless costs. Apart from its complacency, the group is a good one. The people like one another, work well together, and are loyal to the organization. They are not resentful of you, but are waiting to see what you will do and how you will proceed.

6. *A high-producing, self-confident group.* The group members pride themselves on their ability to get the job done quickly and do superior work. On the other hand, they are a bit eccentric. They sometimes step on the toes of other work groups and frequently ignore certain rules and procedures to get the job done well and speedily. They think of themselves as the best group in the organization. Thus, while being cohesive and very supportive of each other, they do not think much of other work groups or associate with them very much.

Formal, Nonformal, and Informal Groups

Most authorities distinguish between formal and informal groups. It might be better to add the nonformal group, as Herbert does.[2] The formal group stems from the administrative system, which structures task-oriented groups to achieve objectives. The source of the informal group is the social system. It is geared to the satisfaction of people's needs and involves tension-reducing activities, friendships, gossip, and conversations about politics, fashion, sports, women's rights, and so on. The informal group is also influenced by banter, horseplay, and worker-sponsored informal social activities. Midway between the two is the nonformal group, which is work-related and stems from common sense. The formal group is static. Policies, procedures, and rules are always somewhat out of sync with working realities; they can rarely cope with sudden changes. Thus, the nonformal group serves two purposes: it supplements the formal group, enabling it to deal with day-to-day contingencies; and it links the formal and informal groups. A well-disposed nonformal group will always develop shortcuts to do the job better, but a hostile one will find ways to undercut the formal organization. The following two incidents illustrate this well.

A Positive Example

In one experiment in the famous Hawthorne studies some 50 years ago, a small group of women was placed in a special room off the production floor. Using their typical production floor output as a base of 100, the experimenters manipulated such variables as hours of work (8¾, 8, 7), group pay rate rather than individual, rest periods (0 to 30 minutes a day), days worked per week (4 to 5½), and even returning the operators to their original work schedules and back to the shop floor. To the surprise of the experimenters, giving rest periods, shortening the hours worked per day, or shortening the length of the work week did *not* lower productivity. Over a period of years, most experimental changes resulted in increased production, with the highest increase being 140, or 40 percent above the base. The nonformal and informal groups supported the organization to its immense benefit.

A Negative Example

Taylor, the father of scientific management, was a superb machinist. As a boss, he knew that production was only about one-third of what it should be. He asked the men to step up production: no result. He then operated a lathe to show that he was not being unreasonable: no result. He brought in new people who promised to do a fair day's work, but they soon succumbed to the pressures of the regular operatives. He finally cut the pay rates. The men first complained to higher management and then began to sabotage the machines to prove that Taylor was requiring them to operate the equipment at too fast a rate. Taylor, however, had foreseen this strategy and had forewarned higher management. With its full support, he announced that anyone whose machine broke down would be disciplined. It was only after three years of struggling that Taylor finally prevailed! Interestingly, before this contest of wills, Taylor and his subordinates had liked each other.[3]

Some Problems with Groups

Groups create some special problems for the manager. Here are some you may encounter.

Conformity

Every group demands that its members conform, to a greater or lesser extent. Most executives think of conformity as negative, but nothing could be further from the truth. It is not the conformity that is bad, but the *quality* of the conformity. For instance, in one department workers may be pressured to do only as little as required, but in another they may be out of step if they are not creative and innovative. The leader must generate a climate that stimulates people to conform to a desire to improve on past performance, to help one another, to come up with better ways of doing things. This is precisely what happens in the best companies, universities, and restaurants.

Togetherness

The perniciousness of a cloying togetherness and group think is evident. Some workers are *personals* who will do almost anything for the sake of harmony. Others are *counterpersonals* who have an anti-authority chip on their shoulders. Most are *interpersonals* who easily adjust to others without sacrificing their ideas and convictions. In addition, some situations require independence: the salmon must swim upstream to preserve the species. Others call for dependence: when autumn comes, the geese line up behind the leaders. Still others require interdependence: bees work together to protect the queen and the hive. If leaders are not clear in their minds which situations require each approach, they will inevitably emphasize one to the neglect of the other two.

Resistance

A body at rest tends to remain at rest: such is the law of inertia. Regardless of the intelligence or educational level of a cohesive group, its vested interests, status, ingrained habits, and deeply embedded attitudes are a formidable obstacle, as every newly elected President of the United States learns to his chagrin. If possible, the manager should get the group's support for any change he or she has in mind. If this is impossible, resistance should be neutralized. Only as a last resort should the leader have a head-to-head confrontation with a resistant group. It has resources to undermine the best of changes, while giving lip service to it.

The Grapevine

"We are happy to announce that Marie Maelken has been promoted to the position of vice president of advertising and public relations," reads the release. You can bet that the affected people knew about the matter long before it was made public. This is the grapevine in action. Formal communications are dull, task-oriented, and dreadfully slow, and they sometimes ignore the topics that are important to the work force. The grapevine fills an information vacuum and is a kind of people's underground network.

Although most managers think of the grapevine as being a negative influence, the research shows that more than 75 percent of the information it conveys is basically true, although usually embroidered to a greater or lesser extent.[4] Eliminating the grapevine is both foolish and impossible. It is equally foolish to ignore it, since it tells the leader what unmet communication needs employees have. Shrewd leaders will try to meet these needs and thus weaken the grapevine. They can tap in on the vine, screening out those items that demand their attention. Finally, they can plug into the network, putting in items that are important to them. The care and feeding of the grapevine is a fine art.

Rumors

"What's this I hear about the company closing this plant and consolidating operations in the North Carolina operation?" Of such stuff are rumors born. Rumors are based on uncertainty, fear, anxiety, or maliciousness. Depending on the amount of emotion at their roots, rumors are like pillow feathers emptied into a brisk November wind. What can the leader do about them? Verbal denials are usually fruitless; they tend to be perceived as a cover-up. Ignoring rumors often works, if events will contradict them. The leader should analyze why the rumors arose in the first place, because rumors represent an information deficit based on dread. If the rumor has to do with character assassination, the leader can act in a manner that undermines it and discredits the rumormonger; for instance, if it is rumored that a key subordinate is going to get the axe, giving him or her a long-term assignment undercuts the false story. Finally, the leader can ensure, either through a hotline or through an open-door policy, that employees have a valid source for obtaining answers to their questions and fears.

On-the-Job Team Building

The usual methods of team building—the Blake-Mouton Managerial Grid®, training, process analysis, questionnaire surveys, and consultant intervention—are generally beyond the typical manager's authority to institute. They require the guidance of a professional consultant. This section concentrates on a sample of simple techniques that can be used to capitalize on the work group's resources without interfering unduly with the current operations.

Comparative Activities Analysis

"I had the darndest time getting two of my vice presidents to work as closely together as they should have," said a president. "Each fellow left some of the nastier parts of his job to the other. So I asked each independently to write down a description of his job as he lived it day-in and day-out. Then I compared the results. As I anticipated, there was a large area of agreement, a couple of gray areas, and a couple that fell through the cracks—each guy thought it was the other fellow's job. I called them in and showed them the two descriptions. Then I gave them a week to clear up the matter. It worked fine."

This technique can be used between a superior and a key subordinate or between two or more people who must work in close cooperation. It can be done as follows.

1. The leader, using the categories of "essential," "important," and "routine," writes down the activities that take up his or her thought, time, and talent, day to day.

2. The leader then describes the activities of the key subordinate, using the same classifications, as he or she perceives them and wants them done.

3. The subordinate, in turn, writes down the activities that make up his or her day-to-day job, using the identical headings.

4. Now the subordinate describes the activities involved in the manager's job, as the subordinate perceives them and is affected by them.

The four sets of descriptions can then be compared in order to pinpoint misunderstandings, duplication of effort, ambiguities, and gaps in jurisdiction. Having a clear idea of the expectations of the other person helps both to coordinate their work better.

Reversal

The shoe division of a large conglomerate sold its products through its own retail outlets and independents. Since fashion in women's shoes comes and goes rapidly, each sales force demanded first priority on the factory's production for the new season. After they had argued for more than an hour to no avail, it was suggested that they reverse roles, each arguing for the other position. Within 20 minutes, one man remarked, "Hey, we're using all the same arguments they were using." In less than an hour, an allocation system that was satisfactory to both parties was agreed upon.

Role reversal can sometimes break a win-lose attitude. Being forced to adopt the other party's point of view can create a more reasonable climate that prompts people to work toward a mutually satisfactory solution. At a minimum, it helps all concerned to understand not only the viewpoint of the other person but also the reasons why he or she takes that position. This is no small achievement.

Jointly Conducted Meetings

The manager started the meeting and covered the first two items on the agenda. She then yielded the chair to one of her subordinates, who conducted the discussion of the third item. Another subordinate took the chair for the fourth item. The manager then chaired the summary and conclusion of the meeting. When asked why she operated in this manner, she replied, "Where is it written that I am the expert on every subject or that I am the best qualified to conduct the discussion of every topic on the agenda?"

Many meetings waste time while boring the attendees, thus frittering away organizational money. They may ignore matters that are significant to the troops while concentrating on those that are important to either the manager or the organization. This can be changed if the leader will adopt some strategy such as the following.

1. Topics of importance to the organization and the manager will of course be included in the agenda.

2. Before finalizing the agenda, the manager can check with a sample of key subordinates to discover any items they feel are worthy of consideration. Those worth the time and thought of the participants should be incorporated.

3. While being sure to chair the agenda items that he or she could handle best, the leader can delegate the discussion of other items to selected subordinates according to their expertise. They must, of course, be notified in advance which item or items will be their responsibility. A reasonable time span should be defined for each subordinate's presentation; once a person gets at the head of the table there is a temptation to run on unendingly.

4. As the consideration of each item on the agenda is concluded, a participant can be asked to summarize the results. The subordinate should be informed in advance that this will be his or her responsibility.

5. One or two participants, who know in advance that this will be their job, can be asked to summarize the major conclusions of the entire meeting.

6. The leader can then wrap up the meeting after exploring with the group potential subjects for the next meeting.

People are born to be active, not merely reactive. If leaders formulate the agenda alone, if they run the entire meeting, if they expect their subordinates to react only to their stimuli, then the leaders are naive to expect subordinates to become involved and to contribute. Subordinates will look for opportunities to slip in their own personal agendas.

Constructive Behavior Exchange

Provincialism is a built-in hindrance to coordination in all organizations. The aim of the following exercise is to reduce parochialism. Although there are many variations of the technique, these steps can be done in four to five hours.[5]

1. Two departments or sections must work in close cooperation. They meet in a general session. The leader explains that
the three purposes of the meeting are to build closer coordination of effort; to get a better idea of how the departments help
each other; and to get a clearer understanding of how the other
departments hinder each other's work. No criticism, personal
or otherwise, is to be tolerated.

2. Each group then meets separately and discusses the behaviors of the other group that facilitate its efforts to do a good
job. A recorder summarizes the findings on flip-chart paper.

3. The groups reconvene, and the recorders make their reports. A general discussion is held about ways to improve
coordination.

4. Each group again meets independently to examine the
behaviors of the other group that make it more difficult for it to
get its job done well.

5. The recorders make their reports and a general discussion
is held with respect to methods of lessening the hampering
effect of each group's behaviors.

6. At the end of the exercise, the leader appoints one or more
project teams, with representatives from both units, to devise
strategies for improving coordination. A deadline is set for
these task forces to report back at a general meeting of both
groups.

An Advisory Committee

The manager can attend to only so many matters at one time.
An advisory committee can serve several purposes. It can
identify innovative, cost-saving, or production-increasing
ideas that are being overlooked. It can recommend solutions
to problems. It can consult with the leader to keep him or her
abreast of employee needs and feelings. It can participate in
making decisions when the manager adopts a group approach.
Finally, it can be a sounding board off which the leader can
bounce ideas or proposals. Composed of a cross section of
subordinates, such a committee can get many people into the
act if the chair is rotated every three to six months, and one-

third of the membership is similarly rotated. It may work on projects of its own selection or those delegated to it by the manager. If it is not to degenerate into becoming merely "another committee," however, the leader must support its efforts vigorously, grant it reasonable freedom, and be responsive to its recommendations and suggestions.

Perceived Activities Exchange

This technique is similar to the Constructive Behavior Exchange, except that it emphasizes perceptions. It can be used between levels of management or between two departments.

1. The groups meet in a brief general session in which it is explained that the perceptions of each group are desired. It is made clear that no criticism, evaluation, or judgment of the other group will be permitted.

2. Each group then meets separately to address itself to two sets of perceptions: how they perceive themselves, and how they perceive the other department. The self-perception section consists in answering the following questions. *What* do we do? (What are our policies, procedures, activities, and rules?) *Why* do we do these things? (What are our objectives, priorities, and reasons for doing the things we do?) *Why is it important* that we operate as we do? The second part of the discussion deals with the other unit and asks what they do; why they do the things they do; and why it is important that they operate as they do.

3. The two groups reconvene, and the recorders make their reports, giving all concerned the four sets of perceptions.

4. A time span is allowed for members of each group to question members of the other. No criticism is allowed. The aim is clearer understanding and increased coordination.

5. Methods are formulated for ensuring closer cooperation and smoother working relations, or the leader appoints a cross-group task force to formulate procedures for increasing the coordination. A deadline is established for it to report back to a second general session of the groups involved.

An adversary posture can often be undermined by having a clearer concept of what the other department is doing, why it operates the way it does, and why it is important for it to do so. It is all too easy in large organizations to deal with stereotypes of another unit. Sometimes it is striking how little one department knows about the other. A fuller understanding not only promotes closer working relationships but allows the parties at least to disagree over substance, not mere feelings, when disagreements do arise.

Using the Group to Solve Problems

Although groups create special problems for the manager, they can also serve as a valuable resource to help solve problems. The following section gives some suggestions on how to use groups effectively.

The Individual and the Group

"Sometimes everyone knows better than anyone" is a truism that the leader should bear in mind but use cautiously. The research tends to support the following conclusions.

1. Most groups require two types of leadership. The first is task-oriented and keeps the group moving to get the job done. The other is relations-oriented and keeps the group on an even keel, defuses tensions, and fosters supportive interaction.

2. Ideally, the leader should have a high concern for task accomplishment, a low need for autonomy, and a high degree of social intelligence (interpersonal skills).

3. If the aim is to cope with the creative or novel, then the better individuals produce more ideas, better ideas, and more unique ideas than the group.

4. Most group solutions are inferior to these produced by the best individual. However, even the best person tends to make more errors than the group.

5. If possible, the group should be composed of members who have homogeneous attitudes, heterogeneous personalities, and different—but not too different—areas of expertise.

6. Groups become ineffective if the members are nonsocial or highly independent individuals; if they allow the social aspects of the interaction to distract them from the task at hand; if they break down into subgroups or cliques; or if they are overly concerned with individual satisfactions and personal agendas.

7. Because of group pressures, groups may restrict the range of ideas that are considered. Moreover, group decisions may be less than the best possible because of the need to compromise and arrive at some element of agreement. On the other hand, the research indicates that groups that have been taught how to operate and reach consensus often produce solutions that are equal to or better than those evolved by even the best individuals.

Capitalizing on Group Resources

Group approaches to problem solving and decision making can be either a potent force for increased productivity and satisfaction or a frustrating waste of time and energy, depending on how skillfully you utilize them. If the critical variables are information sharing, solution acceptance, member satisfaction, and motivation to implement whatever decision is finally made, then the larger the group of affected people the better. However, if the problem is ill-defined and requires intensive exploration, if a creative solution or a high-quality decision is crucial, or if speed is an important consideration, then the smallest possible group of the most expert people available is usually the most effective strategy.

It follows from all this that a group approach has nothing to do with democracy or getting people involved. It is a pragmatic approach that can be either efficiently or inefficiently employed, depending on its purpose, dynamics, and process. In general, groups should be utilized only if there is no better way to resolve the situation. The reason for this is simple: meetings not only eat up time but can be quite costly. For instance, if 15 people meet for two hours, assuming a 35-hour week, then almost a week's work for one person has been lost if the session accomplishes little or nothing. You can estimate for yourself, in your situation, how much money is squandered in some meetings. It is for this reason that the leader calculates the costs and return on investment before using a group approach to problem solving and decision making. If the returns justify the costs, and the participants are reminded of both factors, then a group approach has many advantages.

communicating with impact: do you build bridges or chasms?

Communication or a Dialogue of the Deaf?

The first sentence of Aristotle's *Metaphysics* reads, "Man is by nature made to know." Rousseau once noted that "Man is like a rabbit, you must catch him by his ears." And the Gospel of St. John begins with the sentence, "In the beginning was the Word." These three statements highlight the importance of interpersonal communication better than a year's course. The leader spends half or more of the time communicating with relevant others. Moreover, organizations are information processing systems. Communication networks are their nerve tissue. Unfortunately, strokes sometimes interfere with the messages that should ensure teamwork.

A Systems Approach to the Communication Process

Communication is any form of interaction—words, a smile, an encouraging nod of the head, a rigid body posture, a show of interest—that results in the sharing of meaning, attitudes, or feelings. The key term is *sharing*; if there is no sharing, then a dialogue of the deaf ensues. We are too often concerned about techniques, important as they are, to the neglect of such questions as: Am I sharing with the other person? Am I making it easy for him or her to share with me?

Figure 27 describes what takes place when the leader attempts to communicate with another person. Each step is deceptively simple, so the causes of static will be pointed out. The next section gives methods for reducing the noise that interferes with communication.

The Sender

"What is good for General Motors is good for the country." "The public be damned." "If you don't come to work on Sunday, don't come in on Monday." These are classic examples of the barriers that the sender's attitudes, assumptions, and perceptions can erect. The mutual suspicion with which some unions and some managements view each other illustrates the importance of reviewing your past experience with the receiver before communicating. These four variables (the sender's perceptions, assumptions, attitudes, and past experience with the receiver) are filters through which the message must travel. They can also be blinders that distort the entire process.

The Specific Situation

Reflect on your own experience, and recall incidents when someone told a story that made the rest of the group cringe in embarrassment. An egregious example of this was when ex-President Carter stated that he consulted with his daughter Amy as to the central problem in the world today. There is nothing as ridiculous as seeing a leader communicate in a ponderous manner something that is essentially insignificant; nothing as sad as having a manager communicate in a cavalier or inappropriate way something that is absolutely crucial. When you ignore the requirements of the situation, inevitably you either overreact or underreact.

Figure 27. The communication cycle.

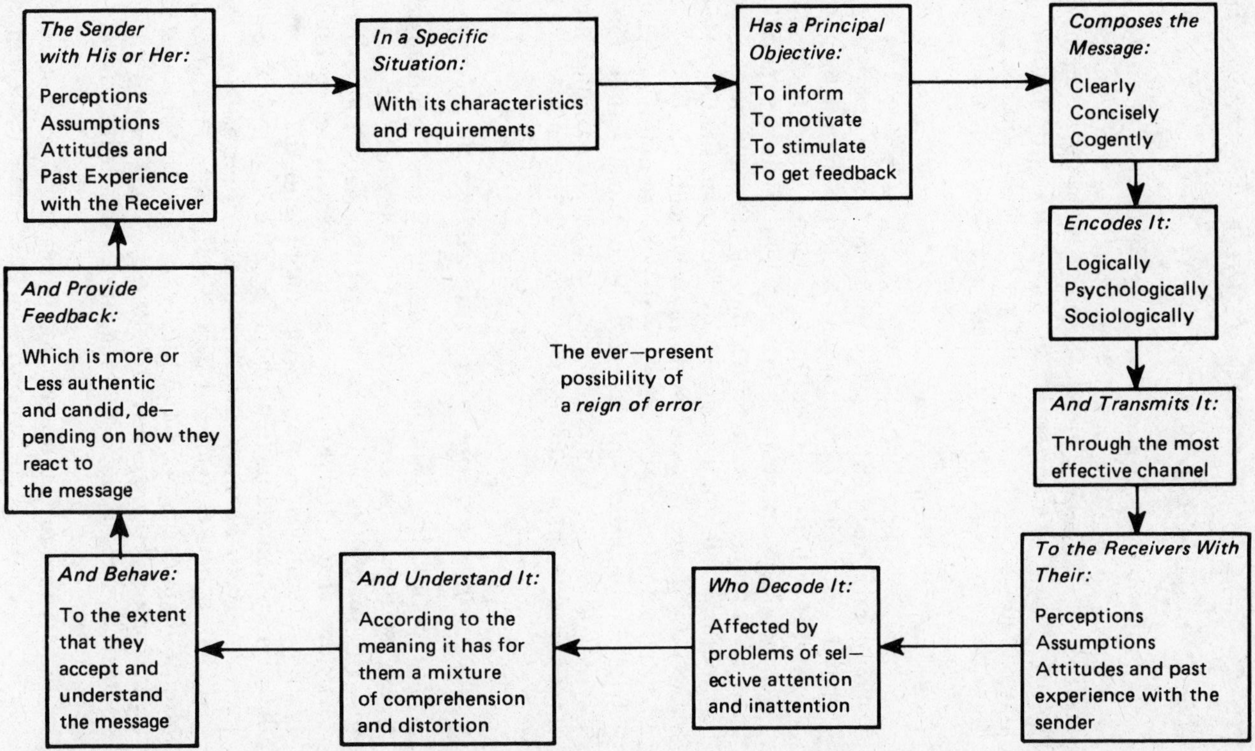

The Sender with His or Her:
Perceptions
Assumptions
Attitudes and
Past Experience
with the Receiver

In a Specific Situation:
With its characteristics and requirements

Has a Principal Objective:
To inform
To motivate
To stimulate
To get feedback

Composes the Message:
Clearly
Concisely
Cogently

Encodes It:
Logically
Psychologically
Sociologically

And Transmits It:
Through the most effective channel

To the Receivers With Their:
Perceptions
Assumptions
Attitudes and past experience with the sender

Who Decode It:
Affected by problems of selective attention and inattention

And Understand It:
According to the meaning it has for them a mixture of comprehension and distortion

And Behave:
To the extent that they accept and understand the message

And Provide Feedback:
Which is more or Less authentic and candid, depending on how they react to the message

The ever—present possibility of a reign of error

The Principal Objective

If you attempt to cover too much ground or attain too many objectives in a single communication, you will confuse the recipient, who cannot get inside your head to ascertain your priorities and relative emphasis. Rarely can you inform, enlighten, motivate, stimulate, and get feedback simultaneously in a single message. Communication is a sharpshooter's proposition, never a shotgun proposition. Failure to sharpen the focus blurs the communication.

> The commencement speaker, on a very hot day, realized that the graduates were more interested in getting on with festivities than in listening to another speech. So he started, "Let's make an agreement. I will limit my remarks to 15 minutes, if you will promise me your undivided attention." He got a round of applause. He then stressed the importance of continuing their education, giving five vivid examples of people who had done so to their advantage, and five well-known examples of those who had not done so to their regret. He finished in 12 minutes and received a standing ovation!

Composing, Encoding, and Transmitting the Message

Most people like parables because they are simple, instructive, easy to understand, and forceful. They are organized so that the readers or listeners can get the point immediately. They are structured to make an impact on the recipients. When you compose a message, it is not the logic of the sender that is important, but that of the receivers; not how well it sounds to you, but how it will sound in their ears; not how stimulating it is to you, but how it will motivate them. Too often a manager expects the receivers to accept the message on his or her terms rather than theirs. You can test this for yourself by making a game of teaching a small child how to tie shoelaces.

Encoding requires translating what is significant to the sender into terms that are acceptable, meaningful, and impactful to the receiver. Unless we are careful, there is a temptation to regress to what is familiar, comfortable, and habitual for us, rather than making the recipient comfortable. This is the pitfall of experts who love to impress others with their mastery of arcane technical jargon. Contrast such an approach with the shrewdness shown by this salesperson.

> She was trying to sell a complex telecommunications system. She had thoroughly explained the advantages of the system, its superiorities over competitive systems, and all its technical details. The buyer was still unconvinced. Then she shifted tactics and said, "Look, your major problem seems to be the fact that you are losing money because receivables are long past due. Suppose we could come up with a program, based on this system, that would add $500,000 each year to your net profit. Would you be interested?" "I sure would be!" came the instant reply. "How can we do this?" After they had carefully worked through the numbers together and seen that the claim was justified, the sale was made on the spot!

The medium may not be the message, but it certainly can distort it. The wrong channel can create needless static. Should it be a one-on-one discussion? a small meeting? a general meeting? an insertion in the house organ? a posting on the bulletin boards? a "for your information" routing? Each may be a suitable vehicle depending on the purpose of the communication.

Decoding and Understanding It

If the sender has filters, the receiver is no less human. Defensiveness, aggressiveness, lack of trust, or absence of confidence can block out the best-intentioned communication. Moreover, receivers are not warm wax on which senders can make whatever impression they prefer. They are very active in the process. They attend carefully to some aspects of the message while being inattentive to others. "Red flag" words that stir up negative emotions can prompt the receiver to reject the entire message. Finally, whatever is received is received according to the mind set of the person taking it in. Is the "Mona Lisa" smiling, smirking, or deep in pensive thought? In communication, meaning and understanding are in the mind of the beholder.

Behaving and Giving Feedback

A newly consecrated Episcopalian bishop was asked how it felt. He replied, "Now that I am a bishop, two things will never happen to me again: I will never eat a poorly prepared meal, and I will never hear the whole truth." This is precisely the way many higher-level managers feel. Without feedback, leaders cannot be certain that the message has gotten through as they intended. The communication loop is complete when subordinates understand, feel, or behave according to the original objective of the communicator.

Reducing Noise in Communication

Your communication skills will surely improve if you implement the following dozen ideas as circumstances allow.

1. Except when giving orders or directions, you are the servant, not the master, regardless of your authority. Your job is that of a midwife, helping the receiver to give birth to the same ideas, data, feelings, or motivations that you have.

2. Remember that the other party has three unverbalized questions: What's in it for me? How will if affect me? How seriously should I take the communication? Answer these questions as best you can.

3. To the other people, your communication involves a struggle for meaning. Facilitate their efforts through the organization, content, length, and mechanics of your message.

4. Become familiar with what things turn the receivers on, tune them out, and tick them off.

5. First be person-minded, situation-minded, objective-minded—and only then, be word-minded.

6. Choose words for their meaning to the receiver. Words are empty cups: what you put in is not nearly so important as knowing what the other person is likely to take out. The most reasonable request may be misinterpreted as an arbitrary demand.

7. Stay in character. Be sensitive to: the way the other party perceives you; his or her trust in you; the reasons why he or she respects you; and the relationship that exists between you.

8. Work into the message the five C's: clarity, completeness, conciseness, candor, and courtesy.

9. Spotlight your major objective, but also be aware of the unintended objectives the recipients are likely to read into the message.

10. Read your communication as it will be perceived through the eyes of the receiver. Listen to your message as it will sound in the ears of the recipient.

11. Words are not only signs; they are sometimes symbols. "The Star-Spangled Banner" is not merely a grouping of words; it is charged with emotion. Avoid buzzwords that can trigger off negative feelings, attitudes, or biases.

12. Communicate with yourself. How congruent is what you say or write with what you really think or feel? You need only be as frank as the situation requires, but you *must* be that candid.

The Art of Listening

Few experiences are as satisfying as that of realizing that one is being listened to and understood. How rare an experience it is! Truly listening to another individual is one of the most difficult tasks for the leader. Most of us would rather speak than listen. Moreover, we can listen three to six times as fast as anyone else can talk. Finally, we sometimes listen "with our fists," all too ready to refute the other person; or we listen marginally, ever open to distraction; or we listen with an evaluative or critical attitude; or we listen incompletely, missing important aspects of the communication. If you doubt this and have children, ask them how true these observations are.

Figure 28. **Your listening IQ.**

	Usually	Sometimes	Rarely
1. I vacuum my mind of all preconceptions, biases, and negative attitudes before listening.	_____	_____	_____
2. I pay strict, undivided attention to the other person.	_____	_____	_____
3. I listen within the other person's frame of reference.	_____	_____	_____
4. I listen with my whole body, showing that what is being said is of interest and concern to me.	_____	_____	_____
5. I listen for both intellectual content and emotional feelings, but keep them distinct.	_____	_____	_____
6. I note, but do not react to, efforts to flatter or needle me.	_____	_____	_____
7. I listen empathically and encouragingly, making it easier for the person to speak freely.	_____	_____	_____
8. I focus on the substance of what is being said, not the manner, unless the manner helps me understand the message more thoroughly.	_____	_____	_____
9. I listen for the major theme of what is being said.	_____	_____	_____
10. I listen in a tripartite way, linking what has been said with what is being said and what is likely to be said.	_____	_____	_____

	Usually	**Sometimes**	**Rarely**
11. I listen to what the person is trying to communicate in spite of the way he or she may express it.	_____	_____	_____
12. I listen to learn. I listen to help.	_____	_____	_____
13. I listen prudently, not allowing the person to say things that he or she is likely to regret later.	_____	_____	_____
14. I hold my tongue. I hear the other person out. I don't interrupt.	_____	_____	_____
15. I give the person feedback to show that I am listening by comments, brief questions, and body language that encourage him or her to continue.	_____	_____	_____
16. I make a genuine effort to discuss, not argue.	_____	_____	_____
17. If I disagree, I first restate the position of the other party before presenting my views.	_____	_____	_____
18. I listen carefully to what is *not* said, because sometimes the real message is here.	_____	_____	_____
19. I listen to the connotations, as well as the denotations, of what is said.	_____	_____	_____
20. I try to listen to my own words as they sound in the ears of the other person.	_____	_____	_____

Children know all too well how distracted and impatient adults can become when they listen.

The leader appreciates the fact that if he or she wishes other people to listen, then the courtesy of first listening to them must be given. You might like to complete the checklist in Figure 28 to discover how sharp your listening skills are and where they require the whetstone of effort.

Fitting the Question to the Quest

One of the greatest assets that leaders have at their disposal is the question, artfully asked. Yet all one has to do is watch the nightly news on television to discover how poorly questions are often used. For instance, a mother has just lost a child in a terrible fire and the TV person inquires, "How do you feel?" Such gaucheness is not for the leader, but some managers are just this maladroit. They ask the same trite questions over and over regardless of the situation, they invade privacy imprudently if not impudently, and they ask the wrong types of questions in the wrong ways, resulting in Pavlovian responses and/or resentment. If questioning is a technique that can be utilized for a wide variety of purposes, it is one that must be used with thoughtful care. Instead of writing at length about questioning skills, it might be more practical to give a sample of the possible kinds of questions that can be used, with illustrations of each type.

To check understanding. "Your contention is that we are overmanned in certain departments but undermanned in others, with a resulting imbalance in the work loads. Is that it?"

To establish reasons. "I realize that it's been customary to handle problems of this sort in the way you've described. But I wonder, why have we dealt with them like this?"

To obtain reactions. "This is how we tentatively plan to go about making the transition. What do you think of it?"

To obtain suggestions. "I think this plan is basically sound, but I also realize it probably has flaws in it that I'm not aware of. Have you any suggestions for making it more foolproof?"

To act as a devil's advocate. "This looks fine on paper. But what unanticipated difficulties are we likely to get into if we establish a zero-defects program in one department but not in the others?"

To draw on past experience. "This is a new one for us. On the other hand, we've been in this business for a long time. Have we ever run into something similar in the past? What can we draw on from our past experience to help us attack this situation?"

To discover the source. "We all know that it's company policy to promote on the basis of merit. How did this rumor get started that minority-group people couldn't make supervisor?"

To focus attention. "We've been talking about several problems. In fact, at times we've bounced back and forth from one to the other. Now, which do you feel is the core problem we should start with?"

To obtain feedback. "We've been following this procedure for some time. What exactly have been the benefits and disadvantages, from your viewpoint as a department head?"

To stimulate reflective thinking. "We've considered a great number of things. But is there a danger that we may have been examining symptoms rather than causes? What do you feel are the root reasons for the things we've been discussing?"

To emphasize ethical considerations. "I realize that what has been proposed would be efficient. But in the long run, would it be fair to everybody concerned?"

To secure opinions. "As you know, it has been proposed to merge department X with department Y. What is your view of this proposal?"

To arouse provocative discussion. "Do you think that a job enrichment program would do anything for the kind of people who work with us?"

To ascertain intensity of feeling. "I realize that you're in favor of this change. But how important is it to you?"

To determine reluctance or eagerness to move ahead. "There seems to be general agreement on the merits of the proposal. Should we start as soon as possible or think it over for a while before committing ourselves to action?"

To test for consensus. "We've looked at this from many angles. Does everybody feel that this is the way we should go, or are there some who have doubts about it?"

To prevent too-quick agreement. "We've all agreed about what should be done. But we seem to have agreed so quickly that I wonder whether we've thought this thing through. Would it be wise for all of us to mull it over for another week and then take it up again?"

To obtain evaluations. "Where do you feel that you've done a superior job? Where might you have fallen down on the job?"

To follow up. "Last time we agreed that you would spend at least 15 percent of your time training your salesmen. How has it worked out?"

To explore resources. "Now we know what we want to do. But what personnel resources do we have to do it effectively?"

Communication at a Deeper Level

If you quietly say to yourself the word "communication," you may be struck by the fact that it is very close in sound to three basic ideas: *common, community,* and *communion.* Where there is nothing in common, there can be no communication. This is the reason physicists from any country can converse easily, so long as they remain in their area of expertise, and why some members of the United Nations rarely communicate with one another. They indulge in a semantic Ping-Pong game of one-upmanship. A sense of community exists when people have shared objectives, values, interests, and concerns, even though each may also have individual goals. This fact is obvious in any family, any cohesive work group, or any sports team. Communing is the highest form of sharing. Overtly, it implies the courtesy of trying to understand the other person and his or her viewpoint. A reciprocal courtesy is usually the fruit of this effort. Nonverbal communication also has its place; you need not always be verbal or active.

Two approaches to interaction can be of particular help to the leader: transactional analysis and the Johari window.

Transactional Analysis

First developed by Berne, Harris, and others, TA has become so popular that it borders on faddism; the expected crop of "armchair psychologists" has been attracted to it.[1] The reasons for its popularity are easy to explain. First, it is based on observable behavior, not exotic theory. Second, its basic concepts are easy to understand. Third, it is devoid of confusing jargon; whenever possible, ideas are expressed in single, descriptive words. Finally, it can be applied immediately to interpersonal relations because it is practical and utilitarian. However, its very simplicity can be a snare, for it is far more complex than it appears to be at first glance. Be that as it may, the major concepts include the following:

1. A transaction is a stimulus-response exchange between two people. TA studies the pattern of these incidents.

2. When two human beings behave toward each other, six "people" get into the act.

— The *Parent* of each is protective, guiding, supportive, nurturing, and advising (the positive aspects), but also critical, judging, rule-enforcing, demanding, disciplining, and hard to please (the negative aspects).

— The *Adult* of each is mature, balanced, reality-oriented, rational, evidence-attuned, and objective.

— The *Child* of each is playful, trusting, imaginative, fun-loving, and venturesome (positive), but also whining, pouting, complaining, demanding, conforming, and frightened (negative).

PAC (for Parent, Adult, Child) is at the heart of TA. These six *ego states* are neither good nor bad, but they get all jumbled up in the interaction between the two people involved. The Parent we assimilate from our real parents from early childhood. We are programmed to perceive, feel, and act in certain ways rather than others because we identify with these parents and relevant others. The Child is the Peter Pan that is in all of us: "I won't grow up, I won't grow up. . . ." The Adult is our own achievement, our mature self.

3. As a result of our preconditioning and life experiences, each of us is somewhere on a continuum between the ex-

tremes of four basic interpersonal orientations. *I'm OK, You're OK* is a very healthy stance and outlook. *I'm OK, You're Not OK* is a posture that stimulates me to be suspicious of you, to use, abuse, or demean you. *You're OK, I'm Not OK* is just the reverse of the previous attitude. Finally, *I'm Not OK, You're Not OK* is a perspective that almost guarantees mutual distrust and conflict.

4. Although we can change according to circumstances, we are programmed to resort to one or other of the ego states and to adopt one of the major orientations in our interpersonal relations. A programmed psychic *tape* represents the life script or scenario that we feel impelled, but not inevitably compelled, to live out in dealing with others.

5. People look for *strokes* in relating to others. Strokes are desired rewards from human interaction.

6. People sometimes play games with each other. A *game* is a form of interaction that involves psychological trickery; it seeks, consciously or unwittingly, to secure a payoff at the expense of the other party. Some 90 games have been identified, each with its own brilliantly descriptive title: "Ain't it Awful?," "Kick Me," "If It Weren't for You, I Could," "Yes, But," "Now I've Got You, You S.O.B.," and so on.

7. TA has two basic laws. The first states that complementary (parallel) transactions can go on indefinitely. They reinforce each other, usually without addressing the real problem. The second law affirms that crossed transactions bring communication to a grinding halt. They become crossed when a person speaks from one ego state—Parent, Adult, or Child—expecting the other person to respond accordingly. When this fails to happen, communication is short-circuited.

Let's illustrate this with a simple example. The following statements are made by pairs of passengers in response to the same situation. Responses 1 through 5 illustrate complementary transactions; responses 6 through 9 show crossed ones.

The Situation: During the morning rush hour, a New York City subway train stops for a few minutes between stations.

1. *Parent–Parent*   "They've done it again. Can't the idiots
                      who run these subways do anything

right?" —"What do you expect? They have graduate degrees in screwing the simplest things up."

2. *Adult –Adult* "I wonder what's gone wrong?" —"I don't know. Why don't we ask the conductor and find out?"

3. *Child –Child* "Oh, no! Why does it always happen to me?" —"Nobody cares about us at all."

4. *Child –Parent* "I'm scared." —"Don't worry. I'll see to it that nothing happens to you."

5. *Parent –Child* "When I get to the office, I'm going to write them a letter that will blister their ears." —"I'm with you. That's right."

6. *Parent –Adult* "New cars, and these incompetents manage to break them." —"Perhaps the trains are backed up momentarily because of the rush hour. Besides, it's Christmas shopping season."

7. *Child –Adult* "I'm scared." —"No need to be frightened. The lights are on, and everything seems OK. We've just stopped for a moment."

8. *Adult –Paent* "I wonder what's happened?" —"Are you kidding? You must be new. Nothing works in this city."

9. *Adult –Child* "I wonder what's causing the delay?" —"It doesn't matter. There's nothing we can do."

As a manager, you can readily see how the principles of TA apply to such important activities as setting objectives, performance reviews, discipline, giving orders and directions, managing friction and conflict, conducting meetings, handling complaints and grievances, coping with criticisms, coaching and counseling subordinates, dealing with superiors and peers, introducing changes, and even to the leadership process itself. However, like all good psychology, TA must start with you before it can be very useful in understanding and interacting with others. It helps you realize where you're coming from. Is your Adult, Parent, or Child in the saddle? It facilitates your efforts to recognize the harmful impact when your Parent or Child controls the reins of the relationship. It reminds you of the need to develop your Adult and see to it that it controls your Parent and Child.

What about the other person? Knowing that you are forced to cope with his or her Parent or Child enables you to devise strategies for so doing without losing your cool; the Child loves strokes and the Parent desires a certain amount of control which your Adult may be able to accommodate, to some degree. Finally, an understanding of the games people play can be a safeguard against being seduced emotionally and becoming entangled in feelings as the other party endeavors to "hook" your Child or Parent. Your Adult responses can often help the other person to rely on his or her Adult, rather than Parent or Child.

The Johari Window

When two people interact or communicate, each is in the position of listening to the ticking of a watch and observing its visible movements with the purpose of trying to fathom its inner workings. Each person has certain advantages and vulnerabilities. You, the leader, know certain things that the subordinate also knows. You know certain things that he or she does not know. The subordinate knows certain things that you are unaware of and there are things that neither of you know about each other. How can you and the subordinate get clear insight into yourselves and each other, so that you can interact and communicate more openly? The Johari window, developed by Joseph Luft and Harry Ingham, helps you to do just that.[2] It is presented in Figure 29.

What follows? It is clear that both you and your subordinate have two options: to work together to enlarge the Open Arena or to play games and try to manipulate each other by magnifying the Hidden Area. It is interesting to examine the four boxes from the point of view of self-disclosure and giving and receiving feedback. In the Open Arena, both parties reveal themselves and are open to feedback. The benefits of this are

Figure 29. **The Johari window.**

	Known to You	Not Known to You
Known to the Subordinate	Open Arena	Blind Spot (Denied)
Not Known to the Subordinate	Hidden Area (Facade) (Deceit)	Unknown

obvious for coordination of effort and teamwork. If you enlarge the Hidden Area, you will seek a great deal of information from the subordinate but give little in return. This will make the subordinate defensive because it is a one-way street: you know where the other person stands, but he or she does not know where you stand. If efforts are made to enhance the Blind Spot, you will be giving a great deal of feedback in terms of expressing your ideas and opinions, but you will irritate the subordinate because you are not open to his or her ideas and feedback. Thus, you may not get to know how you are coming across to the subordinate. The Unknown should be explored cautiously and only within the parameters of the job situation. No one is entitled to the whole truth about another person.

You might like to use the Johari window technique in estimating how well you reveal yourself to your key subordinates, the extent to which they reveal themselves to you, and the type and amount of feedback that takes place between them and you.

chapter thirteen

making change productive: do you optimize or compromise?

Change or Perish

Democritus, the Greek philosopher, claimed that everything was in a state of flux and flow. To the authors of such books as *The Third Wave* and *Managing in Turbulent Times*, he would probably say, "Congratulations! You fellows finally got my message." With more than 90 percent of all the scientists who have ever lived now alive, there is no need to give a long list of the changes that are taking place. One hundred years ago we had neither telephone nor elevator. Who can predict what will happen in the next 20 years? Two facts are evident. First, the leader must bring about changes for the better. Second, those who project and forecast the future should be mindful of Disraeli's statement, "The things we foresee so rarely occur, and the unexpected has a way of intruding itself."

Intellectually, it is easy to acknowledge the need for change, but emotionally, it is far more difficult. One of the psychological defense mechanisms is the "old oaken bucket." This is a tendency on the part of some to resist change by extolling the superiorities of the past, to cling tenaciously to ways of doing things that are no longer adequate. Contrast these two attitudes. An old Navy Chief, in World War II, was heard to say, "When I entered this man's navy, we had wooden ships and iron men. Now we have iron ships and wooden men." But a director of nursing has on her desk a sign that reads "Director of Change." Change has little to do with technology. It is characterized by an inquisitive mind, a venturesome spirit, and an urge to improve on the present.

Wrong Reasons for Change

T. S. Eliot once noted that the highest treason is to do the right thing for the wrong reason. This treason takes four forms: ego-tripping, imitation, overkill, and tinkering.

Ego-Tripping. Near the end of his tenure, the chairman of a large company pushed through the construction of a splendid headquarters, one that went far beyond the current and near future needs of the organization. When asked why such an edifice was necessary, some of the managers replied, "It was the chairman's idea. We call it his last erection." This snide remark may be unfair, but it does highlight the fact that those with power sometimes make changes on the basis of personal preference or caprice. Corporate arrogance and executive arrogance are not unknown. We all like to ego-trip now and then. But when leaders act in this fashion, they leave their followers unmotivated to make the change succeed.

Imitation. Since man is a mimicking animal, there is a natural proclivity to keep up with the Joneses, in organizations as in neighborhoods. There used to be the General Motors, IBM, Du Pont, or General Electric way, which other firms thought they could duplicate to ensure their success. I know of at least three incidents where alumni of these giants had to be replaced because they sought in vain to impose on a medium-size company procedures that worked well for this or that behemoth. The New testament gives some sound advice about putting new wine in old winebags. Prudent people learn from the experience of others, but they must be sensitive to the difference between an *o* and an *a*: Nothing can be adopted because it has worked well for others. It must be adapted to the realities of a given situation.

Overkill. The inexperienced often try to change too much, too soon. This is commonplace in those government programs that start out dramatically and end up failing. The itch to change things also affects some newly appointed managers who are so insecure that they attempt to wipe the slate clean instead of building on the strengths and accomplishments of a department. The old saw still serves: if you want an omelet, you need not hit the eggs with a hammer.

Tinkering. Some managers find it almost impossible to let well enough alone. They are forever tinkering with this or that aspect of a system without realizing that rearrangement is not a synonym for improvement.

> The Ford Mustang was a brilliant recovery from the disaster of the Edsel. Within two years, 1.28 million were built. But as *Time* magazine pointed out, "Detroit cannot keep its hands off a winner." Ford gradually fattened the car, adding some 584 pounds to its weight. The Mustang had been the only car to win a design award from Tiffany & Co., but its sales slowed and it died of obesity. As Lee Iacocca remarked, "We walked away from the market." [1]

Yet the people who recommended and approved the changes in the Mustang's design probably thought their ideas were good. If change is desirable, stability is no less necessary. Tinkering merely ticks people off.

A Return on Investment Approach to Making Changes

Any change, even a minor one, brings with it a variety of costs. It disrupts familiar ways of doing things, it reduces efficiency at the outset, it may offend the status of some, it generally creates a certain amount of resistance, and it takes time and energy to implement. Accordingly, no change should be introduced until a cost/benefit analysis has been made. If the returns do not considerably outweigh the costs, then put the change on the back burner until a more propitious time.

A consultant noticed two envelopes on the president's desk. A month later, they were still there. "Don't you trust the U.S. mail?" asked the consultant. "Open the letters and read," replied the president. In each envelope was the name of a key vice president and a date. "You see," continued the president, "I have a change I would like to make, but they are strongly opposed to it. It's not that important, so I can wait until at least one of them retires. Of course, I could force it on them. But I have to work with these people. I don't want to win a battle and lose a war. That change can keep for a while."

Figure 30 illustrates the steps involved in making any substantial change in current operations. Each box represents a "proceed-stop" state of affairs where the situation can be evaluated. If the realities associated with each step are not favorable, the planned change will not be as successful as it might be.

Symptoms Indicating the Need for Change

The stimulants to change may be positive, negative, or some mix of the two. Negative influences are such factors as loss of competitive position; new legislation or regulations; a system that is buckling under the load; falling productivity; escalating costs and waste; unacceptable morale, absenteeism, and friction; or poor quality of personnel. Positive reasons for changing include the need to implement strategic plans and policies; a desire to capitalize on new opportunities; a plan to introduce old products into new markets or new products into old markets; a determination to capitalize on surplus or underutilized talent; a decision to upgrade the technology of production; the introduction of a management information system; and the start-up of an organization development program.

Figure 30. **Flow chart for implementing change.**

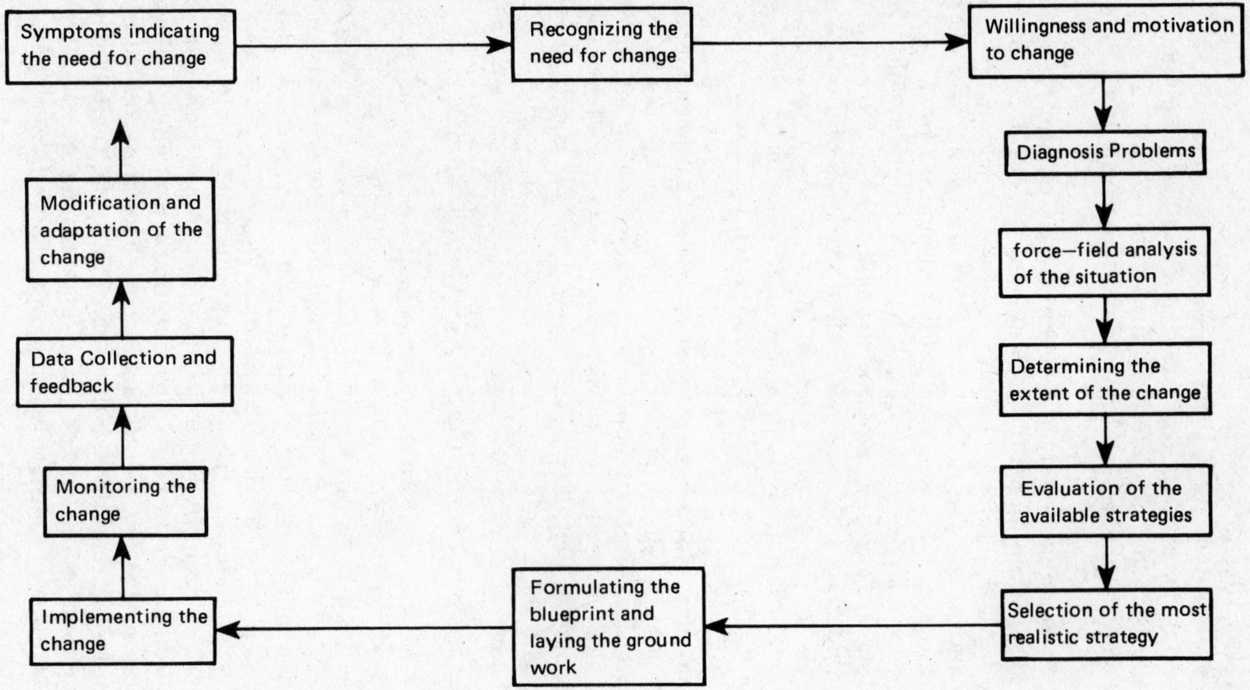

Recognizing the Need for Change

Justice Holmes once remarked, "I no more believe in rapid deformation than I believe in rapid reformation." Few things in an organization happen suddenly. The symptoms are always clear and identifiable, but usually they are initially ignored by those in power. Organizational and personal inertia are very difficult to overcome. Here the problem is psychological rather than intellectual. The stultifying effect of habit and the secure feeling of the familiar blind us to the need to change. If self-deception is not to take over, the leader must frankly admit that the matters requiring attention will not cure themselves.

Diagnosing Problems

With respect to change, there are four types of leaders: those who give lip service to the need to change; those who acknowledge the need but procrastinate; those who adopt half-hearted measures that tranquilize the situation temporarily without resolving it; and those who analyze the situation and then cope with it. It is essential to distinguish between root causes, minor causes, results, concomitant conditions, and symptoms. Unless this is done, the change will fail and you will be left holding the bag. As President Kennedy noted, "Success has many volunteer parents; failure is always an orphan."

A consultant was asked by a company to give a series of supervisory development programs. It seemed that as the company grew rapidly, the supervisors were less than excellent. Before starting the first program, the consultant interviewed a cross section of new employees, supervisors, middle managers, and personnel people. He discovered that the organization was growing so fast that it was difficult to attract enough of the right kind of employees to meet the company's needs. The supervisors were reasonably competent, about on a par with most that the consultant had known. Personnel was trying its best to fill

requisitions. The real problem was not with the supervisors but with the company's failure to plan its manpower requirements as carefully as its financial growth.
The firm almost wasted money on programs that would
have addressed themselves to a result, not the cause.

Referred pain, in medicine, means pain that is felt somewhere other than the source. (For example, one's calf muscles
may ache because of a slight misalignment of the spine.) The
leader must sometimes look beyond the immediate problem to
get at the basic situation. Some organizations use far too much
cosmetology in resolving problems.

Force-Field Analysis

Once the manager is convinced that a change is necessary,
there is a temptation to fall in love with the idea or to go off
half-cocked. Force-field analysis is a method for preventing
emotional entanglement with one's own views. It requires a
hard-headed analysis of the *driving* and *restraining* forces that
the change must take into account. Driving forces are supportive of the change. They may be *external,* such as legislation
that makes affirmative action programs necessary, or the fact
that a competitor is gaining a larger market share. They may be
internal, such as the active interest of key authority figures, or
the need to make changes in order to carry out a new strategic
plan. Similarly, the restraining forces may be either external or
internal.[2]

The manager must calculate the driving forces in order to
capitalize on them. What is to be done with the restraining
forces that are internal to the organization? The quick
answer—overcome them—is often the wrong answer. If you
possess sufficient power, this is possible. However, people
who feel that they have been forced to submit nurture their
resentment, looking for opportunities to sabotage the change.
It's better if the leader can win over, undermine, or at least
neutralize the opposition. Often people are reacting to their
own fears, rather than to the proposed change. Pointing out its
benefits, letting them ventilate their feelings and doubts, and

seeking out their suggestions frequently undermines the emotional base of their resistance.

Although it is helpful to write down the various driving and restraining forces, both internal and external, it is important to concentrate not on their number but rather on their importance and impact. The active support of one key person may be more significant than the disagreement of several people who lack power to help or hinder.

In 1970, John Reed, the youngest senior vice president in First National City Bank's history, decided to reorganize the Operating Group of the bank. This group, among other functions, processed between 1.5 million and 2 million individual items. (A stack of 1.5 million checks stands as high as a 66-story building.) Reed and his assistants determined that the Operating Group was in fact a paper-processing "factory" to which the principles of production management should be applied. This was a radical departure from past precedent in banking. It was met with some opposition, much misunderstanding, and considerable confusion. However, after extraordinary effort, the change was a tremendous success. One wonders how successful it might have been had Reed lacked either the active support of William Spencer, executive vice president in charge of Operations and a prime candidate for the bank's presidency; or the positive change of attitude of top management toward the Operating Group. In this instance, the driving forces far outweighed the restraining ones.[3]

Determining the Extent of the Change

Radical surgery? Minor change? Small modification? Fine tuning? Which is most appropriate to the situation? The law of parsimony should be your guide. Change as little as possible to attain the objectives you have in mind. A second criterion has to do with the benefits that the change will produce in relation to the costs that it will require. Finally, be sensitive to unanticipated consequences. The economic return on the change may be substantial, but if it means that the hidden costs of future interdepartmental or interpersonal conflict will be excessive, then the change may be little more than a Pyrrhic victory.

Strategy Evaluation and Selection

Two myths still live on: that it is necessary to get all the facts, and that the leader must choose the best solution. No one can ever get all the facts. Moreover, getting all the facts, as many computer printouts prove, often serves to blur the meaning of the data. Managers should make sure that they have examined the critical facts, the vital few rather than the trivial many. The best solution, like the best book, is one that will never be found. Managers are paid to make things happen, often under conditions of uncertainty. The change should be the most realistic and practical one that circumstances allow. If it resolves an irksome problem or capitalizes on an unexploited opportunity, while avoiding long-term costs in favor of short-term gains, then it should be implemented. The executive is not like the scientist who can experiment unendingly in a laboratory in the quest for a greater truth. Action must be taken to improve on past performance.

Changing the Blueprint and Laying the Groundwork

Strategy selection means asking, "Will it work in our situation?" Strategy implementation means asking, "How can we make it work? How can we avoid the rocks and shoals of the organization?" Blueprinting is an intellectual task that requires the constant use of the "What if" process. It involves identifying supporters, helpers, make-or-break implementers, hinderers, obstacle builders, potential saboteurs, footdraggers, and lip-servers. Additionally, it requires a careful analysis of organizational climate, mores, attitudes, policies, procedures, status systems, sacred cows, tender nerves, objectives, priorities, needs, foci of interests, permissible limits, and parameters of tolerance and acceptance, not to mention the normal work flow, ways of doing things, and territorial prerogatives. Finally, the currents and eddies of competition, jealousy, power seeking, cooperation, friendship, and jockeying for more favorable positions must be scrutinized. Unless this is done carefully, the leader may encounter unexpected opposition and unpleasantness.

Laying the groundwork for the change is largely psychological and sociological in nature. Those associated with the change usually have lived with it so long that its virtues are self-evident *to them.* To others, it may be not only a novelty but a threat. A state of psychological readiness to accept, or at least not undermine, the change must be created. This can often be done by discussion; by providing opportunities for the reluctant to express their questions, doubts, and fears; by seeking the constructive criticism of "nonparents" of the change; by using others as a sounding board; or by getting those who are likely to resist it to serve as devil's advocates. The ways for spiking the guns of potential and actual opposition are numerous, if the leader perceives doing this as energy invested in the ultimate success of the change rather than a waste of time in responding to petty nitpickers. In Chapter 1 it was noted that it is better to have a change that is only 50 percent technically correct but will be embraced with 90 percent enthusiasm, than to have one that is 90 percent technically correct but which those affected will embrace with only 50 percent, or less, enthusiasm.

Implementing the Change

A very large merchandising corporation is well known for its excellent grooming of its managers. What is not so well known is that the president, now dead, decided years ago to change his managers from "merchants" to professional executives. He studied the corporation's many large stores scattered throughout the country and found one department in one of the units where conditions were most favorable. This is where he started. He could have imposed a management development program on the entire chain by fiat. "What good would that have done?" he asked. "My plan was to have people anxious to get into the program, not force them into it. The best way was to start modestly and make certain that this pilot program was a complete success. That is exactly what happened. Instead of asking, 'Why us?' our best people said, 'Why not us?' This is what I hoped would happen."

Any leader can learn from this president. You must address problems of methods of implementation, sequence of activities, phasing, timing, establishment of time frames and deadlines, and so on.

Monitoring, Feedback, and Modification

No manager can authorize a change and then walk away from it. Any change, even a minor one, should be put into "intensive care" at the outset. Many more problems will crop up than expected, and it will take three to five times as long to get the change on stream smoothly than was estimated. To prevent shocks and unpleasant surprises, the change must be closely monitored. An early warning system must be built into the change so that quick remedial action can be taken before things get out of hand. Thus, in-process, not merely after-the-fact, data collection is a must. This should take the form of numbers. But it is also necessary to obtain personal reactions.

Defusing the Opposition: Making Change Effective

Contrary to popular opinion, people do not fear, resist, or resent change. How many would resist a free vacation, five extra holidays, or a promotion? What they *fear* is the unknown, the unfamiliar, and the uncertain. What they *resist* is being forced to alter well-established habits. What they *react negatively to* is any perceived threat to their authority, status, security, or comfort zones. What they *resent* is being changed by others unilaterally, without the opportunity either to participate in planning the change or to contribute to it. However, people sometimes resist change because they are not intellectually convinced that it is in the best interests of the organization. Figure 31 lists ways to defuse both intellectual and emotional opposition while increasing the chances of success for your proposed change.

Figure 31. **Making change effective.**

	Always	Sometimes	Rarely
Planning the Change			
I make changes only to improve on current performance, not on the basis of personal preference, caprice, or whimsy.	___	___	___
I change as little as must be changed to attain my objectives.	___	___	___
I do not make changes because they are the "in" thing to do. Any ideas I get from other organizations or departments, I adapt to the realities of my situation.	___	___	___
I identify the core opportunity or problem, indulging in neither change overkill nor cosmetology.	___	___	___
I make an objective cost/benefit analysis of the change for the short and long term.	___	___	___
I carefully evaluate the driving and restraining forces before deciding on the type and extent of the proposed change.	___	___	___
I analyze carefully the possible unanticipated consequences of the proposed change.	___	___	___
I make a blueprint of the change process in terms of timing, phasing, methods, strategies, and tactics for the input, throughput, and output of the change.	___	___	___
I try out the change in a pilot study, if possible.	___	___	___
I have a realistic time frame for the change, from start to finish.	___	___	___

	Always	Sometimes	Rarely
I formulate criteria for judging the success of the change.	___	___	___
I devise techniques for detecting deviations, problems, and attempts to sabotage the change.	___	___	___
I draw up contingency strategies for coping with unexpected difficulties and problems.	___	___	___
I establish optimistic, pessimistic, and realistic time deadlines for implementing the various stages of the change.	___	___	___
I have means for monitoring the change and for putting it in intensive care at the outset.	___	___	___
I have methods for gathering valid and useful data with respect to the success of the change, so that I can modify it if necessary.	___	___	___
I realize how the change may force me to behave differently, not merely others.	___	___	___
I am sensitive to the impact that the change may have on the work of other units.	___	___	___

Defusing the Opposition
I avoid becoming so emotionally involved with the change that I am blind to its deficiencies.   ___   ___   ___

I avoid perceiving those who oppose the change as adversaries.   ___   ___   ___

I identify early in the game those who are *intellectually opposed* to the change.   ___   ___   ___

	Always	Sometimes	Rarely
I explain the benefits of the change to those who are intellectually opposed to it.	————	————	————
I invite them to contribute to the change and to point out its disadvantages as they perceive them.	————	————	————
I listen carefully to the reasons why they are intellectually opposed to the change, making any adaptations that are required when their reasons are valid.	————	————	————
I seek their help by asking them to make suggestions to make the change even more effective.	————	————	————
I respect their right to disagree intellectually about the merits of the change.	————	————	————
If all efforts to persuade them fail, I make it clear that they have the right to disagree but not to undermine the change.	————	————	————
As a last resort, I challenge the opposers to come up with a more effective change.	————	————	————
I identify early in the game those who are *emotionally resistant* to the change.	————	————	————
I analyze the reasons for their opposition.	————	————	————
I allow them reasonable opportunity to ventilate their feelings and to voice their opposition.	————	————	————
If possible, I get their views privately before finalizing the change.	————	————	————

	Always	Sometimes	Rarely
If possible, I appoint their major representatives as devil's advocates to detect flaws in the change.	_____	_____	_____
I challenge them to devise a more efficient change.	_____	_____	_____
I demand that emotional opposers change their criticisms into positive suggestions.	_____	_____	_____
I try in every way possible to get the group that is affected by the change to control the emotional resisters.	_____	_____	_____
I have strategies for dealing with the backbiters, nitpickers, petulant critics, delayers, passive resisters, obstacle builders, lip-servers, and foot-draggers.	_____	_____	_____
I make it clear that no undermining or sabotage of the change will be tolerated.	_____	_____	_____
I avoid arguing with emotional resisters.	_____	_____	_____
I have methods for detecting potential saboteurs quickly and for dealing with them immediately.	_____	_____	_____

Making the Change Effective

I do not finalize the change until I am convinced that my superiors will actively support it.	_____	_____	_____
I avoid disrupting the ongoing work flow, to the extent that this is possible.	_____	_____	_____

I forewarn all concerned that
efficiency may decline somewhat at

	Always	Sometimes	Rarely
the outset; the benefits of the change will not be instantaneous.	_____	_____	_____
I try not to threaten the status or prerogatives of key people affected by the change.	_____	_____	_____
I make strenuous efforts to win over key people and groups that can make or break the change.	_____	_____	_____
I get as many helpers and supporters as possible to contribute to the formulation of the change.	_____	_____	_____
I take whatever time is necessary to build as broad a base of support for the change as conditions permit.	_____	_____	_____
If circumstances allow, I let people live with the idea of the change and get accustomed to it before implementing it.	_____	_____	_____
I neither oversell nor undersell the benefits to be derived from the change.	_____	_____	_____
I am sensitive to the nonformal and informal groups in making the change.	_____	_____	_____
I plan the change so that as many as possible will benefit from it.	_____	_____	_____
If the change succeeds, I make it clear that as many as possible will share the credit for its success.	_____	_____	_____
I allow ample time, if possible, for key people to convince themselves of the merits of the change.	_____	_____	_____

managing conflict: do you solve or resolve friction?

Changing Attitudes Toward Conflict

One of the first recorded incidents of conflict ended in Abel's death, and over the centuries human nature has changed very little.

— A president resigns because his philosophy of doing business is rejected by the board.
— Quality assurance and manufacturing are at loggerheads because of a dispute over acceptable standards.
— Two groups in a power struggle do their best to undercut each other.
— Workers slow down production by sticking to the letter of the rule book to lash back at management.
— One department head tries his best to assassinate the character of a competitor for a promotion.

The hidden costs of interpersonal and intergroup friction in large organizations are stunning. Traditionally, companies have *mismanaged* friction in four ways: coercion, dominance, ignoring it in the hope that it will go away, or oiling it over, sweeping it under the rug. Today, they are much more likely to admit its existence and devise strategies to cope with it. The leader who does not become adept at managing conflict will rule over either a madhouse or a lifeless swamp.

Conflict: Golden Opportunity or Inevitable Nuisance?

The typical management reaction to friction is one of annoyance. Yet conflict need not be a bothersome vexation. It has both a positive and a negative face.

The Positive Face of Conflict

Every situation has an optimal level of friction in much the same manner as the brake on an automobile. Too little results in lethargy, apathy, and letting things go unchallenged; too much brings productivity to a grinding halt, to the harm of the organization. When friction remains within reasonable limits, the following beneficial outcomes can result.

1. Catharsis is not only good for the soul, it can be good for the relationship. Once people ventilate their true feelings, they are often in a better frame of mind to resolve the difficulty.

2. A constructive confrontation often brings to the surface feelings that have long lain dormant. One party then appreciates how intensely the other feels about the matter at issue.

3. An honest squabble can bring to the manager's attention disagreements that might otherwise have continued unnoticed.

4. Locking horns often saves time and energy. People are sometimes so polite and etiquette-conscious that little gets done.

5. An eyeball-to-eyeball clash may prompt higher management to evaluate policies, procedures, or rules to prevent a repetition of the situation.

6. As a blade is sharpend by honing it on a whetstone, so a

vigorous disagreement may cause both parties to rethink their positions, producing more effective ideas and ways of doing things.

7. Conflict sometimes stimulates people to work harder and smarter, if for no other reason than to prove that they were right, or that it could be done as they proposed.

8. Seeing individuals frankly disagree often encourages the timid to express their opinions, which might otherwise have been held in silence.

9. Standing up for your viewpoint prevents the other person from unfairly encroaching on your territory. It also prevents the other person from taking you for an easy mark.

10. An altercation frequently enables the leader to identify the nonformal leaders and the various cliques in the work group.

11. An honest dispute often engenders a greater mutual respect and a clearer understanding of the positions of both sides.

12. Conflict can often teach the combatants how to fight cleanly.

These twelve benefits of constructive friction are no mean payoffs, so the leader should not be too impulsive to snuff out all conflicts.

The Negative Face of Conflict

You, as a manager, know from experience how harmful destructive conflict can be. A "he who is not with me is against me" climate takes over, while coordination of effort, job satisfaction, morale, and productivity go down the drain. Organizational objectives yield to provincial victories. People are forced to choose sides whether they want to or not, and fratricidal vendettas become the principal goal of the combatants. Joe Kennedy is reputed to have advised his sons, "Don't get mad; get even." Such an attitude produces lasting enmity that stimulates people to plot how to get the foe, not how to get the job done. Finally, if the conflict festers for any length of time, mutual suspicion and distrust are its offspring no matter how it is handled. These represent severe organizational costs.

Nature and Types of Conflict

The key terms in defining conflict are *incompatibility* and *simultaneity*. A conflict exists when incompatible goals, resources, or rewards are sought simultaneously. This may take any of the following forms.

Intragroup. The older managers want to continue to operate as they have always done, but the newly hired MBAs are eager to innovate and change work processes.

Person-Group. Smith works diligently at his job, goes to night school for a college degree, and plans to get promoted, but his fellow supervisors ridicule him and give him the cold-shoulder treatment.

Intrasender. Jones's superior insists that her work group produce as much and as well as possible, but he also demands that she overlook the poor work of minority subordinates and let them get away with violations of the rules that are not permitted other employees.

Intersender. This is the reason why many foremen feel that they are the man in the middle and the victim of double-talk. Superiors tell them that they are in charge and have the necessary authority to get the job done, but staff specialists demand that they comply with their directions.

The potential for conflict of all four types is enormous.

Role Conflict

A particularly anxiety-provoking form of incompatible simultaneity is role conflict. A role is a pattern of behaviors that a person is expected to engage in as he or she carries out the functions of a given position and interacts with others. As Figure 32 indicates, the network of perceptions and expectations makes role conflict one of the most complicated problems in organizational behavior. There are five variables that influence the leader—organization, superior, peers, subordinates, and off-the-job relations. For each of these, there are three possible sets of roles, perceptions, and expectations that interact: the self-perceived roles of each; how each perceives

Figure 32. **Role network and potential conflict.**

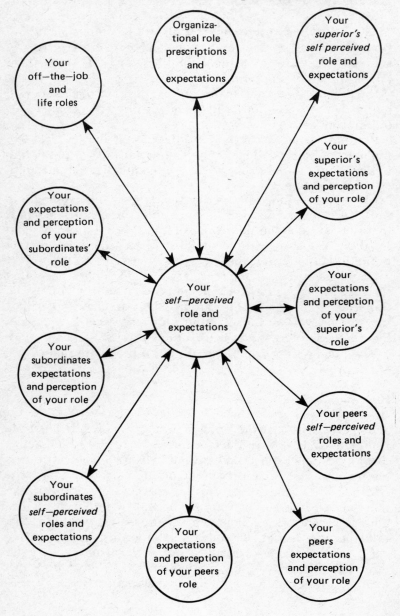

the role of the leader; and how the leader perceives the roles of the others.

Some examples should illustrate the wide range of role conflicts.

1. The organization perceives the role of a manager as that of a maintainer, carrying out orders and working placidly within the system, but he sees his role as that of a change agent.

2. A superior may not define precisely his expectations of subordinates, who will then suffer from *role ambiguity*. A sizable number of lower-level managers find this ambiguity stressful, not to mention those managers who are not sure of the real criteria used for promotions. Conflict will also exist if a superior sees his role as tightly controlling every aspect of the operation, expecting his assistant to carry out his directions, but that assistant sees his role as working closely with the superior, offering ideas and suggestions, being delegated meaningful projects, and participating in at least some decision-making activities. Such conflicts occur frequently.

3. A superior may expect a leader to accomplish more than is reasonably possible. Then the latter suffers from *role overload* and will use whatever strategy she can to cope with the situation.

4. *Sent roles* are behaviors that others expect the leader to exhibit. Peers, such as staff specialists, expect the line manager to consult with them and be open to their counsel. The work group expects the supervisor to be supportive and helpful. All key individuals and groups with whom the leader interacts have their own ideas as to how she should perform her job. Since each set of expectations is more or less self-interested, the potential for anxiety and conflict is impressive.

5. Subordinates not only have their self-defined roles but also have their expectations of how the leader should act. A manager may perceive his role as that of taking care of number one, satisfying the demands of higher management no matter what it takes, cultivating key power figures, and accelerating his career. But his subordinates, most of whom are going nowhere, may define his role as that of a facilitator who removes roadblocks and makes it easier for them to produce. In such an extreme case, conflict of an intense sort is predictable.

6. The leader plays many roles, as Shakespeare proved over and over. He or she has many life roles—spouse, parent, friend, club member, community volunteer. Many a career, and many a marriage, has been debilitated because the parties involved failed to balance out these roles with the occupational roles. In fact, right now many women who are quite successful in business are troubled about their role as mother, despite all the reassurances of psychologists.

Preventing Conflict

Conflict is like a virus. It can never be completely eradicated, but left uncontrolled, it becomes epidemic. Accordingly, the best strategy is to counteract it, and the best preventive method is effective management. Competent planning, organizing, directing, leading, coordinating, and controlling the work force are all musts. Many conflicts stem from ineffectual management. Like weeds, friction flourishes under incompetence. Effective management cuts off its nutrients.

Since some conflicts are positive, it behooves the leader to recognize which kind he or she is managing. DuBrinn gives a simple classification of constructive and destructive conflicts.[1]

Let's look at some examples of these kinds of conflict. An advertising firm and a client are arguing about the design of a new campaign. The former contends that the proposed program is novel and creative; the latter insists that it is not right for what his company wants to get across to the market. After a prickly discussion, they come up with a new design that is better than either conceptualized at the outset. This is a *functional conflict over substance*. On the other hand, when the industrial relations department rides roughshod over the line managers with respect to the interpretation and administration of the union contract, so that the latter feel that their power to cope with the union is minimized, a substantive matter has produced a *dysfunctional conflict*. Two managers find each other abrasive. They have a head-to-head argument. As a result, they still do not like each other, but they have developed mutual respect. The personality clash has been functional. But when subordinates try to get rid of a supervisor who is fair but reasonably demanding, the personal friction is dysfunctional.

One good technique for keeping conflict to a minimum is for the leader to lay down the ground rules for "fighting."

1. People have both a right and a corresponding obligation. They are expected to criticize any activity or procedure that requires improvement. However, they must offer a practical method for improving it. The privilege to criticize is matched by the responsibility to improve.

2. When people disagree over substantive matters, they are to do so in a win-win manner. Disagreeing agreeably but firmly requires tact.

3. Personal attacks, petty sniping, nitpicking, obstacle building, slanderous backbiting, and demeaning attacks will not be tolerated.

4. When there is a personality clash, under no circumstances will it be allowed to hinder production. People may like or dislike whom they will, but this antagonism is not to affect the work flow or coordination or effort.

5. Attempts to divide the work group into antagonistic cliques will be dealt with firmly; efforts to undermine the efficiency of another person or group will be even more severely censured.

6. Disputes are to be resolved by the parties involved. If they wish, the leader will serve as a mediator or arbitrator. However, if they cannot or will not resolve disputes, the leader will do so as fairly as possible.

7. No one will earn Brownie points by succeeding at the expense of another. People will be rewarded for being practically helpful to other units, groups, and individuals.

8. Once a conflict is settled, or a fight ended, it is to become history. Nursing grudges will not be permitted.

The leader can also insist that people keep others informed. This can be done by classifying five types of actions or decisions: (1) those that a person or group can take without informing anyone; (2) those that may be taken but only if related people or units are informed *after the fact*, so that they will not be taken off guard; (3) those that are within the jurisdiction of the individual or group but that cannot be taken until other affected units are informed *before the fact,* since such actions have an impact on their activities; (4) those that may be taken only after the individual has negotiated with related people and the parties involved have *reached agreement,* lest the unilateral action of one create a problem for the other; and (5) those that may not be taken without specific permission of the person's or group's superior. You, as the manager, will know which actions or decisions properly belong to each category.

Strategies for Managing Conflict

Despite the best efforts of the leader to prevent conflict, friction is bound to occur when human beings interact. Discord is always threatening to break out among us. Hence, the manager must have available a spectrum of strategies for *resolving* it.

Least Effective Strategies

Some popular strategies appear to solve the conflict, but in fact they do not *resolve* it for the simple reason that they give only short-term results and breed frustration, distrust, and a feeling of being treated unfairly.

Coercion. Overt or subtle, coercion settles the matter as quickly as it gives birth to resentment. *Intimidation,* naked or implied, produces similar reactions. *Dominance* is a pressure tactic that most people find distasteful.

Procrastination. Putting off a resolution of the disagreement may well cause it to feed on itself.

Persuasion. The difficulty with persuasion is that the persuader is psychologically superior, the persuadee inferior. In addition, it is like heroin: the persuasive "shots" must be progressively more frequent and stronger to keep the other party in line.

Coalitions. Alliances are often necessary to get things done. But as a means for managing conflict, coalitions force people to choose sides. This may lead to all-out warfare.

Distributive Bargaining. Compromise is necessary at times.

The problem with such bargaining, however, is that each antagonist must trade off at least some things that he or she prizes. No one is really satisfied with a compromise. Moreover, after the transient peace has been attained, each party is likely to be beset by two doubts: Did I yield too much too readily? If I had pushed harder or longer, might I have secured more?

More Effective Strategies

In the real world, the perfect resolution to friction will never be found. The partly effective approaches enable the parties to cope with the conflict in an efficient manner, while limiting its negative impact. This is the best that can be done under some circumstances.

Peaceful Coexistence. Neighbors, religions, countries, and in-laws have all learned the advantages of peaceful coexistence. When conditions permit, getting people to stay on their own side of the street is a simple method for managing two individuals or groups that find each other abrasive or disruptive, especially if the leader lays down the ground rules for coexistence and enforces them rigorously.

Two supervisors hated each other's guts, and the bad feeling was beginning to infect both work groups. The manager called the two subordinate supervisors together several times and tried to help them work in a more cooperative manner. When these attempts failed and production was starting to suffer, she called them to her office and said, "Harry, you don't care very much for Tom, right? And, Tom, you couldn't care less for Harry, right? That's OK with me. I can't tell you whom to like and whom to dislike. But this thing is getting out of hand, and production is suffering. I've tried my best to bring you people together but apparently have failed. Now here's the way we're going to run things. Tom, you do your work and stay out of Harry's way. Harry, you do your work and stay out of Tom's way. When you must coordinate your efforts, both of you will do so to the utmost, or else you will *both* hear from me. Is this clear?"

Appeal. Any citizen who feels that an injustice has been done him or her in a lower court has the right to appeal to a higher one. Many organizations, however, have no appeal system. If an organization has a known procedure for taking one's case up the line, the following advantages result. First, such a system protects the subordinate from the bias, caprice, jealousy, or hostility of the superior. Second, it stimulates the parties in a conflict to deal more honestly with each other, since each realizes that the other has an avenue to attain justice. Finally, it allows for a more objective resolution of the problem because those who adjudicate the matter are not emotionally involved with it.

A computer system was to be installed in a medium-size company. The managers of all functional areas had been consulted and had contributed to making the decision regarding the specific system selected. Once the computer was in place, however, a great deal of wrangling ensued. The accounting/finance people wanted first programming priority, but so did manufacturing, sales, export, and administration/personnel. The system could easily handle all these data, but it could not do so all at once. After listening to all the managers plead their cases at a special meeting, the president determined that the rank order would be as follows: accounting/finance, manufacturing, administration/personnel, sales, and export.

An appeal system, however, is hardly a panacea. There are at least eight potential hazards:

1. Upper management may be unwilling to play the role of Solomon.
2. Higher authority tends to be busy and may have little time or inclination to sift through the divergent contentions thoroughly.

3. When the friction involves a manager and subordinate, the higher echelons may habitually support the former regardless of the facts in the case.
4. The assertive person or group may be judged a troublemaker.
5. A few petty or neurotic people will certainly abuse the procedure; their litigious attitude will cause them to magnify every friction molehill into a conflict mountain.
6. Managers whose subordinates make appeals may feel that their judgment or fairness is being questioned.
7. Some subordinates will look upon an appeal system as a means for bypassing the supervisor.
8. Since the appeal pathway is available, people may be less motivated to resolve their differences at the local level.

Despite all this, however, the right of appeal is a guaranteed right of every citizen in a democracy. Appropriate procedures can be formulated to control its abuse.

Mediation. Organizational conflicts are like family arguments. In the absence of countervailing forces, attitudes tend to be polarized, perspectives become set in concrete, a middle ground is ignored, and a win-lose attitude pervades the interaction. All this creates a climate of defensiveness which aborts any inclination to understand the other party's position. To prevent conflict from reaching such an impasse, the intervention of a knowledgeable and trusted third party is helpful. The objective viewpoint of a conciliator or mediator often defuses the emotionality of the combatants and catalyzes their efforts to reach a mutually acceptable resolution.

Years ago, a favorite buzzword was "ombudsman." Ombudsmen were outside the chain of command and brought to the situation concern, detachment, knowledge, and freedom to contact various segments of the organization in their quest for justice. Preferably, they also had a helping attitude, coupled with the requisite negotiation skills. Regardless of the title given, this is an excellent role for a respected manager who is one or two years from retirement. He or she knows the organization, appreciates what can or cannot be done, has no ax to grind, and can deal with clean hands. Moreover, such a manager is concerned not only with the merits of the case but also with the interests of the organization.

A management-development specialist was giving a company program when, during a coffee break, a young woman manager asked him, "Does every company and large department have a chaplain?" "What do you mean?" came the response. "You know," she continued, "someone to whom you can go confidentially when things go wrong, or when you have a problem, or when you and someone else aren't getting along very well." The expert had never heard it put quite this way, but on reflection, he came to the conclusion that this is often the case. In almost every large group, there will be a trusted someone to whom other people turn for advice and help in resolving their problems, especially those they would prefer not to take to a superior.

Constructive Competition. Competition keeps human beings on their toes and stimulates them to do their best. When the disputants are not in a position to undermine one another, they may be allowed to compete according to well-understood rules. Engineers who disagree vehemently over the design of a new product, salespeople who are at odds about the best way to sell, advertising personnel who cannot agree about a layout, managers who are at odds regarding the number, type, and content of various reports—all these situations are sometimes best solved by challenging each of the discordant groups to formulate their best ideas and techniques independently. A lively competition stirs up the brain cells and breaks the binding effect of habit. It also tends to put to positive use the emotional energy that might otherwise be wasted in conflict.

At an annual sales meeting, the afternoon of the last working day was set aside for the customary golf tournament. Unfortunately, it rained so hard that the contest was canceled. By the time the concluding dinner was held, some of the people had imbibed more than a little of the cup that cheers, and a boisterous atmosphere permeated the dinner. While the president was giving his final talk, one group shouted, "The Southwest region bets each of the other regions that we will sell more than they will in each quarter for the coming year. The bet is $1,000 each quarter." Naturally, the challenge was taken up by the other regions with loud shouting and catcalls. The president waited for a few minutes for the noise level to subside. Then he said, "We'll do better than that. Anyone who exceeds quota by 20 percent will get a bonus of $1,000 per quarter. And the group that increases its sales profits by 25 percent over last year will receive a bonus to be decided by the vice president of sales and me." The cheers that followed were deafening.

Most Effective Strategies

A strategy may be termed successful if it produces short-term results and a passing peace at the expense of long-term cooperation. Truly effective strategies, however, manage the problem of the moment while laying a foundation for increasing teamwork.

Superordinate Goal. Russia and the United States worked together to defeat Hitler not out of love for each other but because neither could obtain its objectives without the help of the other. The research has consistently shown that a goal transcending the parochial objectives of both individuals or groups is an excellent way to resolve a conflict. To obtain individual or parochial objectives, both parties must work together for a greater good.

A company found it increasingly difficult to compete because of rejects, reworks, complaints from customers, low productivity, and sloppy work. It decided to relocate to the Sun Belt. The union protested strenuously. The corporation showed the records and the books. Since neither the organization nor the union wanted to force employees to uproot their families and leave their friends for a strange section of the country, basic accommodations were made that enabled the company to remain and be competitive. The union tempered its demands for wage increases, got its membership to improve the quantity and quality of production, and cooperated with management in making the plant a viable operation.

Integrative Bargaining. Some people are so accustomed to the trade-offs required in distributive bargaining that the idea of a different type of negotiation rarely occurs to them. Win-lose attitudes are generated by sports, college debates, court trials, and even by relations between certain religious and political groups. We are so programmed to win at the expense of the other fellow that we sometimes forget that there are many situations in which all concerned can win something. The problem is not one of techniques but one of attitudes.

The heart of integrative bargaining is that it requires no one to yield anything that is essential to him or her. It is a problem-solving process rather than a jousting for victory, and each party comes away from the negotiation with valued outcomes. For example, flexitime allows subordinates to set their own work periods, as long as they satisfy organizational requirements. Work groups can be permitted to devise their own methods for getting the job done, so long as it is well done. And nearly all forms of job enrichment involve integrative bargaining. In all these instances, the employees get something that is important to them, and the organization gets what it requires.

For several months a sales manager had difficulty getting his people to do the paperwork that was so important for analysis, planning, feedback, and control. Call reports, customer data, and other types of intelligence information (but *never* expense accounts) were submitted after the established deadlines. Time and again the manager reminded his sales force of the importance of such data. He tried many approaches: urging, pointing out the advantages to the sales personnel, cajoling, and even threatening. After a temporary improvement, the salespeople fell back to familiar habits. At a meeting, they complained that the paperwork kept them from their primary task— imposing their will on the competition.

After much discussion, the following plan was developed. Each salesperson was given a pocket dictating machine. Either between calls or at the end of the day, the salespeople dictated all information into the machine. In the evening they called a special number in the sales department and played their tapes into the receiver. At the other end, a recording was made of each transmission, and in the morning, a typist came in early and transcribed the messages from all the salespeople. In this way the manager got what he needed: quick, comprehensive data. The salespeople also got what they wanted: avoidance of the chore of writing reports, coupled with additional time to sell.

Mix and Match. Matrix management, task forces, project teams, and rotation of personnel among various units are all forms of mix and match. Divide and conquer may be an efficient Machiavellian technique, but forming new combinations of people is more effective in the long run. People are creatures of habit. Even when they attend the movies, go to church, or watch a sports event, they tend to sit in approximately the same location if possible. We are likely to identify with those who interact with us most frequently. Both these realities give rise to provincialism. Recombining personnel, when advantageous, serves to prevent this. The mix-and-match strategy has the additional plus of bringing to bear on a problem the best expertise available, not to mention the benefits of the cross-fertilization process.

Redesigning the Structure

It has been assumed up to now that the sources of conflict stem primarily from people. Sometimes, however, the root of the problem is in the organizational structure, policies, and procedures. The structure may be inadequate and inappropriate. Policies may be outdated. Procedures may require modification and updating. Jurisdictions may not be clearly defined—they may either overlap or leave gaps. Accountabilities may be crystal-clear in some instances but vague in others. Structure must follow the mission and objectives of the company, and sometimes goals and plans are changed without making corresponding alterations in organizational patterns.

The typical reader is probably not in a position to institute the more complex strategies of organization development. Programs such as the Blake-Mouton Managerial Grid®, Likert's Questionnaire-Feedback Management Systems approach, T-groups and D-groups (sensitivity training), Transactional Analysis, and Focused Exercises usually require strong and major commitments on the part of top management. Organizational renewal seeks to change radically the culture, values, attitudes, climate, and interaction patterns of an organization. The processes involved are complicated, time-consuming, and risky to some extent. They require the guidance of an experienced consultant. For these reasons they are not discussed in detail here. If you are interested, you can study any of the available books on organizational behavior. These will give you leads, should you wish to pursue the matter in depth.

Executives might keep in mind that there are good reasons why the playing area is different for baseball, football, tennis, basketball, and hockey: each is proper to the nature of the sport and its purposes. Organizational structures should match goals and strategies in just the same way.

increasing your creativity: do you get good ideas or profitable ideas?

Your Most Creative Asset—People

According to Yale University biophysicist Harold J. Morowitz, the human body is worth about $6 million. That covers the raw materials—the enzymes, proteins, hormones, and so on. To combine the basic matter into human cells would cost an additional six thousand trillion dollars, he says. And the cost of assembling those cells into a functioning human being is beyond computation. "Each human being," Morowitz states emphatically, "is priceless!"[1]

How fortunate for organizations that this investment has been made for them! How unfortunate that some fail to capitalize on their most valuable asset—the innovative ideas of employees. Economic resources are necessary, but human resources are essential; financial capital is needful, but talent capital is crucial; reindustrialization is desirable, but actualization of human potential is critical. This is what leadership is all about.

The latest buzzwords are Theory Z management, quality of work life, consensus decision making, and quality circles. The concepts are neither new nor revolutionary.[2] There is nothing startlingly new in perceiving employees as a valuable brain-endowed resource, rather than as a mob of mindless hired hands. Some companies have always adopted this perspective, and others are making earnest—if belated—efforts to do so.[3] What *is* new is that a worsening competitive position is forcing organizations to swallow their corporate pride and at least experiment with the concepts and techniques inherent in these terms. The central thrust of this movement is threefold: to build a climate and system that stimulate, welcome, act on, and reward the ideas and suggestions of employees; to share with the work force the responsibility for devising improved ways of doing things and better problem solutions; and to create a common purpose that prompts both management and subordinates to work toward mutually beneficial superordinate objectives rather than provincial concerns.

Why Innovation Is a Must

In a Darwinian universe, the inefficient are devoured by the creative. Few organizations come a cropper because of any single monstrous blunder. Corporate decay is much like tooth decay. The deterioration goes unnoticed until the pain throbs. Then much hustle and bustle ensue, often too late and too unplanned to be effective. The most potent corporate fluoride is a climate that keeps two principles front and center: (1) the worst enemy of the best is the good enough; (2) anything devised can be improved if people are given an opportunity to do so and are rewarded for their contributions.

No need to summarize the grisly data that indicate how far the United States has slipped from its proud preeminence after World War II.

If we can believe the evidence, the rate of productivity growth in the United States has declined markedly since the mid-1960s. The Council of Economic Advisors (CEA), for example, has found that the growth of output per labor hour, which averaged 3.3 percent per year over the 1948–1966 period, declined to 2.1 percent during the 1966–1973 period. Official data for 1973–1977 indicate a further deterioration to 1.2 percent.[4]

The snail has little future in today's productivity race.

Some Necessary Distinctions

The terms performance, improvement, innovation, and creativity are often confused. *Performance* is related to current production methods and techniques. *Improvement* implies the more efficient rearrangement of present ways of doing things in order to increase output; nothing new is added. For instance, the keys of the typewriter are not designed in the most effective manner. Merely rearranging them so that the most commonly used letters are struck by the most powerful fingers would improve matters. *Innovation* involves the creation of new combinations and the addition of new elements. The electric typewriter, the ballpoint pen, and the heat exchanger used in a fireplace are good examples. *Creativity,* in the strict sense, denotes the development of the striking breakthrough that changes the rules of the game or represents a radical departure from current processes. Once the transistor, the jet engine, or the laser is invented, everyone must adapt to it or perish. Creativity, in the broad sense, means perceiving things from a new perspective, mentally juggling new combinations, imagining different arrangements, conceptualizing novel applications. It includes improvement, innovation, and invention and is the meaning used throughout the remainder of the chapter.

What Prevents People from Becoming More Creative

The amazing fact is that improvement and innovation require no great intelligence. How much brains did it take to think of the simple spindle, which greatly increases the efficiency of the fast-food cook while keeping peace among the waitresses as to whose order is first? What genius was required to think of putting a "window" in an oven? wheels on a refrigerator? an eraser on the end of a pencil? What brilliance was needed to develop Pampers? to devise the paper clip? to think of storm windows? How often have you thought, on seeing a novel combination of familiar concepts or processes, "Why didn't I think of that?"

There are five major reasons why subordinates are not more innovative: (1) the climate of the organization; (2) the personality of the individual; (3) peer pressure; (4) lower management attitudes; and (5) lack of training and reinforcement.

The Climate of the Organization

Any change may be a threat to well-established status, territorial rights, and prerogative systems. Among the upper echelons, ingrained habits and comfortable ways of doing things are likely to be upset to some degree. Additionally, the climate may be rejecting of improvement, or the stricture of the organization structure may rebuff it.

For decades AT&T prided itself on its innovative technology and customer service, providing the best telephone system in the world. It did not have a marketing function in the true meaning of the term—what monopoly need market its services? Under the impact of deregulation, increased competition, and an awareness of probable future changes and challenges in the communications industry, top management decided to develop a market orientation. Presumably, none of the executives possessed the necessary talents and experience in this area, so Archie J. McGill was hired away from IBM. One can only imagine the puzzlement, resistance, and perhaps resentment this "new boy on the block" had to contend with because seasoned managers who had spent their whole lives at AT&T saw a new function that they knew little about being placed high on the priority list of the corporation.[5]

At times, the higher echelons send confusing signals to subordinate managers. They say that they are in favor of one thing but then contradict this is their behavior. One CEO complained that no matter how hard he tried to raise quality level he was unsuccessful. But when his subordiantes were questioned, they said, "Of course he's for quality, but he's for everything else, too. We have a theme a month here." [6]

Perhaps most important of all is the fact that suggestions for improvement are neither welcomed nor rewarded. People are hardly stupid. They tend to focus on those activities that please management and gain them "Brownie points." Unless they have the conviction of an Admiral Rickover, they avoid those activities that are likely to go unrecognized. This is an excellent illustration of the expectancy theory of motivation.

The Personality of the Individual

Some people are failure avoiders. They are so lacking in self-confidence that they find the risk involved in innovation too great to bear. They are at ease only when life is structured, predictable, and stable. They lack the "I wonder what would happen, if?" attitude that is at the root of innovation. Without the encouragement of superiors, they will not think of better ways of doing things.

Another group that may have little creative potential consists of those who are overspecialized and preoccupied with a narrow field of endeavor. The tunnel vision of a specialty and the trained incapabilities that it produces make it difficult for such people to shift perceptions and to experiment with new combinations. Everyone is aware of the accountant who is a fine technician but cannot convey to higher management the meaning of the data and recommendations for managerial action.

A third group that cannot be counted on to be innovative consists of those who are at odds with themselves and the world. They have never rationalized authority. They are "agin' the government," carry a chip on their shoulders, go out of their way to be contrary. The salmon swims upstream for the laudable purpose of ensuring the future of the species. These individuals, however, swim against the tide for negative reasons. Emotionally, they are fixated at the rebellious adolescent stage of development.

Because our culture sometimes confuses the truly creative person with the one who merely seeks attention, it is important to distinguish the innovative individual from the mere pretender.

The Innovator	*The Mere Pretender*
Is intellectually inquisitive.	Is cynically doubting.
Is constructively critical.	Is corrosively critical.
Seeks to improve the operation.	Seeks attention.
Listens to his or her own drummer.	Picks the brains of others and pirates their ideas.
Has firm convictions based on evidence as he or she perceives it.	Is stubborn for emotional or self-centered reasons.
Is persistent; carries on well in spite of opposition.	Pouts readily and is easily discouraged; attacks perceived opposition at a personal level.
Is relatively unconcerned with organizational protocol.	May be very sensitive to protocol if it magnifies his or her ego or status.
Sticks with an idea or proposal until it is completed.	Flits from idea to idea, making many starts but few completions.
Often has an appreciation of the comical and a wry sense of humor.	Is dreadfully self-serious or has a caustic sense of humor.
Dislikes disagreement but can cope with it.	Perceives disagreement as a personal affront.
Does not relate well to authority but accepts it as a fact of life.	Resents authority and seeks to fight or circumvent it.
Is zealous for his or her ideas and projects.	Is zealous to stay in the limelight.
Prefers complexity.	Prefers the attention-getting.

The Innovator	*The Mere Pretender*
Deviates when necessary.	Deviates for the sake of being different.
Is not particularly adroit in human relations.	Is often quite adroit in human relations of the manipulative sort.
Is nonconforming in a natural way.	Is nonconforming for purposes of self-display.
Gravitates to the solid and substantive.	Gravitates to the showy and the bizarre.
Is genuinely interested in improving the operation.	Is interested in grinding his or her own ax.

Peer Pressure

It is all too human to project the whole blame for the lack of innovation on higher management. The fact is that creative people are thwarted more by peers than superiors. The improver is perceived as a wavemaker. He or she makes co-workers feel either jealous or guilty, or both. And the reward-punishment system of the peer group is often more immediate and compelling than that available to management. Changing the climate within the work group is a first step to innovation.

Several companies in the steel industry are experimenting with labor-management participation committees. Composed of workers, supervisors, and managers, they cooperate to improve the quality of work life, while reducing costs and increasing production. United Steel Workers vice president Joseph Odorchich has said, "The managers have got to listen to the workers because they know more about the plant than any industrial engineer or boss. This goes way beyond improving productivity. I'm talking about people having confidence in one another." [7]

Lower Management Attitudes

The majority of supervisors are concerned about increasing productivity. Any significant innovative change, however, is likely to be perceived with a wary eye. Supervisors have seen programs come and programs go, after the initial enthusiasm faded. They may adopt a "here we go again" attitude. A goodly number are neither comfortable with nor skilled in a participative management mode. Others may misinterpret any attempt to involve the employees as an encroachment on their authority, a threat to their status, an affront to their right to control their people, or a tacit criticism of the way they are doing their jobs. Above all others, first-line management is in a position to sabotage the best-intentioned efforts of the upper echelons to bring about improvement and innovation. Every strategy must be employed to get lower management to accept changes as being beneficial to them, rather than as needless nuisances that add problems to their already overburdened lives.

Lack of Training and Reinforcement

A few people seem to be born with a lot of curiosity; they enjoy mentally manipulating new arrangements and combinations. The vast majority of us have to be trained to become more improvement-oriented than we currently are. Innovation is a heady wine. Once the principles and a few techniques are mastered, it stimulates itself. These concepts are discussed later in the chapter.

Organizational Strategies to Increase Innovation

For decades, Louis Marx & Company was one of the nation's biggest and most profitable toy makers. Eight years ago Marx sold out to Quaker Oats Company and retired at the age of 80. Things soon went from bad to worse. Now the company is working out a plan to pay its debts under court protection. People joked that the new Marx managers went to toy shows and then raced back to copy what they had seen. "They lost their innovation," says Harold Kamp, a toy buyer. Mr. Marx was a driving, hardworking, and stern but gracious "genius." He invented most of his own toys. He used advanced mass-production methods. He was one of the first to import toys from the Orient.[8]

When Bic entered the U.S. market, Gillette executives regarded the French company as a "pesky nuisance." They took the complacent view that Bic's 19-cent pen was no match for Gillette's best-selling, higher-priced Paper Mate. Soon the Bic pen was outselling its competitor. Ten years later, Bic challenged the Cricket lighter. Gillette executives were not perturbed. But when Bic invaded the core of Gillette's business, the razor-and-blade market, the U.S. company, always known for its innovation, decided to out-Bic Bic. According to *Fortune* magazine, "The competition between the rivals is no longer just a matter of one pen or one lighter, or one razor against another. It is a war on all fronts." [9]

These two incidents, and one could readily include Pepsico and Coca-Cola, show what happens when a company becomes ever so slightly self-satisfied. How can an organization keep its improvement orientation finely tuned? Fortunately, the research is of some help. T. Peters and the staff at McKinsey & Company studied 37 excellent companies, focusing on 10 of them: IBM, Texas Instruments, Hewlett-Packard, 3M, Digital Equipment, Procter & Gamble, Johnson & Johnson, McDonald's, Dana, and Emerson Electric. [10] On the surface, these organizations have little in common. Five are in high technology, one produces packaged foods, one makes medical products, two manufacture mechanical and electrical products, and one operates fast-food restaurants. Yet they were found to share eight characteristics.

A Bias Toward Action. These companies emphasize "Do it, fix it, try it." Sweeping new concepts and the perfect plan are secondary to making small, progressive steps. Ideas are solicited and tested quickly. Those that work are pushed fast. At 3M new-product ideas must be presented in less than five pages. One-page memos are the rule at Procter & Gamble. Objectives for managers are few but central. As one Texas Instruments (TI) executive put it, "More than two objectives is no objective." Task forces are used to identify opportunities and resolve problems. They consist of the best people available, who are volunteers. They are short-lived, usually lasting less than 90 days. Results are reviewed and the manager must justify the time invested. These companies focus on key problems. When Du Pont discovered that transportation amounted to $800 million annually, a "czar" was appointed to work out logistics. Productivity and energy czars are used, each with power to override a division's autonomy.

Simple Form and Lean Staff. "Small is beautiful" is the structural model, despite the fact that all the organizations are large—the smallest, McDonald's, does $1.9 billion a year. Small, manageable entrepreneurial groups are formed to get things done. At the high-technology firms, "champions" shepherd new ideas through the bureaucracy to ensure that they receive the attention of top management.

Closeness to the Customer. At IBM and Digital, top management spends at least 30 days annually conferring with key accounts. At Lanier, most senior executives make sales calls every month. Caterpillar Tractor spends much of its managerial talent to make its motto—"24-hour parts delivery anywhere in the world"—a reality. Boeing does the same. Each company takes to heart Drucker's observation that the justification of a company is to satisfy a customer. With good reason: in a study of two fast-paced industries, Eric Von Hippel found that 100 percent of the major new-product ideas, and 80 percent of the minor ones, came directly from customers!

Productivity Improvement Via Consensus. Motivation, autonomy, and rewards are used to increase productivity. At TI, shop floor teams set production targets. At 3M, a self-sufficient team stays together from the inception of a new product to its national introduction. The emphasis is never on monetary rewards alone. Forms of recognition range from the "corny"—pins, badges, and medals—to TI's practice of allowing outstanding production teams to describe their successes to the board.

Autonomy to Encourage Entrepreneurship. Managers are expected to act like entrepreneurs. Divisions are allowed to reinvest most of their earnings in their own operations. Headquarters staff may not cut off funds for divisional products arbitrarily. TI has a special group of "listeners"—138 senior technical people—who assess ideas. Junior staff are encouraged to meet with these people for a one-on-one evaluation of their ideas. IBM's Fellows Program allows proven senior performers to explore their unique concepts. They are usually highly skilled gadflies who shake things up—almost always to the good of the organization.

Stress on a Key Business Value. These excellent companies have one basic theme and stick to it: Dana focuses on cost reduction and productivity; IBM, on customer satisfaction; TI, 3M, and H-P, on new-product development and research; P&G, on product quality; McDonald's, on quality, cleanliness, and value. Thus a climate is engendered that indoctrinates newcomers, while those rising through the ranks serve as role models.

Capitalizing on What They Know Best. Unlike the Marx–Quaker Oats incident noted above, these organizations capitalize on what they do best. They resist the temptation to get into attractive-looking businesses that require skills they lack. As one former chairman put it, "Never acquire a business you don't know how to run."

Simultaneous Loose-Tight Controls. Whereas bureaucratic organizations tend to control the essential, important, and marginal with the same rigid policies and procedures, these firms tightly control the few essential variables while allowing managers great leeway in conducting day-to-day operations. At 3M, the yardstick is return on sales and the number of employees utilized. When Rene McPherson became president of Dana, he threw out all policy manuals and replaced them with a one-page statement of philosophy. All divisions were required to report costs and revenues daily. Thus these companies avoid the extremes of undue looseness and rigid controls.

Additional guidance comes from the Stanford Research Institute, which for years has been studying the reasons some organizations have outstanding growth records while others merely drift along.[11] Among the major conclusions are:

1. They systematically seek out growth products and markets.
2. They have organized programs for identifying and promoting new business opportunities.
3. They are self-critical about the adequacy of present opera-

tions and therefore demonstrate superior competitive abilities in their present line of business.

4. Their top management slots are staffed by courageous executives who bubble with dissatisfaction and are driven by an energetic zeal to lead rather than to follow.

5. They have formal systems for discovering opportunities and offsetting risks by "planning for the unseeable."

6. The chief executives consciously and conscientiously, by word and deed, establish an organizational climate of ruthless self-examination and effervescent high adventure.

Increasing Your Own Creativity

No one can give what he or she does not have. If you are to serve as a role model, you must give some thought to your own innovative attitudes and skills. The following questions may start you on this path.

What are my on-the-job priorities?	Are they based on effectiveness, or mere habit and personal preference?
How do I manage my time?	How can I invest it more profitably?
How am I using my talents and skills?	Are there better ways of investing them?
What are my work routines?	Are they the result of careful planning, or of custom, firefighting, and reaction to the latest pressure?
What am I handling personally that should be delegated?	How can I gradually delegate these things to key subordinates?
What am I *not* doing that I *should* be doing?	How can I organize my work to include them?
Do I manage work or objectives?	How can I focus on results and more effective ways of attaining them?
How many innovative procedures have I thought of in the past six months?	How can I come up with more and better methods over the next six months?

How accepting am I of subordinates' suggestions?

How can I encourage subordinates to think of improvement-oriented ideas?

To what extent do I reward subordinates' efforts to come up with better ways of doing things?

How can I make sure that their efforts are recognized and appreciated?

Over the past six months, what action have I taken to implement subordinates' suggestions for improving the operation?

How can I ensure that action is taken as quickly as possible?

To what degree have I helped my people become more innovative?

What methods can I use to help them become more innovative?

Stimulating Your People to Be More Innovative

The four great obstacles to increased innovativeness on the part of the work force are (1) subordinates often do not realize how creative they can be; (2) creativity is not demanded of them; (3) they have not been helped to experiment with new combinations and arrangements that force them to break habit and to overcome *functional fixity*—the tendency to view a situation from only one point of view; (4) few organizations systematically provide opportunities for innovative thinking on the part of the work force. Yet there are several simple techniques that can be used to bring about on-the-job improvements.

Brainstorming

Popular in the 1950s, brainstorming became faddish because of the superficial uses to which it was put. Even so, it can be a valuable and enjoyable exercise. The following steps are typical:

1. A work issue is selected that holds promise of improvement. This may involve analysis of work methods, preparation for an emergency that might arise, motivation of employees, or any similar problem or opportunity.

2. The participants are told in advance the nature and purpose of the exercise. It is assumed that those close to the work

situation will have realistic suggestions for coping with or improving it.

3. Participants are urged to let their imaginations run free. The critical terms are combine, eliminate, modify, adapt, rearrange, substitute, put to other uses, change the sequence, and redesign.

4. The purpose is to build a pool of useful ideas. Hence, no criticism is permitted at this stage.

5. When a suitable number of suggestions are secured, they can be classified under three headings: most practical, probably useful, and good but unrealistic.

6. The group then discusses ways of implementing the most valid suggestions and identifies those worthy of further exploration. One of the difficulties with brainstorming in the past has been the lack of follow-through after the pleasant experience of "imagineering."

Improvement Sessions

The improvement session can be held once a quarter or as part of a regular meeting. It consists of the following procedures.

1. You select a part of the operation that can and should be improved. Any job area can be chosen—improvement of work methods, reduction of needless overtime, reduction of waste, cost reduction, improvement of quantity or quality of production.

2. You must chair the first go-round for the simple reason that your people must *experience* your concern for improvement, the limits within which they are to work, and how free they are to challenge the accepted ways of doing things. In later sessions, the chair can be rotated.

3. Before the session, subordinates are informed of the nature and objectives of the session and are asked to come prepared to contribute their constructive ideas. In this respect, the approach differs from brainstorming.

4. The participants are encouraged to voice their suggestions, no matter how radical, as long as all ideas are based on evidence and practicality.

5. When the group has expressed its ideas, each is evaluated in terms of the realities of the work situation.

Barnacle Sessions

Organizations are like saltwater ships. Willy-nilly, they pick up barnacles that reduce their speed. An occasional barnacle session sensitizes people to those small inefficiencies that inevitably take hold in an organization if they are not detected and eliminated promptly. It is obviously the obverse side of the improvement session and the procedural steps are the same. In both cases, however, it is important that *the chair be rotated among your key subordinates.* Each chairperson should be responsible for thinking of a part of the operation that can be improved or in which inefficiencies can be eliminated or minimized. These two simple types of sessions can produce valuable results. Suppose, for instance, that four departments held as few as four meetings of each type per year. At least 32 opportunities or problem areas would receive concentrated study!

Pride Sessions

Eagerness to improve can sometimes have the unanticipated consequence of impelling people to focus on what is wrong rather than take pride in what is well done. Now and then, part of a meeting can be devoted to reinforcing the successes of the work force. This approach emphasizes the positive; strengthens the participants' sense of competence, adequacy, and worth; and enables the leader to tune in on what people regard as their assets. The mechanics are uncomplicated. The leader asks a simple question, "What are the three things we do that make us proud to work in this department?" Each person writes down three ideas. This is followed by feedback and a general discussion of how even the best-done things can be done better. A variation of this technique is to administer a one-page questionnaire to the entire work force. Each employee fills in three open-ended questions anonymously: (1) I like working in this unit because . . . ; (2) I

do not care particularly for . . . ; (3) for the future, I suggest
that . . . . The process takes very little time and the feedback
can be used to help establish action programs for improvement, not to mention agenda items for meetings.

Hot-Seat Sessions

The presentation and defense of a viewpoint is a centuries-
old educational device. It is commonplace in MBA programs,
where a student or team is responsible for the analysis, presentation, and defense of a case study. With a little modification, the technique can be applied to the work situation. A
subordinate manager or supervisor is asked in advance to
present to the work group at least the following items: (1) what
the objectives of his or her group are; (2) what group members
do to attain these goals; (3) what methods they utilize; (4) why
they use these particular methods; (5) what they do well; (6)
what they do acceptably; (7) what they do in less than a desirable manner. The group then serves two functions. It critiques
the content of the presentation with a view to pointing out
things that the presenter may have omitted or minimized. It
offers positive suggestions to help the manager or supervisor.
Being forced to stand in the spotlight and explain what goes on
in a given unit requires the individual to *think*. It is necessary,
of course, to remind the participants that while it is expected
that they be intellectually cruel, they are also to be emotionally supportive.

The Delphi Approach

Several givens militate against complete honesty in a group
situation. The status, authority, and power of some of the participants may be a suppressing factor. The "talkers" may
overwhelm the "thinkers." Members may be inclined to go
along with the majority. The unique suggestion may be lost
because it is perceived as being deviant. Personalities, rather
than ideas, may clash and adversary subgroups may be
formed, each defending a provincial viewpoint. Premature
criticism of suggestions may dry up excellent sources of ideas.

In the Delphi approach, participants do not meet and communicate in writing. Although often employed to write scenarios about the future, Delphi can be adapted to any work situation. It requires little time and need not interrupt the work flow.

1. People are chosen who are competent with respect to the subject under consideration; your key subordinates meet this requirement for such matters as friction between departments, communications problems, and methods of improving production.

2. Each person writes down his or her perceptions of the opportunity or problem, together with proposed strategies for coping with or capitalizing on it. This is best done anonymously.

3. A summary of the central thrust of the responses of all the people involved is sent to each participant.

4. Each person is then allowed to alter his or her ideas but must justify any departure from an initial position or any marked deviation from the general trend of the responses from the other participants.

Usually only two or three rounds are needed to ferret out the best ideas. More important, the research indicates that better decisions and strategies are reached this way than in face-to-face discussions.[12]

The Nominal Group Approach

In the Delphi approach, strictly defined, the participants remain anonymous, never meet face to face, and communicate only in writing. In the nominal group approach, they know each other and meet together. One procedure is as follows.

1. The seven to ten group members meet and are informed of the opportunity or problem, as well as the rules of the game.
2. Each person lists his or her ideas or solutions on a piece of paper privately.
3. A recorder asks each participant to voice one of his or her suggestions. These are written on a flip chart.

4. Step 3 is repeated until all the ideas have been listed.
5. Each idea or proposed solution is discussed and analyzed.
6. Each person ranks the ideas or solutions in order of merit. *This is done privately.* Those ideas that receive the highest ranks are adopted.

The nominal group approach has several advantages. Every idea or proposed solution gets a hearing. Group discussion, critique, and support are stimulating and encouraging. No one person, or small subgroup, can dominate the range of ideas considered. Although problems of status, authority, and power are not eliminated, the private ranking of ideas does minimize them. Finally, the research indicates that this technique is excellent for idea generation and decision making.

stress management:
are you master or victim?

The Surge of Stress

Tension, frustration, fear, worry, conflict, and anxiety have become buzzwords for three reasons: organizational, individual, and societal. Organizational complexities, administrative trivia and pettiness, undue pressures to conform, political in-fighting, inappropriate bureaucratic structures, maladaptive management styles, power struggles, provincial defense of territorial rights, increased social distance, burdensome computer-generated data, nettlesome interruptions, keener competition for advancement, ill-defined criteria for promotion, tighter deadlines, restrictive budgets, poorly designed jobs, less certain job security, increased work loads, more impersonal production methods—all are the fruitful soil of stress.

The individual, too, makes his or her own input. Unrealistic expectations, unreasonable levels of aspiration, career blocks, distorted perceptions of success, self-defeating attitudes, hampering habits, financial problems, status incongruence, absence of valid priorities, conflict between work and family roles, increasing age, lack of purpose and direction in life, an ethical code of putty, obsessive concern for work, failure to keep up with one's specialty, and the unfinished business of early development—all are the chemicals that make the soil of stress fertile.

Finally, society is often of little help. Role models are con- tradictory. A confused ethos produces perplexed people. Prin- ciples are blurred. Relativism governs values. Narcissism dominates standards. Group support for consistent action is fragmented. Clear demarcations between the permissible and the prohibited are vague. Consensus is notable by its absence. Thus numerators abound, but a bonding common de- nominator is often lacking. The combination of all three fac- tors makes stress not only inevitable but acute for most leaders at one time or another.

The Executive Facade

Behind the imperturbable executive mask lies a very fallible and fragile human being. Hidden from public scrutiny are the turbulent ingredients of the manager's personality. Since every leader must wrestle with his or her inner dynamics, the wisest course is to have a constructive confronta- tion with the self. If the leader fails to do so, he or she is likely to pay an inordinate price for whatever career success is achieved, derive small satisfaction from it, and project per- sonal problems on others. This does not call for a do-it- yourself form of psychiatry, nor does it involve lastering homemade band-aids on the results of self-punishing intro- spections. It does require that the leader, before seeking to understand others, make some investment in gaining self- insight. Many managers are eager to learn what makes others tick, while neglecting the more challenging task of coming to grips with what makes thm tick.

Stress: Fulcrum or Folly?

Stress, like happiness, is not easy to define, though it is all too easy to experience. The common elements in the various types of stress are feelings of threat, discomfort, and at least some degree of helplessness and confusion. Such feelings may range from a mild disquiet, to a stimulating motivation, to a disabling anxiety. Hence, certain distinctions should be made. Stresses are experienced feelings; they are not the stressors that give rise to these feelings. Every individual has three basic drives: to maintain equilibrium, to strive for self-enhancement, and to avoid any diminution of his or her prized states. Any perceived threat creates tension. It is the perception of threat, not necessarily the reality, that is important. Intensity of the reaction is also significant. Mild tension is often an incentive, stirring us to meet the challenge or to overcome the obstacle, as every salesperson well knows. Acute, prolonged stress can be not only disorganizing but disabling. Finally, the absence of all tension is not a sign of happiness; rather, it indicates apathy or an ignorance of what is taking place. As in all other things, there is an optimum level of stress for each situation.

Hans Selye, the noted authority on stress, has described the general adaptation syndrome: (1) the alarm reaction; (2) the resistance stage; (3) the stage of exhaustion.[1] At the perception of threat, the individual mobilizes his or her resources to deal with it—the well-known fight-or-flight reaction. If these efforts succeed, or perhaps if the source of the stress is simply removed, equilibrium is restored. If the stress persists, most likely mounting in its intensity, then the inappropriate coping tactics the person uses leave him or her exhausted. Effective management of the stress-producing situation, on the other hand, not only resolves the problem but increases resistance to future onsets of strain. Thus, stress can be either a fulcrum for growth or an instrument of folly.

The somatic manifestations of undue stress are manifold. Figure 33 lists some of the more common, and less serious, ones. The total number of items that you check is not nearly as important as their frequency, combination, and disruptive impact. Moreover, two ideas must be borne in mind: (1) when it comes to the sources of stress, one person's meat is another's poison; (2) some people have developed stratgies for coping with great stress, while others have difficulty handling even

Figure 33. **Indicators of undue stress.**

Indicator	Rarely	Sometimes	Frequently
Chain smoking.	___	___	___
Overdependence on liquor to unwind.	___	___	___
Overdependence on pills of various sorts.	___	___	___
Headaches with no apparent organic cause.	___	___	___
Feelings of fatigue with no justifiable reason.	___	___	___
Inability to sleep, fitful and interrupted sleep.	___	___	___
"Nervous stomach," diarrhea with no evident cause.	___	___	___
Restiveness, need to be ever on the go, inability to relax or to be alone.	___	___	___
Excessive reliance on work for satisfaction and distraction.	___	___	___
Edginess, hypersensitivity, emotional outbursts over minor matters.	___	___	___
Periods of moodiness, loss of self-confidence, feelings of inadequacy.	___	___	___
Difficulty in concentrating on or completing a task.	___	___	___
Persistent low-level feelings of tension.	___	___	___
Little time for physical exercise, leisure pursuits, and friendship activities.	___	___	___
Illogical fears and worries.	___	___	___

moderate stress. Levels of stress tolerance vary markedly from person to person, and from situation to situation with respect to the same individual.

A Few Caveats

The number of items checked should give you some idea of the amount of stress that affects you. It will not tell you its intensity or causes. If you checked "frequently" more than a few times, you might be wise to reexamine your coping strategies, and perhaps even talk the matter over with a specialist.

Most managers are able to handle moderate stress. In fact, they seem to need it for stimulation. A well-known consultant, Rosalind A. Forbes, has called them "adrenalin freaks." However, the phenomenon of "burnout" or "flameout" is becoming more common as some people rush out irrationally in hot pursuit of what Veblen called "that bitch goddess Success."

The so-called Type A personality is likely to bear a needless burden of stress because he or she tends to have the following characteristics: (1) an intense sense of urgency; (2) an unreasonably high level of competitiveness and aggression—Type A's must *always* win, no matter what they do; (3) overachievement motivation—they force themselves onward and upward; (4) "polyphasic behavior"—they are involved in many things at once and are inclined to be restive, restless, and unendingly on the go; (5) "success stress"—they become addicted to the cause of their stress as each achievement, after momentary satisfaction, impels them to drive themselves harder.

The manifestations of undue stress over a long period can take many forms, ranging from allergies and frequent illnesses, to depression and a lack of zest for life's activities. Acute stress cannot be resolved by activities that are merely distracting. Techniques for cause identification and problem solving must be used, in extreme cases with professional assistance.

The Robbers of Inner Peace

The major enemies of personal tranquility are frustration, fear, worry, anxiety, conflict, and irrational guilt.

Frustration

When Dwight D. Eisenhower was elected President, Harry Truman was reported to have commented, "I feel sorry for Ike. When he was a general, he gave orders and was pretty sure that they'd be carried out. Now that he's President, he's going to sit in the Oval Office and give orders, but not a damn thing is going to happen."

Frustration is an emotional reaction to being thwarted. A bright woman supervisor cannot secure a cherished promotion because the company has come on hard times and no one is being advanced—the impediment is situational. A vice president cannot make needed changes because of the opposition of the union leadership—the hindrance is human. Since the cause of frustration is external, self-control and problem-solving techniques are usually adequate to cope with it. The woman can change jobs; the vice president can plan to change the union contract in the next round of negotiations, living within its constraints or around them for the time being. We have all learned to adjust to those realities that we cannot alter

Fear

Fear is produced by a perceived specific and identifiable threat that prompts us to flee if flight is possible. The fear reaction may be rational or irrational; it may be proportionate to the perceived threat or all out of proportion. If a reduction in the work force has been ordered, employees who have been malingerers rightly should fear losing their jobs, but it would be silly for the best producers to suffer the same fear. Fears that are proportionate to their causes are adaptive; they

motivate us to do something constructive about them. Dispro-
portionate fears, on the side of either excess or deficiency, are
psychologically and emotionally harmful.

Worry

Fears can usually be managed in a straightforward manner,
even when they are somewhat irrational in nature. Worries are
a different matter. Worries are fears projected into the future,
accompanied by a feeling of foreboding about some dread
eventuality. They are ideal for stirring up the emotional pot
because they are oriented to the future, about which we have
only incomplete knowledge and incomplete, or no, control.
Worry, in a sense, is like a rocking chair. It keeps us busy but it
doesn't get us anywhere. Or, to change the metaphor, the
treadmill of worry can keep us running without geting anywhere.

Some people are chronic worriers. They keep the emotional
stew simmering, stirring up one worry after the next. Then,
with the illogical rationality of the worrywart, they interpret
the resulting physical and psychological symptoms as confir-
mations of their initial foreboding. Thus, the worry cycle goes
round and round. Other people are more fretful than worriers.
They continually seem to be upset about this or that. If you
observe their behavior, however, you soon discover that their
so-called worries are quite superficial, in no way disruptive.
They are not content unless they have something minor to fuss
about. Serious worries, on the other hand, are debilitating and
disorganizing. Normal worries can be dealt with by the nonoc-
currence of the calamitous event and the realization that it is
foolish to waste precious time, thought, and energy on such
matters. Disabling worries require the assistance of a professionally trained counselor.

Anxiety

Like fear and frustration, anxiety has two faces. Mild fear,
frustration, and anxiety are stimulating; they impel us to do

something positive about the situation. This is the healthy face. The unhealthy face of anxiety is a pervasive, diffuse, and painful form of stress that the person finds difficult to analyze, define, or pinpoint. It is difficult to speak in any rational way about acute anxieties, for they have a logic of their own. Moreover, one feels "just rotten," "terribly depressed," "helpless," or "stupid." To make matters worse, the person has usually developed ineffective tactics for allaying his or her anxiety. At best, they provide only short-term quiescence. At worst, they make matters more difficult because they do not get anywhere near the real source of the anxiety. Eventually, feelings of inadequacy, self-doubt, self-anger, guilt, and isolation set in.

Managers who feel hostile toward superiors because they have never worked through their resentment of authority can twist and turn as they will. Sooner or later, their latent animosity will break through their contrived defenses, ultimately to their harm. The same applies to insecure, dependent managers who are placed in a position that requires making crucial decisions, taking forceful action, or effecting radical changes. Not everyone has what it takes to sit behind the desk that bears the sign "The buck stops here." Severe anxieties cannot be resolved without the guidance of an experienced professional counselor.

Conflict

The twin roots of conflict are incompatibility and simultaneity. The individual aspires to or desires two antithetical "goods" at the same time. Although conflict, like Satan, can take many forms, three major types have been identified.

Approach–Approach. This is a kind of "I want–I want" dilemma. A manager wishes to be popular and liked by her subordinates, but she also wishes to be perceived by her superiors as an outstanding producer and performer. Under certain conditions, the tuggings are in opposite directions. The father who yearns to be intimately involved in the upbringing of his young children and wants also to accelerate his career; the supervisor who feels that she must adhere to her strict ethical code and also feels pressured by her peers to cut corners here and there; the senior executive who is attracted by the idea of retirement and is also drawn by the possibility of retaining his power and status as long as possible—all suffer from the same type of conflict: no one can have his cake and eat it too.

Avoidance–Avoidance. This is an "I don't want–I don't want" quandary. The individual is caught between two unpleasant situations, one of which must be chosen. In a divorce, children often do not want to lose either the father or the mother, but one parent will generally get custody. The following incident illustrates how bothersome this kind of conflict can be.

"I have a rough decision to make," said a president. "I hate to get rid of a vice president who not only broke me into the business but is a personal friend. Yet he cannot stay. He's way behind the times. Two of his key people are more competent than he is. We have no place to shift him. We've just run out of options, except to give him the 'golden handshake.' I'm damned if I do, and damned if I don't."

Approach–Avoidance. This is an "I want–I don't want" conflict, as the following story shows.

"He's a real pain, in some ways," observed a young manager of his boss. "He's tough as nails, he's very demanding, sometimes he has the velvet touch of sandpaper. He rarely accepts excuses; he wants results and you'd better produce them for him. On the other hand, he knows more about this business than anyone I've ever worked for. His experience is tremendous. He's brilliant. I've learned more from him in one year than from anyone else in three. Besides, he's great for recommending his people for better positions in the company."

All of us have had the bittersweet experience of working for the task master who pressed and pushed us hard but also helped us learn and grow. Again, this type of conflict can take many forms. Managers eager to achieve executive status but reluctant to take on some of its less pleasant chores; career-women eager to have children but bothered that infants insist on acting like infants; married people rising in an organization who are titillated by the prospects of an office romance but fearful of its potential harmful consequences—all experience this push-pull force.

Guilt

Guilt occurs when we have acted against our values, convictions, or "best self." Although we *feel* guilty, guilt is a judgment we make regarding our own behavior. It may be mature and genuine, or immature and irrational. It is healthy when it forces us to admit to ourselves that we have acted in less than a laudable manner and stimulates us to improve our behavior. It is false and unhealthy when it has no objective basis and diminishes our self-regard. The person who pads his or her expense account should feel guilty. The person who has done his best and failed need feel no guilt. The guilt-laden usually carry burdens imposed on them, consciously, unconsciously, or deliberately, by others.

Ineffective Adjustment Strategies

Figure 34 lists some of the more common self-deceptive techniques for coping with the robbers of interior contentment. Given a nettlesome situation, one can run against it (hostility), run away from it (flight), or run around it (compromise). Or one can manage it effectively. Hostility is self-hurtful, flight self-weakening, compromise self-delusive. All yield distractive short-term quiescence at the expense of long-term benefits. Moreover, they waste much energy. However, it is essential to remember that only the habitual use of such tactics is deleterious. We all resort to them from time to time.

Figure 34. **Ineffective stress strategies.**

Strategy	Description	Example
Running Against: Hostility		
Negativism	The habitual naysayer with an "agin' the government" attitude.	The expert critic who opposes almost everything but offers no positive suggestions.
Nagging	Forever on people's backs, never on their side.	The fault-finding supervisor who nitpicks and nudges unendingly.
Aggression	Intimidating, bullying behavior.	The punitive executive who relies on threats and ultimatums.
Displacement	Venting feelings on a convenient, vulnerable target rather than on the real cause.	The boss who vents his spleen on his people after being turned down for a promotion.
Decompensation	Flying off the handle for no sufficient reason.	The employee who stalks out of a meeting in anger because someone disagreed with him.
Revenge	Implacable vindictiveness.	The manager who plots to undermine her superior who treated her unfairly.
Running Away: Flight		
Overindulgence	Eating, drinking, sleeping, taking pills to excess.	The manager who uses uppers and downers to keep going.
Procrastination	Putting off reality.	The manager who delays making important decisions that must be made.
Hypochondria	Escaping through illness.	The worker who gets "convenient fever" when the workload becomes heavy.

The format of this figure was taken from T. Costello and S. Zalkind, *Psychology in Administration: A Research Orientation* (Englewood Cliffs, N.J.: Prentice-Hall, 1963). The content and discussion are the author's responsibility.

Strategy	Description	Example
Denial	Refusing to face up to reality.	The manager in the acquired firm who continues to act as though no merger had taken place.
Isolation	Intellectually compartmentalizing situations that cause stress or conflict.	The manager who says that business and ethical behavior don't mix.
Regression	Retreating to behavior that was appropriate to an earlier developmental stage but is now ineffective.	The department head who knows that she is a poor manager and so gets involved in minor tasks that others should do.
Fixation	Rigid adherence to self-defeating behavior patterns.	The manager who uses outmoded leadership techniques even though they rarely work well.
Withdrawal	Apathy or resignation.	The greatly underutilized engineer who daydreams of his hobbies while on the job.
Repression	Self-protective, unconscious forgetfulness.	The assistant who "forgets" to tell her boss about a very embarrassing blunder she had made.

Running Around: Compromise

Positive

Compensation	Gaining substitute satisfactions when prevented from attaining those we really want.	The manager who cannot get a promotion and so runs for office in local politics.
Sublimation	Channeling a thwarted need or goal into a constructive path.	The manager who never married and becomes very active in the Big Brother movement.
Identification	Basking in reflected glory.	The assistant who gets vicarious pleasure from the achievements of his boss, takes on his manner, thinking, and attitudes.

Strategy	Description	Example
Negative		
Projection 1	Blaming others for our own deficiencies.	The manager who blames her mistakes on her secretary.
Projection 2	Attributing our faults to others.	The manager "on the take" who sees all her peers as crooked.
Rationalization: Sweet Lemon	Giving a socially acceptable reason for the true reason—preferring our present state to what we cannot get.	The manager who says that he prefers his current position to a desired promotion he cannot get.
Rationalization: Sour Grapes	Giving a plausible reason for the true reason—denegrating what is unattainable.	The supervisor who cannot advance and claims that he would not want to because of the increased problems that come with promotion.
Sympathism	Attempting to get commiseration for our unhappy lot.	The manager who constantly tries to get associates to feel sorry for his troubles with the boss.
Egocentricism	Constant self-references.	The ineffective manager who constantly talks of her great achievements in her former company.

Techniques for Managing Stress

Like Gilbert and Sullivan's policeman, the executive's lot is not always a happy one. He or she is forever wrestling to balance out a series of antagonistic forces: independence and interdependence, competition and cooperation, friendship and social distance, assertiveness and obedience, self-interest and concern for others, quest for success and fear of failure, a wholesome pride and hubris. Small wonder that Aristotle observed that all vice stems from either an excess or a deficiency of a virtue. Not surprising that most cultures have extolled a sound mind in a sound body!

Given the torque produced by these antithetical forces, how do leaders continue to be masters of their fate, if not captains of their soul? The following 20 suggestions may help. Keep in mind, however, that what works well for one person may not be effective for another. For instance, some managers find great tension relief from talking over business matters with their spouses, whereas others would consider this a last resort.

1. Accept the fact that tension, sometimes great tension, is a natural part of life. There is nothing wrong in feeling confused or even helpless in the face of a perplexing problem or situation.

2. Control your "cool." The greater the strain, the greater your need to "stay loose." Have a basic confidence in your ability to work your way through the difficulty, perhaps with some help.

3. Prevention is better than cure. Make sure that your regimen includes good health habits, physical examinations, regular sleep and exercise, social activities, and quiet time for self-renewal.

4. Analyze the *real* causes of your stress, not merely the symptoms or results. Analyze why you are so upset—it well may be that you are overreacting because you are uptight.

5. Don't let the tension envelop you. Never race your motor about it. Put it in perspective, as far as your total life is concerned.

6. Be wary of your feelings. Emotions make excellent servants but tyrannical masters. Never act on the basis of emotion alone.

7. Schedule a definite time and place to think through your stress and its causes. Do not think about it at any other time. This will take some effort until it becomes a habit. If you let the emotional effects of stress intrude willy-nilly, they will make you spin endlessly.

8. Avoid false guilt. Do not allow others to make you feel guilty. Do not judge, criticize, or devalue yourself and your sense of adequacy.

9. Learn to shift gears. Engage in tension-reducing activities, knowing full well that you will address the situation when you have had some respite from it.

10.   Be cautious of the "crutches" you are inclined to use when tension becomes stressful—pills, drinking, sleeping, eating, compulsive working. More important, realize that they are crutches.

11.   If the stress stems from job conditions, talk it over with trusted associates who are gifted with zippered lips. The catharsis you derive and the understanding you receive can be helpful. But do not seek the counsel of the ignorant or the incompetent.

12.   Get outside yourself. Giving of yourself altruistically to community groups, within the bounds of prudence, can be an excellent source of self-regeneration.

13.   Develop one or more off-the-job hobbies in which you can immerse yourself. All work and no play may make lots of jack, but it also makes Jack dull beyond words.

14.   Formulate a reasoned set of values, principles, and convictions. This will enable you to be consistent and to bear up under stress without self-condemnation.

15.   From your experience, build up a system of constructive stress-coping strategies that work for you. Then, as best you can, try to anticipate the conditions that signal the onset of undue strain.

16.   After a stressful situation has been resolved, analyze exactly what transpired so that you will build up your resistance to future strain and be better able to manage it.

17.   When a clear course of action is indicated, follow it no matter how you feel.

18.   If the stress becomes too heavy for you to bear alone, seek out the help of the professionally trained, but use such resources as facilitating agents, not gods.

19.   Do your best to maintain your sense of the comical, especially with reference to yourself.

20.   Remember that Thucydides once noted that happiness depends on being free and freedom depends on being courageous. This applies to stress as well as to democracy.

your leadership values: do you stand for something or fall for anything?

The Ethical Tower of Babel

The most bothersome executive problem is ethical behavior. High-sounding platitudes abound. Clear ideas are notable by their absence. Absolutists rigidly insist that everything is either right or wrong. Relativists elastically contend that life consist of variables, not constants. Skeptics doubt that a workable ethical code can be formulated. Cynics snicker at the lofty proposals of the CEOs of megacorporations that securely straddle their markets. Realists question whether marginal firms can afford the luxury of ethics. Naysayers reject the entire concept, claiming that business is a zero-sum game in which bluffing, deception, and corner cutting are acceptable. Pragmatists affirm that it is sufficient to stay within the letter of the law; ethics is for people and the corporation is merely a legal, fictitious "person."

Small wonder that managers are confused, especially when the value-forming institutions—churches and schools—are themselves in a state of transition. For instance, the new dean of the nation's most prestigious business school has made one of his priorities "honing a new field—business ethics!" The school has two trained ethicists who are learning the business environment. He hopes "they'll be around long enough to develop a field." [1] When ethics in industry is considered a new field, the public is rightly puzzled.

The Difficulties of Ethical Behavior

If you are persuaded that ethics is much ado about nothing, complete the inventory in Figure 35, thinking of the harm that a radically erroneous course of action might cause. It may make you a bit more empathic for the practicing manager who is neither lawyer nor ethicist.

The Ethics Dilemma

Fortune studied 1,043 of the outstanding corporations in the United States. It was found that between 1970 and 1980 117 were involved in some type of domestic delinquency—bribery, kickbacks, tax evasion, illegal rebates and political contributions, price fixing and other violations of antitrust. One executive of this 11 percent commented, "We didn't do these things for our own behalf . . . [but] for the betterment of the company." And the SEC's enforcement chief noted, "In many instances where people are not lining their own pockets, you can only explain corporate crime in terms of 'produce or perish.' " [2]

John H. McArthur, dean of the Harvard Business School, has said, "MBAs find ethics Mickey Mouse, but as people move toward the top, the legal-moral-ethical constraints become more important." [3]

In the 1925 U.S. Open, Bobby Jones penalized himself a

Figure 35. **Inventory of ethical choices.**

Directions: In the space provided at the left of each statement, enter the number that best represents your overall conviction regarding each incident. It is assumed that specific circumstances would affect your decision. This granted, give your general reaction to each statement, using the following system as a guide: (1) Strongly Agree, (2) Agree, (3) Disagree, (4) Strongly Disagree, (5) Not Sure.

1. ____ In making decisions having ethical implications, the manager should be guided primarily by corporate policies and procedures, only secondarily by his or her code of conduct.

2. ____ It is ethical for a company to require applicants for an important managerial position to take so-called projective tests, which probe their deeper personality dynamics.

3. ____ It is ethical for a company to require that the spouse of an applicant for a vice presidential position be interviewed by a clinical psychologist.

4. ____ It is company policy that buyers for key accounts be provided with every possible hospitality. One buyer asks that you set him up with a "call girl." It is ethical for you to do so, provided you take no part in the proceedings.

5. ____ You discover that your sales have been falling off with certain key accounts because a competitor has been giving kickbacks. It is ethical for you to "fight fire with fire."

6. ____ It is ethical for a firm to require applicants for nonsensitive positions to undergo a polygraph test.

7. ____ It is ethical for a company to pay its employees less than a living wage if the alternative is going out of business or else firing some employees who would not find a job in the foreseeable future.

8. ____ It is ethical for a company to hire a private detective agency to "keep tabs" on its key executives, even though it has no evidence of wrongdoing.

9. ____ The various data banks maintained by the government, credit agencies, and other organizations are basically unethical because they collect information without the individual's permission— often without his knowledge.

10. _____ The manager should not concern himself with questions of ethics. It is sufficient if he or she abides by the laws.

11. _____ Business is so competitive these days that, willingly or unwillingly, the manager must act unethically from time to time.

12. _____ A key subordinate is "hooked" on criminal drugs but is above average in performance. It would be unethical for you to bring this matter to the attention of your boss.

13. _____ It is ethical for a firm to undercut a competitor and take a loss to drive the competitor out of business.

1⁻. _____ A competitor has a brilliant scientist who is just on the verge of a "breakthrough." It would be ethical on your part to offer the scientist an attractive job offer in order to capitalize on the near discovery.

---

stroke when his ball moved after he had addressed it. This dropped him into a tie with Willie Macfarlane, who won the playoff. Fifty-three years later, Tom Kite did the same thing in the Hall of Fame Classic at Pinehurst. The self-imposed penalty caused him to finish one stroke behind Tom Watson. Kite received the USGA's Bob Jones Award for Sportsmanship at its annual meeting. Kite's reaction was, "I only did what many others golfers have done. Golf is different from other sports." Golf has created a level of ethics above that of other sports. In the absence of officials, the golfer's conscience is his or her guide.[4]

These three incidents illustrate the problems associated with ethical behavior. The behavioral norms of golf, despite all the jokes, make it easier for a contestant to play fair. This is not always the case in industry. Some executives think of moral behavior as Mickey Mouse because winners are rewarded and losers are punished. Many managers feel that they are caught in a vise. They are acting not just for their own benefit but for that of the organization.

The Love-Hate Perceptions of Business

Throughout history business leaders have been admired for their knowledge, skills, risk-taking ability, drive, innovativeness, and opportunism. Yet the rewards that these traits have produced make them objects of distrust and fear. The Greeks made Hermes the sponsoring god of both thieves and merchants. Kings have used businessmen. Patricians have scorned them. Intellectuals have derided them for knowing the price of everything and the value of nothing. Artists have lampooned them. Authors have excoriated them. Theologians have threatened them. Radicals have made them the primal original sin. Politicians have made them scapegoats.[5]

Moreover, when corporations do well by society, they are perceived as doing too little. When they stumble, their "sins" are magnified out of all proportion. Not surprisingly, many have responded with an attitude of "We'll stay within the law; we'll do the best we can. That's all we can do." What are the realities? Although few executives qualify for sainthood, the fact is that never have so few controlled so much power, for the benefit of so many, with such great self-restraint. It is difficult to think of any other group that would be so disciplined. The shock caused by the crimes of the several is a tribute to the basic honesty of the overwhelming majority.

The Problem Will Not Go Away

Trying to ignore the ethical aspects of business behavior is much like trying to get rid of a boomerang by throwing it away. Like neuroses, ethical problems keep intruding no matter how hard we try to suppress them. A mature approach involves the candid admission of four realities: (1) ethics is a nuisance—the questions are plentiful, the sure answers few, the gray areas many; (2) ethics is oblique—it has little direct impact on profit; (3) ethics is perplexing—like any developing science it is incomplete, so that there are situations where people of equal goodwill disagree; (4) ethics is vexing—it counsels managers to do what should be done rather than what they may prefer to do.

This said, ethics is inevitable. Business operates with the

consent of society. Should the public turn on it, government-imposed constraints will be ever more constipating. Private enterprise is becoming ever less private, and prosperous obscurity is a luxury no longer granted to any sizable organization. Additionally, like democracy, ethics is an aggravation until one considers the alternative—a return of Hobbes's *Leviathan,* in which the predatory devour the defenseless. Finally, the executive must live in a moral cosmos, not a chaos. He or she must maintain a certain degree of inner self-congruence.

The Possible Options

There are numerous sources of behavioral guidelines: the state, law, humanistic tradition, the situation, religion, duty, custom, social contract, individual convictions, pragmatism. Helpful as these are, they are incomplete, singly or in combination. They are often man-made and therefore subject to all the foibles of their creators or past-oriented and thus incapable of coping with new situations. Or they may be highly subjective and of use only to the people involved, or after-the-fact and too late to prevent injustice, or too general to direct specific day-to-day actions, or so flexible as to be overly elastic.

Some Buoys for The Ethical Channel

The purpose of buoys is to mark the safe channel so that the captain can sail smoothly while knowing when he is endangering his ship and crew. For the sailor, buoys mark clearly the limits of permissible behavior. Ethics should serve the same purpose. By what shall behavioral norms be buoyed? Reluctantly, perhaps unwillingly, one is forced back to the nature of mankind. People of all cultures share at least five characteristics:

1. *They are rational;* the ability to reason, judge, and decide with respect to the moral quality of human behavior is universal.

2. *They are self-determining;* despite the influences of previous conditioning and subconscious motivations, they are accountable for at least many of their deliberate actions.
3. *They experience self-approval and guilt;* granted that at times these are vague or even neurotic feelings, still self-judgment is often a mature acknowledgment that a given behavior has been either contrary to one's nature or unjust to others.
4. *They live in community* and have obligations to their fellows.
5. *They have certain human rights* that may not be violated—or else everything that has been said is meaningless.

Sensitivity to human rights is the glue that binds a society. What are these so-called natural rights? It is impossible to enumerate them all, but surely the following are not unimportant: to justice, to freedom of movement, to privacy, to truth from others, to one's character and good name, to adequate education, to health care and housing, to a job, to joining with others to attain common goals, to protection from unfair intrusions, to opportunities to actualize one's potential. Two other considerations are important: (1) every right has a corollary obligation—the right to a decent wage implies the responsibility to give a fair day's work; (2) the extent to which such rights are exercised is a function of the resources of the community and the corresponding rights of others.

Ethics and Principles

Rules are mandatory. Principles are adaptive. Rules make for rigidity. Principles provide consistency and flexibility by allowing for adaptation to different situations. Accordingly, the leader does not need a long list of rules. He or she needs a brief set of coherent and valid principles.

The Primary Principle

The basic principle is to do good and avoid evil. The difficulty is that different people, groups, and cultures may define good and bad in diverse ways. It is for this reason, Baumhart[6] found, that executives accept the Golden Rule but find it less than adequate in coping with particular problems. Even so, the principle remains. It requires development and refinement, not rejection. This is the task of education, corporate climate, philosophy, policies, and especially the modeling behavior of higher management.

The Secondary Principles

The categorical imperative to do good and avoid doing evil is obvious to all but the morally deaf, dumb, and blind. However, its simplicity is flawed by its generality. It requires specification to particular situations. This is the purpose of the secondary principles. Although it is not always obvious how these principles should be applied, people with a reasonable amount of intelligence, education, and experience can usually come to some type of agreement about them. You do not have to be a logical genius to realize that bugging a competitor's telephone, operating a sweatshop by abusing illegal aliens price collusion, and padding expense accounts are bad. On the other hand, respecting the rights of customers, advertising products honestly, treating employees in a humane manner, and refusing either to bribe others or to take bribes are good.

The Tertiary Principles

Here is where the problems really occur for the simple reason that individuals with equal intelligence, education, experience, and goodwill can come to different conclusions regarding the same behaviors. Such situations usually involve a conflict of rights. A company has a right to know about its employees, but when does the exercise of this right become an invasion of privacy? Lying is wrong, but under what conditions is a manager free to tell an incomplete truth? The collection of debts due is a right of any firm, but under what conditions do the methods for doing so become a form of terrorization? The list is well-nigh endless. The situation is worsened by the fact that the leader is not an impersonal, rational computer. Reason is often a lonely stranger in the psychological world of feelings, habits, pressures, desires, and passions where the irrational forces are always at home and in the majority. However, the situation is hardly hopeless. Given the proper support, the laser beam of reason can still pierce the smog created by emotional pyrotechnics, especially if the pervading climate is supportive to doing the decent thing. Informed, prudent, experienced managers can nearly always draw the line between ethical and unethical behavior in a given organization or industry. If they fail to do so, then a declining curve of ethical behavior is inevitable.

A Practical Illustration

In 1952 the American Psychological Association designated a committee to draw up a set of ethical principles. Using an empirical, inductive, critical-incident, content-analysis approach, it produced *Ethical Standards of Psychologists*. This document has been revised and updated ever since. The result of all this work is a viable pattern of ethical practice guidelines, coupled with a *Casebook on Ethical Standards of Psychologists*, to which all can refer in time of doubt.[7] No fewer than 18 significant behavioral areas are covered. A procedure is in place whereby violations of ethics can be brought to the attention of the association and adjudicated. Perhaps more important, the importance of ethics is reinforced continually in the journals of the association.

It would be ideal if industry, trade, and management associations asked their most experienced leaders to do something similar. Executives would welcome such an idea: (1) it would spell out the rules of the game; (2) it would make it easier to resist the unethical demands of customers and other constituencies; (3) it would help control those who are morally insensitive. Moreover, such codes, however imperfect, would be a strong countervailing influence on government regulation. Historically, government has usually entered the picture only after business and industry have failed to police themselves and their unethical practitioners. Codes would serve to prevent the many honest organizations from paying for the derelictions of the few in terms of public image and the ability to operate freely.

Ethics and Individual Conduct

Theodore Roosevelt once noted that a tramp will steal a ride on a railroad car, but if you send him to college and educate him, he will steal the railroad. Canon Frederick Lewis Donaldson summarized the seven deadly sins of modern society in the following terms:

Policies without principles
Wealth without work
Pleasure without conscience
Industry without morality
Knowledge without character
Science without humanity
Worship without sacrifice

Although these concepts are enlightening, they lack the specificity that the leader needs in his or her daily behavior. The following dozen suggestions, drawn from a variety of sources, may be of assistance.

1. Do not perform an action unless you would be willing to have it become a law binding all mankind.
2. Never use another human being as a mere means to your personal ends, and never permit anyone to use you in this manner.
3. Before engaging in a given behavior, ask yourself, "Would I be willing to justify my action before an objective, competent board of inquiry?"
4. Would you perform the act if you were certain that it would be on the six o'clock television news?
5. How would you judge the action that you propose to take if it were done by your worst enemy?
6. If you excuse yourself on the grounds that everybody's doing it, would you do it if no one else did?
7. How would you feel if, after you had performed the proposed act, you were forced to justify your motives and behavior to your children?
8. Would you be content if your superiors and associates

were to behave toward you as you propose to act toward
someone else?

9. Since people learn what they live and little else, would
you be willing to have each of your subordinates act in
the precise manner that you intend?

10. If you feel that the pressures are too great to resist, how
would you judge the behavior of a competitor who used
the same justification?

11. If you reason that the damage done someone else by your
behavior is small, what would your judgment be if
everyone in your company or industry behaved in a similar way?

12. If you were to make a habit of doing what you propose to
do, what kind of person would you become?

Moral Knowledge or Moral Courage?

To know what is the right thing to do is usually far easier
than to do it. The manager-leader is not expected to be any
more perfect than the general run of mankind. On the other
hand, expectations and mandates rise as authority, power, and
influence accrue to a person. What might be frowned upon in a
private citizen can become intolerable if that same citizen
were a candidate for a seat on the Supreme Court. Rank has
not only its privileges but its increased responsibility to give
an example of impeccable conduct. Human frailties in high
places are understandable. They cannot be considered mere
peccadilloes as they might be in people of lower station. To
paraphrase President Truman, if the executive cannot bear the
ethical heat, let him stay out of the organizational kitchen.

What can conscientious manager-leaders do who desire to
combine, as best they can within their all too human limitations, ethical behavior and practical actions that produce
growth and profits?

They can develop an informed conscience. In the final
analysis, everyone must follow his or her conscience. Conscience, contrary to popular belief, is not a matter of feelings
or emotions. It is an intellectual process whereby a person

judges whether an act or course of action is good and therefore should be done, or bad and therefore should be avoided. It is also the function of conscience to compel a person to experience guilt *consequent* to an act that is contrary to his or her convictions. In the first role, feelings and emotions have little to do with conscience; in the second, they play an important part. But the executive's conscience must be informed: managers must seriously undertake to discover what makes for ethical and unethical behavior. Additionally, the executive's conscience must be mature, realistic, and sensitive. Managers must avoid a primitive absolutism that makes them rigid and a rubberband relativism that makes them a moral zero. Like mathematics, ethics has constants and variables. The intellectual constants give managers a sense of direction and purpose; the variables must be taken into account for a specific decision. But the constants cannot be sacrificed to the variables.

They can do their best to seek justice. Justice obtains when each person is rendered his or her due. *Exchange* or *contract* justice exists between people who are equal with respect to the matter at hand. Its purpose is to protect the rights of individuals. It is evident whenever a person endeavors to be fair in dealing with others. This is a minimum requisite in the manager-leader's conduct. *Distributive* justice is involved in the relationship between a society and its members. It requires the fair distribution of both the benefits and the burdens of a given community among its members. *Corrective* justice endeavors to rectify wrongs that have been done and to redress legitimate grievances. *Social* justice requires that every person contribute to the common good of society. Executives must be alert to their responsibilities in these areas if they are to act in a generally ethical manner.

They can develop a realistic personal code of conduct. The typical manager does not need intellectual enlightenment nearly so much as he or she needs the intestinal fortitude to live by a personal code that is reasonably valid and operationally effective. Managers are not meant to be holier than thou. On the other hand, they are not too admirable if they habitually take refuge behind the specious defense that "everyone else is doing it"; in fact, this is exactly what managers often complain about in their children. Circumstances, it is true, may at times impel or compel managers to act contrary to their code. Ultimately, however, they will have to decide which is better: to live with success at any price or to live with themselves.

Values Are Broader Than Ethics

A value is an enduring belief that a specific mode of conduct or an existence end-state is preferable to others. Every value has a cognitive, affective, and behavioral aspect. Accordingly, ethics is only one component of a person's value system, which includes cultural, political, class, race, nationality, and religious beliefs. Some values are *core* in the sense that they are most important to the individual, such as freedom might be. Others are instrumental in that they lead to values of a central nature. Instrumental values, for example, may deal with *competence*, being logical; or with *morality*, behaving in an honest manner. Rokeach has studied the nature of human values.[8] He has concluded that there are 18 core values, and 18 of an instrumental nature, that are very important to the American people. These values are presented in Figures 36 and 37. You might find it revealing to rank them first as to their importance to you, and then as you think your associates might order them. Space is provided for you to add any other values that are central to your value system.

Corporate Social Responsibility

The public has always admired business and distrusted big business. Critics have always existed, but with the growth of conglomerates, agglomerates, and transnationals, they are now "coming out of the woodwork." Every aspect of corporate life has been grist for their mill. Companies have been censured for gobbling up scarce resources, polluting the environment, and ignoring consumerism. They have been berated for suppressing competition, aborting innovation, and monopolizing markets. They have been rebuked for conducting their affairs

Figure 36. Your core value system.

Core Value	My Ranking	As My Associates Would Rank Them
A comfortable life	————	————
An exciting life	————	————
A sense of accomplishment	————	————
A world at peace	————	————
A world of beauty	————	————
Equality	————	————
Family security	————	————
Freedom	————	————
Happiness	————	————
Inner harmony	————	————
Mature love	————	————
National security	————	————
Pleasure	————	————
Salvation	————	————
Self-respect	————	————
Social recognition	————	————
True friendship	————	————
Wisdom	————	————
————————	————	————
————————	————	————
————————	————	————
————————	————	————
————————	————	————

Figure 37. **Your instrumental value system.**

Instrumental Value	My Ranking	As My Associates Would Rank Them
Ambitious	_____	_____
Broadminded	_____	_____
Capable	_____	_____
Cheerful	_____	_____
Clean	_____	_____
Courageous	_____	_____
Forgiving	_____	_____
Helpful	_____	_____
Honest	_____	_____
Imaginative	_____	_____
Independent	_____	_____
Intellectual	_____	_____
Logical	_____	_____
Loving	_____	_____
Obedient	_____	_____
Polite	_____	_____
Responsible	_____	_____
Self-controlled	_____	_____
_____	_____	_____
_____	_____	_____
_____	_____	_____
_____	_____	_____
_____	_____	_____

like Renaissance states, under the control of a self-perpetuating oligarchy, accountable to no one so long as they stay within the generously permissive limits of law. They have been accused of subverting the political process, while ignoring the poor. They heve been denounced for depriving employees of due process, imposing rigid conformity, and rewarding groupthink.

It has been suggested that corporations be broken up into smaller units, that they be chartered by the federal government, that they be allotted only a defined life span. It has been recommended that employees be given a bill of rights, that they participate in some type of codetermination, that their jobs be considered a form of private property after a specified time. Firms have been advised to place representatives of the public interest on their boards. They have been more and more tightly constrained by the regulators. They have been forced to spend time and money in litigation, much of it petty. They have been blamed for much that is wrong with society and given little credit for what is right. In short, no institution has been so analyzed, studied, evaluated, picked at, and picked over as the megacorporation, not always with the purest of intentions.

In response to all this, corporations have become to an increasing degree social institutions. Stirred by the many critics nipping at their heels, the threat of government domination, and sheer self-interest, they have gradually devoted more of their talent, time, energy, and potential profits to the amelioration of social problems. It has been an admirable effort, especially since most top executives are ill-equipped for the task in terms of prior experience, philosophical bent, personality, and intellectual preference.

Historically, organization leaders have been neither grossly worse nor notably better than the societies in which they have functioned. As societal demands, expectations, and norms have become more exacting, executives have conformed to the new requirements. We have come a long way from the dog-eat-dog robber barons; the day of the profit-maximizing entrepreneur is dead. The future belongs to leaders who are convinced of the merits of *humanistic capitalism*. They accept their accountability as trustees of society's natural resources, as guardians of the nation's prosperity. They recognize that profit is not a dirty word, but rather is the reward that the community bestows for meeting its needs more effectively than the competition. Such leaders work, whenever possible, with government and private groups to improve the quality of life, to contribute to the common good. Humanistic capitalism is at once the litmus test of the private enterprise system and its most exhilarating leadership challenge!

references

Chapter 1

1. "To End the Public-Private War," *Time*, August 18, 1980.
2. W. Abernathy and R. Hayes, "Economic Scene," *The New York Times*, August 20, 1980.
3. "Engineering a Hi-Tech World," *New York Daily News*, May 27, 1981.
4. D. Schultz, *Psychology and Industry Today*, 2nd ed. (New York: Macmillan, 1978), p. 88.
5. Quoted in G. Lodge, "Managerial Implications of Ideological Change," *The Ethics of Corporate Conduct*, C. Walton, ed. (Englewood Cliffs, N.J.: Prentice-Hall, 1977), p. 80.
6. *Ibid.*, p. 103.
7. "Ford's World Car in Debut," *The New York Times*, September 2, 1980.
8. *The New York Times*, August 24, 1980.
9. H. Koontz, C. O'Donnell, and H. Weihrich, *Management*, 7th ed. (New York: McGraw-Hill, 1980), p. 665.
10. R. Stogdill, *Handbook of Leadership: A Survey of Theory and Research* (New York: The Free Press, 1974), pp. 80–82.
11. S. Crowther, "If I Were an Employer: An Interview with Samuel Gompers," *System*, April 1920, in A. Nash and J. Miner, *Personnel and Labor Relations: An Evolutionary Approach* (New York: Macmillan, 1973), pp. 455–465.

Chapter 2

1. R. Likert, *New Patterns of Management* (New York: McGraw-Hill, 1961); and *The Human Organization* (New York: McGraw-Hill, 1967). Also, E. Fleishman, "The Description of Supervisory Behavior," *Journal of Applied Psychology*, 38 (1953), pp. 1–6; and "Leadership, Climate, Human Relations Training, and Supervisory Behavior," *Personnel Psychology*, 6 (1955), pp. 205–222. Also, E. Fleishman and E. Harris, "Patterns of Leadership Behavior Related to Employee Grievance and Turnover," *Personnel Psychology*, 15 (1962), pp. 43–56.
2. A. Zaleznik, *Human Dilemmas of Leadership* (New York: Harper & Row, 1966); and "Managers and Leaders: Are They Different?" *Harvard Business Review*, May–June 1977, pp. 67–78.
3. F. Fiedler, *A Theory of Leadership Effectiveness* (New York: McGraw-Hill, 1967). Also, F. Fiedler and M. Chemers, *Leadership and Effective Management* (Glenview, Ill.: Scott, Foresman, 1974).
4. M. Evans, "The Effects of Supervisory Behavior upon Worker Perception of Their Path-Goal Relationships" (Ph.D. diss., Yale University, 1968). Also, R. House, "A Path-Goal Theory of Leadership Effectiveness," *Administrative Science Quarterly*, September 1971, pp. 321–338.
5. P. Hersey and K. Blanchard, *Management of Organization Behavior*, 3rd ed. (Englewood Cliffs, N.J.: Prentice-Hall, 1977).
6. V. Vroom and P. Yetton, *Leadership and Decision Making* (Pittsburgh: University of Pittsburgh Press, 1973).
7. R. Tannenbaum and W. Schmidt, "How to Choose a Leadership Pattern," *Harvard Business Review*, May–June 1973, pp. 162–180.

Chapter 3

1. M. Mintzberg, *The Nature of Managerial Work* (New York: Harper & Row, 1973).
2. T. Peters, "Leadership: Sad Facts and Silver Linings," *Harvard Business Review*, November–December 1979, pp. 164–172.
3. E. Jennings, *The Executive in Crisis* (East Lansing: Michigan

State University, Graduate School of Business Administration, 1965); and *Routes to the Executive Suite* (New York: McGraw-Hill, 1971); and *The Mobile Executive: A Study of the New Generation of Top Executives* (Ann Arbor: University of Michigan Press, 1967). Also, A. Jay, *Corporate Man* (New York: Random House, 1971). Also, A. Downes, *Inside Bureaucracy* (Boston: Little, Brown, 1967). Also, P. Drucker, *The Effective Executive* (New York: Harper & Row, 1967). Also, E. Fromm, *Man for Himself* (New York: Henry Holt, 1947). Also, J. Campbell, M. Dunnette, E. Lawler, and K. Weick, *Managerial Behavior, Performance, and Effectiveness* (New York: McGraw-Hill, 1970). Finally, R. Murray, "Power and the Ambitious Executive," *Harvard Business Review*, November–December 1973, pp. 140–145.
4. V. Thompson, *Modern Organization* (New York: Knopf, 1961).
5. R. Christie and F. Geis, *Studies in Machiavellianism* (New York: Academic Press, 1970).
6. M. Maccoby, *The Gamesman: The New Corporate Leaders* (New York: Simon & Schuster, 1976).

Chapter 4

1. L. Bennetts, "Many Widows Find a New Life Running Husband's Business," *The New York Times*, September 24, 1979.
2. F. French and B. Raven, "The Bases of Social Power," in *Studies in Social Power*, D. Cartwright, ed. (Ann Arbor: University of Michigan Press, 1959).
3. D. McClelland, "The Two Faces of Power," *Journal of International Affairs*, 24 (1970), pp. 29–47.

Chapter 5

1. The forms in this chapter are drawn largely from the following AMACOM publications: Mack Hanan, James Cribbin, and Herman Heiser, *Consultative Selling*, 1973; Mack Hanan, James Cribbin, and Howard Berrian, *Sales Negotiation Strategies*, 1977; and Mack Hanan, James Cribbin, and Jack Donis, *Systems Selling Strategies*, 1978.

Chapter 6

1. R. Plunkett, Jr., "When the Late Bird Gets the Worm," *New York Daily News*, September 30, 1980.

Chapter 7

1. M. Rokeach, *The Nature of Human Values* (New York: The Free Press, 1973), Chapter 6.

Chapter 8

1. Much of the material in this chapter has been adapted from Mack Hanan, James Cribbin, and Howard Berrian, *Sales Negotiation Strategies* (New York: AMACOM, 1977).

Chapter 9

1. This section is based on a variety of sources, especially R. Steers and R. Mowday, "The Motivational Properties of Tasks," *Academy of Management Review*, October 1977; and J. Hackman, G. Oldham, R. Janson, and K. Purdy, "A New Strategy for Job Enrichment," *California Management Review*, Summer 1975.

2. D. Hampton, C. Summer, and R. Webber, *Organizational Behavior and the Practice of Management*, 3rd ed. (Glenview, Ill.: Scott, Foresman, 1978), pp. 382–396.

3. F. Herzberg, *Work and the Nature of Man* (Cleveland: The World Publishing Company, 1969). Also, A. Alber, "How (and How Not) to Approach Job Enrichment," *Personnel Journal*, December 1979, pp. 837–841. Also, P. Champagne and C. Tausky, "When Job Enrichment Doesn't Pay," *Personnel*, January–February 1978, pp. 30–41. Finally, J. Hackman and J. Suttle, *Improving Life at Work* (Pacific Palisades, Cal.: Goodyear Publishing Company, 1976).

4. M. Fein, "Job Enrichment: A Reevaluation," *Sloane Management Review*, Winter 1974, pp. 69–88.

5. P. Drucker, "Behind Japan's Success," *Harvard Business Review*, January–February 1981, pp. 83–90.

Chapter 10

1. "What Are They Teaching in the B-Schools?" *Business Week,* November 10, 1980.
2. "The Autobiography of Benjamin Franklin," *Reader's Digest Family Treasury of Great Biographies,* vol. 1 (Pleasantville, N.Y.: Reader's Digest Association, 1970), p. 390.
3. C. Alderfer, *Existence, Relatedness, and Growth* (New York: The Free Press, 1972).
4. R. Stagner, "Training and Experience of Some Distinguished Industrial Psychologists," *American Psychologist,* May 1981, pp. 501–502.
5. F. Herzberg, "One More Time: How Do You Motivate Employees?" *Harvard Business Review,* January–February 1968, pp. 53–68.
6. D. McClelland, "The Two Faces of Power," *Journal of International Affairs,* 24 (1970), pp. 29–47; and *The Achieving Society* (New York: Van Nostrand, 1961). Also, "To Know Why Men Do What They Do: A Conversation with David C. McClelland and T. George Harris," *Psychology Today,* January 1971, pp. 35–39.
7. J. Campbell, M. Dunnette, E. Lawler, and K. Weick, *Managerial Behavior, Performance, and Effectiveness* (New York: McGraw-Hill, 1970), pp. 343–348.
8. T. Herbert, *Dimensions of Organizational Behavior* (New York: Macmillan, 1976), pp. 438–446.
9. G. Homans, *The Human Group* (New York: Harcourt, Brace, 1950); and "Social Behavior as Exchange," *American Journal of Sociology,* May 1958, pp. 597–606.

Chapter 11

1. D. Hampton, C. Summer, and R. Webber, *Organizational Behavior and the Practice of Management,* revised ed. (Glenview, Ill.: Scott, Foresman, 1973), pp. 139–140.
2. T. Herbert, *Dimensions of Organizational Behavior* (New York: Macmillan, 1976), Chapter 15.
3. E. Dale, *Management: Theory and Practice,* 2nd ed. (New York: McGraw-Hill, 1969), pp. 132–133.
4. K. Davis, *Human Behavior at Work: Human Relations and Or-*

ganizational Behavior, 5th ed. (New York: McGraw-Hill, 1977), p. 280.
5. The Constructive Behavior Exchange and the Perceived Activities Exchange are rooted in R. Beckhard, *Organization Development: Strategies and Models* (Reading, Mass.: Addison-Wesley, 1969); and "The Confrontation Meeting," *Harvard Business Review,* March–April 1967, pp. 149–155.

Chapter 12

1. T. Harris, *I'm OK—You're OK: A Practical Guide to Transactional Analysis* (New York: Harper & Row, 1969). Also, M. Zivan, *Transactional Analysis for Managers* (New York: American Management Associations, 1975).
2. J. Luft, *Group Processes: An Introduction to Group Dynamics* (Palo Alto, Calif.: National Press, 1963).

Chapter 13

1. "American as All Hell," *Time,* December 1, 1980.
2. K. Lewin, *The Conceptual Representation and Measurement of Psychological Forces* (Durham, N.C.: Duke University Press, 1938).
3. *First National City Bank Operating Group A & B* (Boston: Intercollegiate Clearing House, 1970).

Chapter 14

1. A. DuBrinn, *Fundamentals of Organizational Behavior* (New York: Pergamon Press, 1974).

Chapter 15

1. "Priceless Possession," *Intermountain Express,* Village Square, Hillsdale, New York, March 23, 1979.

2. D. Jenkins, *Job Power: Blue- and White-Collar Democracy* (Garden City, N.Y.: Doubleday, 1973).

3. W. Ouchi, *Theory Z: How American Business Can Meet the Japanese Challenge* (Reading, Mass.: Addison-Wesley, 1981). Also, R. Pascale and A. Athos, *The Art of Japanese Management* (New York: Simon & Schuster, 1981). See "Working Smarter: A New *Fortune* Series," *Fortune,* June 15, 1981. This includes "Westinghouse's Cultural Revolution," pp. 74–93, and "How the Japanese Manage in the U.S.," pp. 97–103.

4. C. McConnell, "Keeping Informed," *Harvard Business Review,* March–April 1979, pp. 36–38.

5. T. Peters, "Putting Excellence into Management," *Business Week,* July 21, 1980.

6. *Ibid.*

7. "Steel Seeks Higher Output Via Workplace Reform," *Business Week,* August 18, 1980.

8. "Successors Couldn't Match His Genius, So Louis Marx' Empire Crumbled," *The Wall Street Journal,* February 8, 1980.

9. "Gillette Takes the Wraps Off," *Fortune,* February 25, 1980.

10. Peters, *op. cit.*

11. Adapted from D. Hussey, *Corporate Planning: Theory and Practice* (New York: Pergamon Press, 1974), p. 16.

12. A. Delbecq, A. van de Ven, and D. Gustafson, *Group Techniques for Program Planning: A Guide to Nominal and Delphi Processes* (Glenview, Ill.: Scott, Foresman, 1975), pp. 7–10, 17–18.

Chapter 16

1. H. Selye, *Stress Without Distress* (New York: Lippincott, 1974). Also, F. Bartolome and P. Evans, "Must Success Cost So Much?" *Harvard Business Review,* March–April 1980, pp. 137–148.

Chapter 17

1. "Business Dean Sets New Harvard Style," *The New York Times,* October 6, 1980.

2. I. Ross, "How Lawless Are Big Corporations?" *Fortune,* December 1, 1980.

3. "Business Dean Sets New Harvard Style," *loc. cit.*

4. D. Anderson, "One Stroke for Sportsmanship," *The New York Times*, January 26, 1979.

5. C. Walton, "Critics of Business: Stonethrowers and Gravediggers," *Columbia Journal of World Business*, Fall 1966, in G. Steiner, ed., *Issues in Business and Society* (New York: Random House, 1972), pp. 5–23.

6. R. Baumhart, S. J., *Ethics in Business* (New York: Holt, Rinehart & Winston, 1968).

7. American Psychological Association, *Casebook on Ethical Standards of Psychologists* (Washington, D.C.: APA, 1967).

8. M. Rokeach, *The Nature of Human Values* (New York: The Free Press, 1973). Adapted with permission.

index